EDUCATING FOR HUMAN RIGHTS

AND

GLOBAL CITIZENSHIP

Educating for Human Rights

and

Global Citizenship

Edited by

Ali A. Abdi and Lynette Shultz

STATE UNIVERSITY OF NEW YORK PRESS

Published by

STATE UNIVERSITY OF NEW YORK PRESS, ALBANY

© 2008 State University of New York

For information, contact
State University of New York Press, Albany, NY
www.sunypress.edu

Production, Laurie Searl
Marketing, Michael Campochiaro

Library of Congress Cataloging-in-Publication Data

Educating for human rights and global citizenship / edited by Ali A. Abdi, Lynette Shultz.
   p. cm.
  Includes bibliographical references and index.
  ISBN 978-0-7914-7373-3 (hardcover : alk. paper)
  1. International education. 2. Human rights—Study and teaching. 3. World citizenship—
Study and teaching. I. Abdi, Ali A., 1955– II. Shultz, Lynette.

LC1090.E217 2008
370.116—dc22

                                                                                                    2007025400

10   9   8   7   6   5   4   3   2   1

Contents

Dedicated to the late Lee Ellis,
scholar, social justice activist, and friend.

Acknowledgments

As in any project of this magnitude, the completion of this book involved the constructive intervention of more people than the editors or contributors. The idea of the book started with our concern for a more inclusive and humanely located global understanding of the rights of all people, and the role education could play in achieving this. It was an idea later corroborated by the undertaking of this project that is about a global context where billions of people are deprived of their rights and by extension, the livelihood possibilities that would have been realized through the achievement of those rights. With this in mind, therefore, we decided to organize a conference entitled, "Educating for Human Rights and Global Citizenship," and invited scholars and practitioners to submit papers and workshop projects. The enthusiasm for the conference was remarkable as people gathered from around the world at the Faculty of Education at the University of Alberta. As this gathering of scholars and activists was taking place and people were discussing their individual and collaborative projects, we were very impressed, not only with the quality of presentations, but also with the commitment of the participants to engaging in transformational practice. It is this commitment by these educators and the communities in which they are working to create change, that we would like to acknowledge as this book becomes a reality. It was also our encounters with these participants that helped us understand that we should not limit our human rights education project to the conference, but should go at least several steps beyond . With that understanding, we chose some of the most important works that were presented, divided those into three categories which led to this edited volume and two special issues of academic journals that are in now "in press."

Our main reason for delineating all of the above is two fold. First, to establish some appreciation for the initiation as well as the conceptualizations of this project, but more importantly to state that while we were doing all of this, we greatly benefited and are grateful for the support of many people. Our first note of gratitude, therefore, goes to those graduate students from our Department of Educational Policy Studies who did so much for the successful undertaking of the conference and related scholarly projects that followed it. At the constant risk of missing someone, we would like to identify particular people to thank, starting with our late friend and colleague Lee Ellis, to whom this book is dedicated, and who passed away unexpectedly in 2007. Lee was an outstanding scholar and activist intellectual. He was a key organizer for the conference as well as working with Ali A. Abdi as a guest co-editor in one of the forthcoming journal special issues. We would also like to thank, Luis D'Elia, Jeff Baker, Carolina Cambre, Lynn Sutankayo, Diane Leard, and Jean Walrond. We are grateful for the financial support of our Department, Educational Policy Studies, as well as the Human Rights, Citizenship and Multiculturalism Department of the Province of Alberta, Rights & Democracy Network in Montreal and the Gandhi Foundation. From SUNY Press, we would like to say "thank you" to Senior Acquisitions Editor, Michael Rinella for his support of this work and for the collaborative spirit he showed throughout the project. Also, thanks to Laurie Searl, Senior Production Editor, who was very helpful and forthcoming with the information we needed as the book publishing was being completed. Finally, we must thank the several anonymous reviewers who gave a number of important suggestions and insights for the amelioration of this project; their notes, comments and criticisms were very useful. As a result of these reviewers, this is a better reader that we hope will encourage others to research and critically interrogate the myriad of disjunctures and conjectures in the important areas of citizenship and human rights education. Finally, we thank our families for their continuous support and patience. Lynette Shultz would like to, particularly, thank her daughters Amelia and Gillian for their energetic and creative support.

ONE

Educating for Human Rights and Global Citizenship

An Introduction

Ali A. Abdi and Lynette Shultz

INTRODUCTION

IT IS NOW ABOUT 60 years since the adoption of the Universal Declaration of Human Rights by the United Nations General Assembly. With the destructive forces of the two world wars behind us, complemented by the demise (legally speaking) of the evils of slavery about 120 years earlier, and the new winds of decolonization sweeping many parts of the globe, all societies should presumably have been more informed about the need for a stable and just world, and it was, indeed, fitting to see the prospects of upholding the main tenets of basic human rights in 1948. And who could not have welcomed such powerful components of the declaration (thirty articles in total) as Article 1: *All human beings are born free and equal in dignity and rights*; Article2: *Everyone is entitled to all . . . rights . . . without distinction of any kind*; Article 3: *Everyone has the right to life, liberty and security of person*; or Article 4, which prohibits slavery.

These were, of course, the ideals of possible human practices, and they should still remain so, but our actions, in more zones of our world than we can count, tell a different story. Indeed, George Santanya's enduring maxim, "Those who cannot remember the past are condemned to repeat it," reflects so much that human beings have been doing to each other since 1948. The above stated articles and all of the remaining twenty-six that comprise the

1

Universal Declaration have been violated, almost at will, in every continent and such terrible practices as lack of equality, racism, religious persecution, gender-based oppression, torture, and slavery still abound in our midst. As Kevin Bales has stated in his seminal work, *Disposable People* (2002), there are tens of millions of slaves in our so-called postindustrial, technologically advanced world.

Moreover, millions of people have been and are still being persecuted, tortured, and killed based on who they are, or which groups they were born into. The killing fields of Cambodia, the genocide in Rwanda, the blood-stained hillsides of Bosnia-Herzegovina, the tragedy in Darfur, Sudan, and yes, the HIV/AIDS pandemic in sub-Saharan Africa (and potentially forth-coming in India and China), among a myriad of other failures, are sympto-matic of a global human rights agenda that has betrayed many of the world's citizens. Indeed, Stephen Lewis, the UN Special Envoy on HIV/AIDS for Africa, could have been speaking for all of us when he told students at McGill University in Montreal that "[In HIV/AIDS devastated countries in Africa], you hear the screams of women mourning their dead, and you feel that the world has gone mad; you wonder how we in the international community have allowed it to come to this." Concerning the Rwanda genocide specifi-cally, Lewis, in his new book *Race against Time* (2005, p. 1) shares these haunting observations with us:

> Between 1998 and 2000, I participated in a study of the Rwandan genocide commissioned by the organization of African Unity. Visits to commemora-tive sites reminiscent of Auschwitz, encounters with survivors, interviews with women who had been raped repeatedly during the genocide—it felt like a descent into depravity from which there was no escape. And yet, somehow, because it came to an end, because the little country of Rwanda is managing to piece itself together, step by painful step, there is a sense that at least the horrific events are rendered unto history. That is not to say that we should ever forget, only to say that it is over.

As should be derived from these horrific problems of diminished citizen-ship (and some that may be more benign in their effect on human life) that both the conceptual and practical implications and realities of citizenship should, indeed, be considered in as wide a context as possible. And when we problematize the case, we should see that for all pragmatic undertakings, the contours as well as the corners of denatured citizenship (fragmented, even destroyed—assuming that people are born as free and naturally enfranchised citizens) have so many forms and characteristics that all nonlegal depriva-tions and suffering could be categorized as lack of citizenship. The fact is that beyond the millions who have been killed, there are billions who are still alive but whose fundamental citizenship rights to education, health, and a viable standard of living have been taken away by those who control access to either state or market resources. In spaces and relationships such as these, citizenship, instead of being created and achieved (see Callan, 1997) is actually being denied, and one can see, as Mamdani (1996) noted, the continuing "subjectification" of so many in presumably decolonized landscapes. Indeed, the overall picture is anything but encouraging. As has been abundantly reported in recent UN publications, close to half of the world's population lives on less than two dollars a day, nearly a billion people cannot read and write, between eight and nine hundred million lack clean drinking water, and an estimated 350 million school-age children do not have access to education, while, in fact, less than 1 percent of the money spent on weapons could educate all the children in the world.

These sites of struggle are collectively an indication of the multicentric nature of the work that is being carried out to address the realities and effects of marginalization, and they lead us to understand the need for a universal approach to human rights. Where some people argue that human rights are particular, necessarily differing according to group and context, we take as a key position that, at many sites, efforts to universalize rights have been the outcome of oppression and the struggle for liberation. The power of the vision and the enactment of universal rights as legal, political, social, cultural, and economic entitlements enables marginalized individuals and groups in particular contexts to challenge claims to power by oppressors. Therefore, our position is that universal human rights creates a vision of a world of diversity where all humans have an equitable claim to the rewards and privileges of their social, economic, political, and cultural context.

Reporting on the depressing state of the world could continue into many more pages; suffice it to say here that as educators and researchers it is incumbent upon us to seek a permanent platform for the attainment by all of viable citizenship rights. These rights, while they may not immediately accord us the noble guarantees we need to avoid the likes of Cambodia in the early 1970s or Rwanda in the early 1990s, should at least help us reclaim some relief for the hundreds of millions of our contemporaries who are exposed to malaise and suffering. The potential for human rights as a common vision of human dignity to be the catalyst for change is significant. As one small component of that overall project, this book aims to minimally and initially diffuse the meaning as well as the possible practices of the rights of all citizens across the world. To achieve some measure of this, we should not underestimate the role of education in instilling in the minds of people core human rights values and the sanctity of a global citizenship ethic. Global citizenship aims to expand inclusion and power and provides the ethical and normative framework to make this a legitimate and far-reaching project whereby citizenship is a product of diversity rather than an institutional tool serving particular groups. This global ethic should affirm, for all of us, that citizenship is not just a mechanism to claim rights that are based on membership in a particular polity, but that human rights are based on membership beyond any state or national boundaries, inherent to all individuals and groups in all places and times. Even in global spaces where fragile or nonexistent states (e.g., Afghanistan, Somalia, Zaire) cannot guarantee the rights of citizens, or in the case where refugees are on the move or located in an "in-between" geographical and political status, people must be still protected by the international community from the pervasiveness of structural violence.

It was with respect to these and related issues, especially in response to the theoretical and analytical exigencies of the case, that we brought together a number of prominent researchers and activist scholars to create a multicentric forum that should, in our understanding, highlight the urgent need to educate for human rights and global citizenship. The chapters contained in this book reflect the struggles and complexity of various projects linked to the universal struggle for human rights based on human dignity, and their themes, while not exhaustive, speak to some of the most important areas of human rights and global citizenship. In addition, the aim of the book is not to deal directly with ways of, for example, alleviating HIV/AIDS, or explicit ways to account for and address the cluster of human failures alluded to above. Rather, its main contribution is to focus on analyzing general issues of global citizenship and educational rights, and to suggest ways of educating people about these issues so that they may not only overcome the liabilities in the short term, but also and as importantly, inform themselves about the situation, and acquire a broader set of definitions of the problems so as to consciously create new spaces of social and educational possibility for enfranchising the disenfranchised.

The book contains sixteen chapters that locate the issues of our time within the human rights frame, and by connecting to global citizenship, indicate how the entitlements of these human rights might be accessed particularly by those who are most marginalized. Contributors address topics ranging from general discussions of human rights and global citizenship to how these and related practices affect knowledge formations, charter rights, cultural intersections and relationships, the role of indigenous knowledges, women's rights and education, governance and politics, and new themes of antiracism education as human rights education. The contributors are mostly university-based researchers and teachers but also include several community leaders whose works are internationally recognized. The analyses encoded in this work should represent an important and timely introduction to the now discursively active but referentially deprived area of human rights and global citizenship education. As should be clear from the contents of the book, there is much that needs to be analyzed and understood in the context of this and related works in the future. Needless to add that beyond the clear expansiveness of the topics under consideration, the saliency of the role of schooling in educating for human rights and global citizenship should be of the utmost importance if twenty-first-century humans are to achieve a more viable human rights and citizenship project than was the case in the last century. As John Dewey (1966 [1916]) told us many decades ago, education by itself should have that inherent element of assuring the pragmatic project of conviviality where all can achieve a democratic space. In that space, there should be the potential, as Paulo Freire (2000 [1970]) would have it, of the oppressor and the oppressed both freeing themselves from their de-conscientizing amnesia.

Indeed, as Shulamith Koenig, one of the contributors to this work and founder of Peoples Movement for Human Rights Education International in New York and winner of the UN Human Rights Prize in 2003, notes, any project that aims to achieve inclusive human rights has to be a collaborative one with groups and individuals seeing the protection of others as their own protection. That collaborative effort should also involve human beings learning together and from each other, which is one important point of emphasis in this work. This last point actually brings to mind the important philosophical and cultural praxis of *Ubuntu*, a Zulu term, which in the African space speaks of the sacred desire to see our own humanity through the humanity of others. Undoubtedly, such a disposition, if some of us could achieve it, would constitute a powerful prescription which, if inclusively operationalized, would do away with much that sustains human bondage and degradation.

CHAPTERS IN THE BOOK

The book brings together expressions from many sites where people's struggles for dignity are located and frames these in the context of human rights and global citizenship. After this short introduction, the second chapter of the book has two important qualities that make it unique in the context of this work. First, the chapter does not rely mainly on the generalizable scholarly research that other segments of the book employ. Here, Hilaria Supa Huaman, a Quechua (Peru) indigenous leader, and Shulamith Koenig, a New Yorker who is the founder of the People's Decade of Human Rights Education, relate their experiences, concerns, and aspirations for the achievement of global rights projects that impact and benefit all. As their own experiences inform their aspirations in this regard, representing a kind of yearning for more humane perspectives, we present this contribution both as a valuable experiential program and an instructional celebratory project. Indeed, even when human achievements are short of our expectations and needs, the individual and community desire to strive for better possibilities is itself worthy of celebration.

In the third chapter, Derek Evans engages, both descriptively and analytically, the historical transactions as well as the qualitative shifts that have characterized the emergence and operationalization of the human rights project. To do so, Evans addresses the enactment of the key principles of universal human dignity and what he terms the "four generations of human rights practice," prospectively and powerfully analyzing such issues as the establishment of the "original" human right principles and other developments that have been achieved since then. In chapter 4, Nigel Dower poses the very important question: Are we all global citizens, or are only some of us global citizens? Dower pursues these points by focusing on the educational implications of the issue and how select learning programs, primarily in the form of citizenship education, should address the questions. Central to Dower's analysis is the desire to deploy global citizenship possibilities that aim for the achievement of a global ethic, which could transform the way people, across national boundaries and continents, relate to and care for each other.

In chapter 5, George Richardson, in speaking about global citizenship in the presence of persistent national realities, starts his analysis with an anecdote that relates to his own teaching in Ukraine and locates that simple story within the contours of a national space that refuses to cede too much currency to the outside world. Following this introduction on nationalisms and citizenship, Richardson poses select questions on the issue and addresses them in the remainder of the chapter. In the sixth chapter, Ali A. Abdi undertakes a select historical investigation of the origins of subjecting non-European populations, and how this has established a global project wherein the majority of the world's populations were deliberately "de-citizenized" via the combined programs of conquest, slavery, and colonization. Abdi points out that despite the termination of some or all of these practices, the damage that has been done to people's citizenship has become of *longue durée*. To deal with the handicap this has imposed in these times of rapidly globalizing spaces, Abdi proposes new educational arrangements and possibilities that aim for the mental and material decolonization of subject populations.

In chapter 7, Ratna Ghosh presents a short history of women's rights in the context of globalization and presents the challenges that women face in their efforts for equity. She points out that while there has been significant acknowledgment of women's exclusion from political, economic, and social power in international conventions, progress has been slower than hoped as select regimes of oppression have prevented the long-awaited recognition of women's rights. Ghosh emphasizes the potential of human rights education, complemented by fully entrenched legal statutes that directly protect the rights of women, as a key mechanism for addressing the continued violence, poverty, and exclusion that limit the life possibilities of women across the globe. In the eighth chapter, Carl James problematizes notions of racism as these are presented in public discourses in Canada. James points out that while general discussions on racism may focus more on select historical or currently observable practices, racism that is inherent in institutional settings, or institutional racism, is one form of racism that poses the greatest challenge to effectively dealing with the issue. In addition, James emphasizes the role education can play in lessening the destructive platforms of racism, and in achieving more inclusive and equitable sociocultural and institutional spaces for all Canadians.

In chapter 9, Dip Kapoor focuses on problems of development and related institutional oppression that negatively affect the lives of Adivasi (original dweller) movements and counterhegemonic struggles in India. Kapoor discusses the role education might play in establishing a viable project in which Adivasis could have a stake, not only in their own educational and social development, but as well in the formation and operationalization of a public discourse that, at the end of the day, might serve as transformational processes to improve the lives of this group of indigenous people. When that is achieved, Kapoor indicates, tribal peoples will be able to appropriate viable praxes of rights and citizenship that will offset the hegemonic forces that impinge upon their lives. In the tenth chapter, Lynette Shultz, in addressing the pressing issue of contemporary slavery, introduces us to the highly problematic and multidimensionally painful world of child slaves, who are subjected, in almost all continents and countries of the world, to levels of exploitation and oppression that cannot be acceptable under any circumstances. In addition, Shultz points out that as both local communities and international institutions have apparently failed these children and with the practice of child slavery increasing in recent years, the freedom as well as the rightful protection of children should become a new global priority for all. Shultz presents a project of education for liberation that serves as an inclusive type of human rights education that aims to dismantle, once and for all, the networks of child slavery in all parts of the world.

In chapter 11, Shibao Guo discusses minority rights and inclusive citizenship in the context of immigrants. He focuses, as a case study, on one voluntary organization in Vancouver, Canada. Guo highlights the role such organizations can play in multicultural and multiethnic democracies such as Canada, and how their contributions are commonly misunderstood. Indeed, based on their familiarity with the history, culture, and language of immigrants, this and similar organizations can enhance not only the quality of services provided to new immigrants, but also the all too crucial understanding and coexistence that is needed among groups. In chapter 12, Makere Stewart-Harawira critically examines how prevalent political systems and institutions construct notions of citizenship that, by and large, fit globalist imperial endeavors that continue to marginalize the rights as well as the needs of indigenous peoples worldwide. Drawing on historical and social notions of citizenship, Stewart-Harawira calls for the immediate recasting of how we understand and practice citizenship, which should help us reshape current anomalies in human rights and relationships.

In chapter 13, Jerrold Kachur continues the theme of citizenship as a project of empire and looks at what he terms "human rights imperialism." Here, Kachur describes how the meaning and, by extension, the possible practice of human rights have been diluted, even corrupted, so that in recent years Western powers have invaded a number of countries under the false pretext of protecting human rights. Kachur problematizes the proliferation of such interventions and proposes what he calls "critical realist humanism" to address current violations of human rights in our world. In the fourteenth chapter, Cora Weber-Pillwax focuses on citizenship and its exclusions in the history as well as the current context of Métis peoples in Canada. Using mainly the story of a family living in Alberta, complemented by her own experience and socio-legalistic understanding of the issues, Weber-Pillwax weaves together personal narrative, theoretical perspectives, and close-range analysis of the lives of people to delineate the problems, and calls for the "righting" of historical wrongs that have continuously been committed against the Métis.

In chapter 15, Toni Samek discusses the importance of creating and defending public spaces as human rights arenas and invites us to view libraries as one of the few remaining open public spaces where the critical work of democracy can be carried out. She links attempts to control and destroy ideas with similar attempts to control and destroy groups of people and their cultures. She challenges learners of all backgrounds and levels, educators and educational managers and other stakeholders in institutions, to reconceptualize their understanding of the important role librarians play in learning spaces and outcomes, and in the wider society. She adds that this process should not be necessarily a one-way street. Samek notes that, through libraries and their attached information study programs, communities can benefit from learning projects such as democratic education, the politics of the textbook and the curriculum, and much-needed platforms of human rights education. In all, Samek proposes to achieve librarianships for human rights, the project has to be a collective one undertaken collaboratively by educators and librarians. In the final and sixteenth chapter, Graham Pike discusses how the idea of global citizenship education has been around for at least a century, and how different areas of education and educational institutions have all contributed to its formation and characteristics. Pike then questions why there is so little global citizenship education on the ground. To achieve more, there may have to be a new kind of schooling and indeed education, which assumes a wider view of life, a type of schooling that cannot be born out of the institutional and policy rigidity that now characterizes most institutions of primary or higher learning.

In sum, therefore, to achieve more inclusive, socially responsible, and pedagogically transformative spaces of schooling (to use Deweyan and Freirean perspectives), the global ethic project that Nigel Dower calls for, in his chapter, should permeate the lives of all people. After all, schools are reflections of the communities that create them in the first place, and it is these communities that continually set the agenda of learning and, when deemed useful, change the policies and relationships that pertain to learning and the attendant possibility for social development. Schools are places where people learn inclusiveness, civil courage, and how to live in communities encompassing diverse relationships. While the aim of this book is not to itemize the articles constituted in the 1948 Universal Declaration of Human Rights and prescribe institutional or socio-legalistic remedies, its authors desire more than what has been harvested for humanity thus far. It is in the spirit of that noble desire, therefore, and via the collective findings, analyses, and propositions of its contributors, that the reader is invited to pursue a more inclusive and intelligent understanding of human rights issues, complemented by new ways to deploy educational programs to alleviate the currently unpleasant but expansive pressures that affect the lives of so many people who still await that elusive promise of humanely located, livelihood possibilities.

Finally, we hope that the book will be useful for students, teachers, and researchers in all areas of education and international development. It might also have some pragmatic value for those in the social sciences, to legal and public policy researchers and practitioners, as well as to specialized interest groups and the general public. At minimum, we expect this book to energize the debate on human rights and global citizenship. More ambitiously, we hope it contributes to the shaping of a more humane global agenda in the coming years and decades.

REFERENCES

Bales, K. (2002). *Disposable people: new slavery in the global economy*. Berkeley: University of California Press.

Callan, E. (1997). *Creating citizens: political education and liberal democracy*. Oxford: Oxford University Press.

Dewey, J. (1966[1916]). *Democracy and education*. New York: Free Press.

Freire, P. (2000[1970]). *Pedagogy of the oppressed*. New York: Continuum.

Lewis, S. (2005). *Race against time*. Toronto: Anansi Press.

Mamdani, M. (1996). *Citizen and subject: contemporary Africa and the legacy of late colonialism*. Princeton: Princeton University Press.

TWO

A Call and Response

Human Rights as a Tool of Dignity and Transformation

———————————————

Hilaria Supa Huaman and Shulamith Koenig
Introduction by Lynette Shultz

INTRODUCTION

THIS CHAPTER BEGINS our look into how human rights provide a transformational response to local struggles against oppression. In this, human rights becomes a global citizenship frame, creating the means for marginalized people to claim those things that will allow them to live with dignity and with a full range of human possibilities. It is not the goal to homogenize human experience but rather, through the extension of relationships of dignity across constructed binaries and boundaries, the commonality of our humanness becomes the response to the call of the oppressed. In this extension, we are jolted from complacency: How can this be? Who are these people who are so disadvantaged? Who are the victimizers and how can they be held to account? What conceptualization provides a response that creates possibilities for liberation and transformation?

Clarence Dias (1993) challenges the myths of Western conceptualizations of human rights, including the myth of harmony, the myth of universality, the myth of equality, and the myth of government lawfulness. He concludes that what is needed is to create strategies that will hold abusers to account, including:

> empowering the victims through organizing countervailing people power;
> imposition of legal and social accountability through the generation of outrage,

11

indignation and shame regarding gross human rights violations; articulating and living the vision and values of a new humane society founded on the most basic and fundamental of human rights, the right to be human. (p. 709)

The following two excerpts provide a stereoscopic view of this approach in action. First, we present the call for justice. Hilaria Supa Huaman, a Quechua woman and community leader, tells her story of rights that have been denied in the forced sterilization of indigenous women by state and international players, during the 1990s, in Peru. Her call for justice is rooted in an indigenous knowledge of common human dignity. In response, we hear from an international human rights activist who declares that the diminishment of a few is the diminishment of the whole. Shulamith Koenig responds to the abuse and struggle of other humans with a declaration of connection through human dignity. This ability of being in community with others based on an understanding of the human rights declaration is the foundation for Koenig's transformational community work. By bringing these stories together we see Dias's strategies at work: organizing the power of local people, connection through outrage, and building a new vision of human relations based on equity, justice, and dignity.

THE CALL: THREADS OF MY LIFE

Hilaria Supa Huaman

Pachamama. Divine Mother God. *Pachakamaq*. Divine Father God. Be with us here, I ask for your presence here with us. Along with all of the ancestors, illuminate us with your wisdom, your balance, your equilibrium and your love. I ask that all human beings of all colors, of all cultures understand equilibrium. We are all together. We are brothers and sisters. There is no kind of discrimination when there are no differences. We are equal; we have the same feelings. In equilibrium there is love, respect, self-esteem. We love ourselves, just as we are. We do not need to feel ashamed of ourselves. We need to take care of ourselves. I ask that each one of us would understand each other. That there be comprehension. That we would enter into the equilibrium of understanding. Thank you Pachamama, Divine Mother, thank you Pachakamaq, Divine Father.

In the times of our grandparents, children were taught from the time they were in the mother's womb. Both boys and girls were educated. They were told: "You are intelligent, you have a good heart." In Quechua we say, "*sama sonco*." The new human beings were told to be noble, to have a good heart, and to be good workers. In the evenings, the elders would talk to the children, the little boys and girls, both, about many things. This is how the children were educated. This is how the leaders, the wise ones were formed.

In the love between the couple, love is seeded. We have always lived like this. With a good example set by the parents to the children, in love and in work to be honest, noble, and wise. This is how the generations resisted the [Spanish] invasion. This still exists in many communities. It is the mutual respect between men and women that brings equilibrium. Dignity is the personality of each human being. Why are we losing this balance? We have to recuperate it. In my community, the women ask themselves, How did they manage to operate on us? Why did we allow them to do this to us? We are strong, what happened? We are a noble people. When the nurses came to the homes, we treated them with love and respect, as we always do. We trusted them. With family planning we saw the possibility of progress, a way to get out of our material misery. They cheated us. The first women to get sterilized were the ones who had confidence in the medical post. They began to convince the rest of the population. They are sorry today and ask themselves, "Why did I accept?" They did not accept; they were forced. "Why did they do this to me, why did they fool me? Who sent them to lie to us?"

Over the last ten years with the sterilizations, I have seen the women age prematurely. With the tubal ligation, they are no longer young; they have a deep sadness. The women try to hide the pain. Recently some French reporters came to visit. When the women told their stories, they cried along with the reporters. Each time I meet with the women, we talk and we cry. We do not show our pain. Silently, we carry our burden. We turn to the Pachamama and Pachakamaq.

A psychological treatment is required. They are beaten by their partners. The justice system pays no attention to them. There is no justice in the sterilizations. In Peru, women do not find justice. The women who were harmed by the sterilizations are mistreated by their health and by their husbands. When the women go to complain about the abuse to the authorities, they are ignored. They do not find justice in the abuse of their human rights—the right to live in health, the right to live in happiness, the right to work and the right to live in dignity. In my community, two of the sterilized women left their families. Due to the insults and the abuse, their character changed. They are traumatized. All of the community feels badly; this has caused harm throughout the community. Many families sold their animals for medical care. They are left without animals and without any means to earn a living. There are many orphans.

It was a group of twelve women from Anta who denounced the sterilizations. The husband of one of the women became an alcoholic. He beat his wife and eventually killed himself leaving the woman with seven children. She lives nine hours away from the medical center. She went to the center for health care for her children. The nurse talked to her about being sterilized. She did not want this. The nurse went to her home and told the husband that he would be put in jail if his wife did not agree to have her tubes tied. From that moment, she felt fear every time she went to the center. On that day she was called into an inner room in the center; when she realized what was happening, she tried to escape. She and ten other women were locked in the room, and sterilized. The next day she went, by foot, to her community without explanations and without medications. Walking nine hours in the sun, her wound became infected. After three or four days at home, she went back to the center. She said, "*Señorita*, something is wrong."

"Liar, you are dirty, that is why you are sick," replied the nurse and gave her an injection. The woman felt her leg go to sleep. They sent her home; she walked the nine hours home. She could not walk any more. In putting in the injection, the nerve in the buttock was pinched. She has been handicapped ever since. They sold the animals to try to cure her. In the end, her husband poisoned himself; they could do no more. She was left alone with her pain and her heartache. She cannot work; her children cannot study. She had to send the children to the city to work as domestic servants.

We are all born with dignity. Dignity of the spirit is always present. What we do not have is economy. In the ten years between 1995 and 2005, the Decade of Human Rights, there are more families, more poverty. In men and women, both, there is more poverty and misery. Where does this come from? Those who have money want more money. They wage wars, they throw away food, and they misspend the money while the people die of hunger and poverty. They do not know any other worlds. We are strong; this is why we survive. When you do not know where to find a piece of bread for your child; you do not have a home; you have nothing. We need a solid investment so that there can be production. What does one live from if there is no production? In all aspects, what are we to live from? We have to live, no? When there is no economy, there is no production. There is no economy, this is certain. Before, production always existed. We did not know money. Yes, there was production. This is how we lived in balance. We produced without any fertilizers. Without any chemicals, we produced naturally and the environment was respected. We had the harvest to feed ourselves healthily and to live in health.

Self-esteem existed. One can know oneself—where are you from, why did you come, what do you do? This is to care for oneself. To feel that one is capable of all things. To feel oneself as intelligent and in service to others. To feel love in one's heart. To share that love; and also to care for oneself. We need all of us. We even need the bad ones—to get to know them, to change them. The white man must be healed.

I will end with a story. The bear is from the underworld, the inner world [of three worlds of Andean cosmology: inner, earthly, and outer]. All that the people throw away, the bear will clean up. Two Peruvian brothers and I came to Canada a few years ago. We wanted to meet the bear. We called a black bear to our camp; we were so happy to watch him and to know him. The bear stayed for three days in the camp; he began to eat the garbage. In the end, with bullets, the white men shot the bear. I felt so bad. I felt so guilty because we had called the bear. What can we learn from this? We humans must not throw away garbage. We are guilty because we throw away the garbage. Every person has garbage in the heart. While one lives in the darkness, one has garbage. May no more bears die, and no other animal. We must not kill our environment. Garbage gets in when we are weak, without love and without spirit. When we are weak, the bad spirit called garbage can easily enter. If one is strong, with love and with faith, and with a strong spirit full of love, no garbage can enter. We must help the children and the grandparents to remember. They must remember the wisdom, the knowledge of how to look after nature. We must teach the children. The grandparents must share their wisdom; share their life experiences with the children. The grandparents are the best books. They are the teachers of life.

I call on Pachamama and Pachakamaq. Help us all to be strong. Thank you.

(For Spanish original, see Appendix A)

THE RESPONSE: A HOLISTIC VISION OF HUMAN RIGHTS AS A STRATEGY FOR ENABLING MEANINGFUL CHANGE

Shulamith Koenig

INTRODUCTION

My Name is Shulamith. In Hebrew "Shulamith" means: a woman of Jerusalem, a woman of peace. The Biblical Jerusalem was called Yru'shalem, where the people will see wholeness, synonymous with peace-Shalom. A woman of Jerusalem is called Shulamith. I speak of my name as it has a deep meaning to the commitments I have made to promote, worldwide, human rights learning at the community level. Having lived in southern Tel Aviv on the outskirts of Jaffa, my parents had owned a metal foundry jointly with an Arab family. I used to play with their children, which was unusual at the time, and unfortunately it is still unusual today for Jewish Israeli children to play with Arab Israeli children. Having had this experience I was very uncomfortable with what I was taught at school: that the Jews are the "The Chosen people." "What about our Arab friends?" I asked my father who was a Talmudic scholar. "Yes," he said, "you are chosen for social responsibility—for Tikkun Olam [mending the world]." It marked my life for all that it is.

HUMAN RIGHTS LEARNING

I write about human rights and human rights learning and I must make sure that we have a common understanding of what human rights is and what human rights are. Many speak of human rights as either "individual rights" or "group rights." This is superfluous and artificial. There is no difference between the human rights of individuals and the human rights of communities. Human rights is being in community in dignity with others. Human rights are political and moral, and protected by the legal. It is true that with regard to indigenous people in Canada and other places "community human rights" are very important and place an obligation on the state; but they are clearly not different from individual human rights of the individual indigenous people. No one human rights can violate another. (Article 30 of the UDHR, as interpreted by me.)

Very rarely do I teach in schools. I usually hold workshops in grassroots communities. However, I did meet with three hundred young children in Rosario, Argentina. I needed a translator; I don't speak Spanish. I had a simple idea of how to share with these young minds what human rights are. I asked two boys and two girls to join me, and asked them to stand ninety degrees to one another. I described each of the pairs as follows: "Two of you are cars, and two of you are pedestrians. When I say 'Go,' go!" Then I called out: "Go," and indeed they collided into each other. Everybody clapped and laughed. I looked around innocently and asked: "What happened?"

"An accident," they called out.

"Oh," I said, "I forgot to tell you to watch the green and red lights. Do you know what this is called?"

One of the children said, "It's the law."

"So let's take it the next step," I suggested, "Were the boys hurt more or less than the girls?"

"No," was the answer in a roar!!

"Okay," I said, "Now we understand: We call this democracy, equality for all. Whether we are a boy or a girl, a man or woman, we want to move in freedom. But to do so we must obey the law. We need to know that when we move no one will restrict us, and neither will we stand in the way of others." As we continued the conversation, the children developed the universal declaration of human rights on their own. They began thinking out loud about where they wanted to go and how they wanted to move ahead. They spoke about the need for shoes and about clothing, about the rain and shelter and about their parents not having enough money, and about how their fathers are treating their mothers. It was an absolutely unbelievable experience. They took the whole Universal Declaration of Human Rights, and the whole body of instruments, and they gave us the essence of how they want to move in dignity in the world. Allow me to refer to the important social concepts of Alfred Adler, as I have noted: human beings have only one drive, which is to belong in community in dignity with others. Indeed, we can say that Adler was the psychologist of human rights.

I believe that what happened at the UN in the last fifty years is a miracle. Each member state, starting with forty-five states in 1948, and as of today

191, was struck by a moral authority and reached a consensus—giving us covenants and conventions that, if implemented, can change the world. Each one of these countries was a human rights violator of one kind or another. Yet, for fifty years, member states joined and harvested from their historic memories, and cultures, hopes and expectations of humanity and invoked the covenants of political, civil, economic, social, and cultural rights. It did not contradict their basic religious belief; it made them richer.

When I speak of historic memory I can't but recall the many discussions I had during the years, reiterating again and again that the one universal desire of all human beings is to be in dignity with others. If this assumption is correct then much of humanity's historic memory is about people's struggles, expectations, and hopes to achieve dignity. It is therefore very clear that the many nations that joined in creating and adopting the Universal Declaration of Human Rights, and then for the last fifty years toiled to introduce it into international law, were guided by a moral authority that grew out of all religions and struggles for economic and social justice that have gone on for as long as humanity can remember. Some speak of human rights as a secular religion, which in itself brings serious unresolved issues such as patriarchy to the discussion table. Such concerns can, when attended to from a human rights perspective and across society, horizontalize society and bring new values to religious thought in the twenty-first century and make it richer for all women, men, youth, and children. I believe all religions in the future will be tested by educated followers as to their handling of equality and nondiscrimination.

Human rights inform a universal value system protected by law. In this context it is important to call attention to the fact that the two major human rights instruments are called "covenants"! In my perception they are covenants with morality, advocating a higher state of being in community, in dignity, with trust, or if you wish, with unconditional love. We are all aware of the fact that human rights reflect the aspirations and hopes of humanity from its beginning. So do the prophecy and teaching of most religions. The downside is that all religions have a patriarchal perspective, which is a way of life that human rights attempt to change for women and marginalized groups—the "unwanted" or the subordinated "others." It should therefore be understood that human rights do not deny religion but simply widen and enrich religion by recognizing women, the excluded, and subordinated "others" as equal members of humanity.

In the early fifties, I had the honor to accompany a group of young Jesuit students to a meeting with Martin Buber. One of them, after listening to this wise man said, timidly, "Professor Buber, allow me to ask you a stupid question: When will there be peace in the world?" Smiling, Buber answered: "There are no stupid questions my son, only stupid answers. Allow me to give you one: If one morning every man and woman alive will say to the first person they meet

that day: 'Good Morning' and mean it, this will be the first morning of peace."
In the last fifty years the struggles of people for economic and social justice
fueled and invigorated the development of international human rights law, and
this included women who were fighting to eliminate discrimination. They were
insisting on the right to participate as equals in the decisions that determine
their lives. They advocated to change harmful conditions in which children
grow; the endless, shameful and painful discrimination and racism throughout
the world; and the criminal acts of torture. These were carefully attended to in
various and detailed human rights conventions, each reflecting the spirit of the
Universal Declaration of Human Rights and the two covenants.

These enunciations of human rights are not always perfect. They are
often not detailed enough, but they are perfect in their call for justice, for a
world guided by human rights. Even if no new convention or resolution is
added to this excellent overarching body of international law and if we
attend only to the implementation of human rights as encoded to date, the
world will be transformed. If, from today on, we demand that our governments stand by all the commitments they have made and the obligations they
have undertaken in the international arena, we will be close to having a perfect world. To achieve this dream it is our responsibility, first, to take action
to have all people know human rights, and have them join in "reminding"
governments and, if necessary, shame them by holding them accountable to
the many "Plans of Action" they have signed on to, the conventions and
covenants they have ratified, undertaking a clear obligation for human rights
to become the law of the land.

What is tragic in my eyes is that the people in struggle for whom human
rights were encoded and whose oppressions, impoverishment, and pain the
system of human rights is meant to alleviate, do not know that human rights
exist nor do they understand the power and meaning of human rights for
their lives. In the hope of changing this unfortunate and very sad situation
People's Decade for Human Rights Education (PDHRE) has made the commitment to develop a movement for human rights education. In essence,
human rights education is about hope and learning about justice. It is about
people transforming systems in which differences are liabilities into systems
where differences and diversity bring joy and richness to our lives. But mostly,
human rights education is political education that leads to people taking
active part in their own economic and social development guided by the
human rights framework. When people ask me: "How do you define human
rights education?" I sum it up as follows: a human rights educator is a person,
a woman or man, who is capable of evoking critical thinking and systemic
analysis in a gender perspective about political, civil, economic, social, and
cultural concerns, within a human rights framework that leads to action. No
more, no less, because we have no other option but human rights. During the
years, the world had learned to understand the meaning of human rights from

the eyes of Amnesty International (AI). Indeed, they are doing a fantastic job to eliminate very specific violations, but on the other hand we read and learn that one billion people in the world live on less than one dollar a day, and the statistics get worse: two billion live on fewer than two dollars a day. Who will advocate for these people's human rights? AI has, by choice, a limited human rights mandate, which historically was absolutely necessary as new nations were and are still establishing themselves within a political and civil human rights framework. However, it is obvious that people have to eat, they need a place to live in, work to support their families, healthcare when sick, and education to grow to their full potential. In the past these were noted as "needs" but are now recognized by international law as very distinct human rights issues. The power that Amnesty International has gained during the years as a human rights organization is often an obstacle to those promoting economic, social, and cultural human rights and the indivisibility and interconnectedness of human rights. In a way, those who fight for the human right to development, are worried that centering on *violation* will undermine the concept of *realization*. However, through a community learning process this narrow understanding of the meaning of human rights can be changed. People may start seeing human rights as a framework that guides them toward the realization of economic and social justice and not only as attending to political and civil violations.

I will never forget visiting the chief of police in Rosario, Argentina, who doesn't know much English, and I don't know any Spanish. He said to me in English, "Madam Koenig, there is no other option but human rights." And just a few years before, they were all members of the Junta. This is the magic that human rights learning can create. It did not happen in a vacuum. It happened while Argentina was recreating and reimagining its democracy and justice. Learning about human rights strengthened this process as people emerged from a dark period in their lives. It gave a deeper meaning to what democracy is, namely, a delivery system of human rights. This new perception in the city of Rosario, where the police were once hunting gays and lesbians, has brought them together to talk about their humanity. There are even groups of policemen, gays, and lesbians who have gone together into the community to teach human rights. These experiences have made me an enthusiast. Yes, I am an evangelist for human rights learning at all levels of society. The voices, the language, the words flowing along the high roads and low pavements of information must be thoughtfully equipped, defined, and designed to break through the vicious cycle of humiliation, which causes endless pain, confusion, frustration, violence, and desolation. Where injustice is justice and where people exchange their equality for survival, a bleak future can be easily reversed if we simply abide by the commitment and obligations made to uphold the moral, political, and legal vision of human rights. There is no other option.

LEARNING THE RIGHTS OF WOMEN

In today's complicated dialogue about the responsibility of the information society, oscillating between form and content, the first inquiry must be into what kind of society we want to develop that will be serviced in a meaningful way by tools of information. The answer for human rights educators working toward economic and social transformation at the community level is: a society where the tools of information enable women and men to transform the prevailing oppressive and egocentric hierarchical system to a horizontal human rights system of equality and lack of discrimination for all. A human rights society where information evokes critical thinking and systemic analysis with a gender perspective about civil, cultural, economic, political, and social concerns, applies knowledge about the human rights framework, and uses it as a powerful transformative tool.

The women's convention the Convention on the Elimination of all Forms of Discrimination against Women—CEDAW—is the only official document anywhere in the world that recognizes women as full and equal human beings. It is a revolutionary human rights document, for it gives women what was never given to them before: the ability to participate in decisions that determine their life. CEDAW makes this point succinctly. In many direct and indirect ways, CEDAW challenges and inquires into the mindset, behaviors, and social institutions that have separated and maintained human inequality between women and men. We call it patriarchy, the most fundamental and universal form of human inequality, which has contributed to a general pattern of hierarchical organization of most social institutions and myriad forms of inequality among all human beings throughout the world. Patriarchy has been the template of the authoritarian, elitist forms of social organization and governance that have tolerated, sanctioned, or committed such systematic and perpetual human rights violations as sexism, racism, exploitation, and oppression, and other such egregious insults to human dignity. This mindset, and its constituent behaviors and social institutions, comprises contemporary forms of patriarchy that deny true and complete human dignity to all men, women, and children. I believe that through a process of learning to understand the holistic vision of human rights, societies can transcend patriarchy and bring forth alternative relationships, behaviors, and social institutions moving closer toward the universal realization of human rights. It is with this conviction that I founded PDHRE fifteen years ago. I am proud to say that we are leaders in developing a worldwide movement for human rights education and learning and toward social and economic transformation by, with, and for the people.

We need to look and distinguish between what human rights IS—a way of life—and what human rights ARE—the law by which we live. Human rights IS a concept that informs a way of life in dignity protected by law. This is something that all humanity desires and hopes for: a way out of humiliation and deprivation and toward acceptance and trust. Human rights laws protect the desired condition that permits the pursuit of social, economic, and political justice by means other than coercion, intimidation, the force of arms, or the imposition of dysfunctional or harmful cultural traditions. The spirit that informs the principles of and movements for human rights is one that aspires to convivial human societies in which men and women of various cultures, political and religious beliefs, and social systems can live together in mutual respect and cooperate in the struggle to overcome all the obstacles to human dignity that perpetuate the human suffering that characterizes the present world order.

THE HUMAN RIGHTS CITIES INITIATIVE

As educators we often ask ourselves: Whose knowledge do we hope to evoke? How do we define knowledge? What type of information leads to creative, viable knowledge? What are the moral and political roots on which the information society relies and/or limits itself to the "production" of information? The knowledge of human rights, which includes vision, mission, and practical solutions for achieving global public good, is crucial to democracy and thus to participatory governance. The holistic vision of human rights must be constantly supported by many forms of delivery of information to strengthen human rights, like the banks of the river in which life flows freely. Two billion people live in cities today where the information society is most active. The forecast says that four billion people will live in cities within fifteen to twenty years. There is no inherent knowledge of how to live with the massive number of people and issues one has not known before. Cities are microcosms of states. They carry all the burdens, struggles, concerns, and hopes for well-being of their inhabitants, very similar to those of a state. They carry the search for a life free from fear and free from want, for women and men alike. People in cities yearn to belong in dignity in these often-alien large communities. They need to know the promise of human rights for food, education, housing, healthcare, and work at livable wages. They need to own human rights and claim them. And we must remember that more then half of them are under twenty-five, who see through communication technology what society can offer that many of them will never have. The Human Rights Cities initiative poses an important challenge to the information society and gives direction as to the contributions that must be made so that all people will learn and know human rights as a way of life. The success of this initiative depends on the good will of society to integrate the understanding of human rights as a guideline for its development. Its vitality could radiate throughout the world, giving us solutions for the future and a new political culture based on human rights. It is from the human rights cities that we are now developing a meaningful analysis for real change. We hope that human rights learning will inform the campaign to transform patriarchy, which we ask you to join.

We offer our extensive experience in the initiation and implementation of human rights education at the community level, formal and informal learning. We have held vigorous discussion with human rights educators of all kinds, learning with them about the meaning and possibilities for human fulfillment and social advancement that lie in human rights, empowering people at all levels of society to struggle for and realize long-sought enjoyment of human dignity. Our work as human rights educators, for people who learn with us, is designed to break through the vicious cycle of humiliation and develop a human rights culture. We have to understand that politically we are in a very difficult time. Communism killed socialism. Socialism was a big vision for the world. I know it personally. Israel was a socialist country, now a growing capitalism. Global capitalism is killing democracy. The only thing we have left, the only viable ideology we have is human rights which takes the best from socialism and the best from democracy.

I believe that human rights is the truth and I like to call on Emmanuel Levinas, a noted French philosopher, who said: "If one person was missing from the world, the *absolute truth* would be different." I tell it with great humility, because I appropriate his thoughts by saying: If one person was missing from the world, human rights would be different. Human rights is about all people! Human rights is, in my opinion, the absolute truth, but a "truth" that evolves as human concerns and conditions change And as many people make up society and define its needs, the truth of human rights is imagined and reimagined to serve in the call for justice for all humanity. This idea gives tremendous value to each human being in the multitudes of six billion. Each one of us adds to the definition of this truth which we embrace individually and communally.

CONCLUSION

Transformational forms of learning produce inner change as well as contribute to the development of capacities that empower learners to bring changes in the social groups and structures of which they are a part. Human rights learning capacitates learners to function as agents of social justice so as to protect and implement human rights, moving to realization to avoid violations, for example, proactive actions to sustain justice. The most effective forms of human rights learning are those that engage learners in the implementation of human rights principles that concern their own lives. We have to move, to work, and to understand, that we move in the world as free yet responsible people. The river continues to flow and we gain our freedom as human rights protects us as we move in the world. Yet, we all need guidance in this noble quest, we need to learn how to move along the walks of life in dignity while protecting the dignity of each other. We need to examine the constraints, which we must consider with humility to avoid humiliation. In this process, guided by the human rights framework, we will make, hopefully, the correct decision about the kind of society we want to create for the future of humanity. We have no other option.

NOTE

Thank you to Satya Das for his assistance in preparing this article.

REFERENCES

Dias, C. (1993). Rural development: Grassroots education and human rights: Some Asian perspectives. In Mahoney & Mahoney (Eds.), *Human rights in the twenty-first century: A global challenge*. Dordecht/Boston/London: Martinus Nijhoff.

THREE

Human Rights

Four Generations of Practice and Development

Derek G. Evans

INTRODUCTION

THE PAST TWO CENTURIES have constituted one of the most turbulent periods in human social and political development. Efforts by historians to capture the essential character of this era invariably resort to the use of terms such as "revolution," "imperialism," and "extremes" (Hobsbawm, 1962; 1975; 1987; 1994).[1] Transformations in the structure and distribution of wealth and power, accompanied by the emergence of new paradigms competing for intellectual dominance and ideological hegemony, led ultimately to various forms of totalitarianism and, in terms of the real lives of ordinary people throughout the world, mass repression, suffering, and genocide.

At the same time, the democratic and humanist movements of this period established the moral basis and philosophical framework for the development of a common vision of human dignity. Through a wide range of struggles—such as the campaigns to abolish slavery, to establish child welfare and labor standards, to achieve electoral enfranchisement, the early decolonization movements in Latin America and parts of Asia, and the efforts to elaborate rules governing the conduct of war—"human rights" were increasingly recognized, defined, and extended to include ever-wider sectors of the human family. Further, the legal, social, and political standards required to implement and protect newly secured rights were increasingly put in place, particularly following World War II.[2]

Of course, the notion and valuing of human dignity, or even more specific principles such as equality, were not new. These ideas have found fundamental

25

expression and even practical support in various forms in all cultures and spiritual traditions through several millennia of human history. However, the notion of these moral assertions or values being defined and described legally as "rights"—universal entitlements that should be both realized and guaranteed—is quite new. As a global concept and undertaking, human rights in this sense has been part of our experience as a species only for the past three or four generations—the historical period present within the living memory of humanity—since the adoption of the UN Charter in 1945.

So pervasive is this "rights consciousness," and so powerful in shaping not only what we do but also how we understand and define ourselves both as individual persons and societies, defining our society, that it is easy to forget how recent a development the "rights revolution" has been (Ignatieff, 2000).[3] Indeed, the revolution is ongoing as our understanding of and approach to human rights continues to evolve and challenge us, both in terms of theory and in relation to practical implementation. This chapter will offer a conceptual framework for understanding the evolution of human rights theory and practice during the past half-century, and examine some of critical practical human rights challenges that will need to be addressed in the coming decades if the revolution is to survive and succeed.

Taking the Universal Declaration of Human Rights of 1948 as our starting point, the conceptual framework proposed will use the word *generation* in two different ways that will interweave somewhat. In one sense, generation refers to historical transitions—as in the changes that occur because of the passage of time from a passing generation to an emergent one. In another sense, we sometimes use generation to refer to deepening layers or significant qualitative shifts—as in the computer industry when a new approach to the shape or design of a processing system fundamentally alters the scene, and we speak of a fourth generation personal computer. That is the case also in the field of human rights—people speak of first, second, third, and fourth generation rights to refer to different types or categories of rights. In the case of human rights, these shifts tend to be inclusive as well as developmental—that is, emergent rights depend on and expand the overall framework, rather than make the former set of rights obsolete.

THE FIRST GENERATION: ESTABLISHING PRINCIPLES

Thinking in terms of historical transitions to begin with, the first generation consists of an approximately twenty-year period beginning with the end of World War II and the founding of the United Nations. This may be regarded as a period focused on establishing basic principles which are reflected in a number of key documents, notably the UN Charter itself,[4] which established that all member states undertake to "reaffirm faith in fundamental human rights, in the dignity and worth of the human person, in the equal rights of men and women and of nations large and small," and, through the UN, to promote "universal respect for, and observance of, human rights and fundamental freedoms for all without distinction as to race, sex, language, or religion."

The Universal Declaration of Human Rights (UDHR) of 1948 carried these general provisions farther by specifying what was actually understood to comprise these fundamental rights. Although only thirty articles in length, the UDHR is by any standard an astonishing document and a significant achievement; it is also a real pity that it is not read more widely, and that it does not appear more regularly as part of our public discourse. Part of its power rests in its unambiguous clarity:

> No one shall be subjected to torture or to cruel, inhuman or degrading treatment or punishment. (Article 5)
> No one shall be subjected to arbitrary arrest, detention or exile. (Article 9)
> Everyone, without any discrimination, has the right to equal pay for equal work. (Article 23)
> Everyone has the right to education. Education shall be free, at least in the elementary and fundamental stages. Elementary education shall be compulsory. Technical and professional education shall be made generally available and higher education shall be equally accessible to all on the basis of merit. (Article 26)

In setting out these fundamental rights, the declaration never uses the words *unless* or *except* to qualify or restrict their application—as in, unless you are suspected of being a terrorist, except if you are a woman, or except if you are poor. In the world of human rights, the term *universal* does not simply mean everywhere, but also is meant to include everyone.

This first generation was very conscious that it was working to establish human rights as a new language and ideology in an international context emerging from the rubble of global war and genocide. Because of this, they tended to focus on rights that asserted the dignity, integrity, and equality of the person—what are sometimes referred to as individual civil and political rights. These are also commonly referred to as "first generation rights" (Waltz, 2001).[5]

Aside from the charter and the declaration, the other developments during this period tended to be elaborations of them (such as the Genocide Convention, which accompanied the declaration in 1948, or the Convention on the Political Rights of Women in 1952) or previous standards (such as the Standard Minimum Rules on the Treatment of Prisoners in 1957, building on the Geneva Conventions). Perhaps most importantly, the work of this period established three principles that have guided all future human rights developments—or at least shaped the debate:

1. OWNERSHIP: that human rights belong to us, and to all of us—the ordinary people, individually and collectively. Just as the UN Charter and the
   Universal Declaration are not treaties agreed to by states, but are procla-
   mations made in the name of "We the People," so the rights set out are to
   be understood not as gifts bestowed or privileges granted by governments,
   but as entitlements that we possess as—and simply because we are—
   human beings;
2. OBLIGATION: that states or governments have an obligation to actively
   promote and protect these rights, and a responsibility to act to prevent
   violation of these rights internationally, and to be accountable to each
   other for their achievement and performance. Fulfillment of their obligations in relation to human rights is understood as the fundamental crite-
   rion for membership in the international community of nations;
3. INTEGRATION: that respect for human rights is the basis of peace and justice, that there is no hierarchy of rights, one more important than another.
   Rather, all rights set out in the UDHR are deemed to be fundamental, and
   the various forms of human rights are to be understood as "interdependent
   and indivisible."

THE SECOND GENERATION: STANDARD SETTING

These principles were significant achievements, but their practical effect in
concrete situations was very limited. The character of the Universal Declaration as a moral statement of the "human family" may have been one of its
virtues in some respects, but it also meant that it expressed only an "aspiration" and lacked any force of law to back it up. The work of the second generation was standard setting, translating the moral force of the UDHR into
legal instruments that "We the People" could not only believe in but could
actually use to realize and protect our rights and those of our neighbors.

The language of declarations and charters gave way to covenants, conventions and treaties. During the 1960s, '70s, and '80s, the bulk of what is
now referred to as "international human rights law" was formulated, and the
organization of movements and systems to begin to address real human rights
cases and concerns emerged. Means were established through the UN Commission on Human Rights and its specialized mechanisms to enable people
throughout the world to participate directly in claiming and defending their
rights, and to support others in doing so. Largely though the building of
regional and global Nongovernmental Organizations (NGOs) such as
Amnesty International, ordinary citizens began to find a place at the tables
traditionally reserved for states and diplomats, demanding opportunities to
hold their governments accountable to the standards of the international
community.[6] Indeed, many of the key legal safeguards developed during this
period, such as the Convention Against Torture, were the result of cam-

paigning initiatives, both in terms of substance and the generation of impetus, launched by NGOs.

The most significant components of the new statutory framework were the two covenants adopted as legal treaties in 1966: the International Covenant on Civil and Political Rights (ICCPR) and the International Covenant on Economic, Social and Cultural Rights (ICESCR). From these additional, more specific standards and instruments emerged (such as, respectively, the Convention Against Torture—1984—or the Convention for the Elimination of All Forms of Discrimination Against Women—1981). Although originally envisioned, according to the principle of integration, as a single, unified "Covenant on Human Rights," a decision was taken in the backrooms of the UN to produce two separate standards, a "Political Covenant" and an "Economic Covenant." The usual explanation of this development is that the treaties needed to be treated separately in order to facilitate gradual or progressive implementation, as it was deemed impossible to establish systems for guaranteeing economic rights. However, this appears to be more of a post facto justification, and the actual reason is probably that many governments found it more politically convenient or ideologically comfortable not even to try to do so.

As with the first generation, context is important in understanding and assessing the achievements of the second. This was the time of the cold war, the dismantling of colonialism, and the construction of a new polarized division of power based on proxy dictatorships allied with either the East or the West. The two covenants came to represent the competing sides—the United States and its allies championing the supposedly individual rights of the ICCPR; the Soviet Union and its allies championing the supposedly collective rights of the ICESCR.

Despite the significant progress made in formulating standards, human rights remained largely a theoretical proposition for many people around the world. Whether by design or chance, the two sides in the cold war conspired to denigrate the very notion of human rights, turning it into simply another ideological weapon with which to assert their superiority, attack their enemies, and, worse, to shield, excuse, and encourage the increasingly vicious repressions of their friends—both at home and throughout the ravaged and repressed "third world." This tacit conspiracy between the superpowers also resulted in an undermining of the integration principle of the indivisibility and interdependence of human rights by:

- establishing fundamentally different approaches to understanding and implementing the two sets of rights;
- establishing, for all practical intents and purposes, the preeminence of the individual, civil, and political rights;
- marginalizing the whole field of social, economic, and cultural rights from international scrutiny and accountability just as famine, poverty, and the

struggle for survival of unrecognized national groups increasingly became prevalent and even predominant characteristics and sources of crisis for the international community.

Perhaps ironically, or perhaps because the challenge they presented had become increasingly unavoidable, these economic, social, and cultural rights are also referred to as "second generation rights."

THE THIRD GENERATION:
COPING WITH THE "NEW WORLD ORDER"

Earlier we suggested that these two ways of thinking about the "generations" of human rights would weave together, and we have just seen that even considering only the historical progression is not a discrete undertaking. Matters of principle are not just a matter of the first generation, but are continually emerging as issues of struggle. It serves to remind us that we cannot take anything about human rights for granted—any achievements have been secured, and continue to be sustained, only through continuing vigilance and dedicated effort. It also forces us to recognize that the issues of principle are not abstractions. They have real consequences for real people, and compel us to take seriously the concrete and changing realities of human rights in our situation: What is the emerging nature of violations? What are the characteristics of the perpetrators? Who is being targeted? What forms of protection will be effective?

The decade of the 1990s was a period of massive change in the field of human rights. It has become commonplace for our society to point to September 11, 2001, as a pivotal moment when the world changed. For most of humanity, the world really did change in significant ways in recent times, in the period immediately following the collapse of another iconic structure of Western architecture in 1989—the Berlin Wall. It is true that we live in a radically different political environment than that into which most of us were born and in which our attitudes were shaped; however, it would appear that 9/11 marks the end of this transformation more than its beginning (Evans, 2004).

The end of the cold war created a vital opportunity to remove the ideological barriers that had served as the great excuse for not moving forward in the practical implementation of human rights and realizing a safer and healthier world for all humanity. In some ways, the so-called peace dividend did make a meaningful contribution to fulfilling these hopes. A range of positive measures were initiated: a formal reaffirmation of the Universal Declaration (Vienna Declaration—1993); the reform of the UN and other international agencies on the basis of "human rights mainstreaming" and the strengthening of civil society; a commitment to the promotion and protection of the rights of women (Beijing Action Plan—1995); and movement toward addressing impunity, through the establishment of an International Criminal Court (Statute of Rome—1999). The international community began to open up some important new fields for policy debate and decision making, such as the question of the responsibility and accountability of business, transnational corporations, armed opposition groups, and other non-state actors in relation to the promotion of human rights and the protection of the environment. Some nations, such as post-Apartheid South Africa, began to explicitly include elements of social, economic, and cultural rights, such as the right to education, within their constitutional frameworks.

The end of the cold war also meant, however, that whole regions of the world—such as sub-Saharan Africa and Central Asia—ceased overnight to hold any strategic interest for those with political and economic power, and were summarily marginalized and then abandoned. Just as suddenly, warlords and dictators who had served as superpower surrogates—created, sponsored, and to some extent controlled by either the Soviet Union or the United States—were loosed upon their peoples to pursue their own interests or private grievances without restraint, sometimes acting as agents of convenience for corporations and other forces of globalization in an increasingly unregulated world. Although the "cold" international war was over, the number of "hot" domestic conflicts proliferated from about thirty to more than eighty within the first five years of the decade.

These developments brought a significant change to the nature of the human rights violations experienced by ordinary people around the world. The pattern of violations no longer tended to be primarily one in which individuals were targeted by repressive governments because of their ideological beliefs or political involvements to be punished with arbitrary imprisonment and torture. Over the course of the 1990s, human rights violations escalated in severity and scale, and changed from being focused on the repression of beliefs to an assault on identities—whether gender, language, religion, or ethnicity. Violations occurred less as a strategy to achieve political hegemony or institutional control, and more as a characteristic of situations of social and structural and environmental breakdown.

In the wars that increasingly defined the lives of more and more people, the key question changed from being "What side are you on?" to simply "Who are you?" (Huntington, 1993). Instead of attempting simply to control or repress their enemies, the perpetrators of human rights violations increasingly sought to eliminate them. The forms of mass terrorism that the whole body of international human rights law was created to ensure would "never again" be part of the human experience erupted again throughout the world: genocide in Central Africa, ethnic cleansing in Eastern Europe, the slavery of women and children in large parts of Africa and Asia. For most people in much of the world, the world of the "peace dividend" turned out to be a much harsher and more dangerous place at the beginning of the new millennium than it had been at the beginning of the 1990s.

The decade between the fall of the Soviet Union in 1991 and the collapse of the Twin Towers in 2001 brought into effect a fundamental reorganization of the structure of power internationally, and of the experience of suffering. Since 1991 a peculiar and dangerous "new world order" took shape in which direction was based almost entirely on the interests of the sole remaining superpower. There was no alternative vision or competing authority to balance or restrain the will of the United States of America. In an environment often described as "globalization," many people became disillusioned with traditional politics, especially at the national level, because they felt it offered little opportunity to really make an effective difference. Globalization means, fundamentally, not some faceless blending into a worldwide cultural conformity but that the repressions, exploitations, and conflicts that may previously have been seen as characteristics of a distant "third world" have become shared realities for communities everywhere. Concerned citizens increasingly focused their efforts either in their local communities, or at the level of global movements. It was left to ordinary people around the world to form networks of local initiative, such as the antiglobalization movement or the World Social Forum, to try to express or "constitute" an alternative basis of power (Lukacs, 2005).[7]

Every age is guided by a dominant cultural ideology or social myth. Though it is usually easier to recognize in retrospect, the dominant social myth reveals the key assumptions, preoccupations, and perspectives of an era. A hundred years ago, the social myth reflected a vision of inexorable progress and might have been something like: "Every day in every way things are getting better and better." During the 1960s and 1970s, a period of creativity and activism, it might have been a hopeful blend of "give peace a chance," "the global village," and "think globally act locally." We seem to have just passed from a time when the dominant social myth, at least in certain places, was reflected in phrases such as "having it all." How would we name the dominant social myth in the world we share today? It would appear that we are increasingly presented with and persuaded to adopt a view of the world as "a place of scarcity, threat, and isolation." Interestingly, in the human rights field the term *third generation rights* refers to collective, environmental, and development rights.

THE FOURTH GENERATION: MAKING RIGHTS REAL

A decade ago, the international community gathered in the largest human rights conference ever convened in the history of the UN. The purpose of the conference was, ostensibly, to examine the current status and challenges facing the development of human rights and to agree a strategy for overcoming them. The formal outcome of the Vienna Conference was that the international community joined together to reaffirm its unanimous commitment to the Universal Declaration on Human Rights and the principles that underlie it. This was no small achievement or mere diplomatic formality; the very survival of the UDHR, in fact, was under serious threat.

As in the case in 1966 when the political and economic covenants were set apart in the back rooms of the Cold War, the conference in 1993 was a behind-the-scenes battleground of serious attempts to either ditch or significantly dilute the UDHR and the definitions of human rights that are available to us. Strange, perhaps uncomfortable, and certainly temporary alliances were formed. Governments such as of those of the United States, Cuba, and Iran sought to undermine the authority of the UDHR, apparently because they wanted to limit the role of activist human rights defenders in civil society. Governments such as that of India sought to restrict the UDHR, purportedly in order to assert the preeminence of social and economic rights over individual and political rights. Governments such as that of Indonesia, at the time, sought to reduce the influence of the UDHR in order to assert the predominance of particular religious or cultural values in interpreting universal standards such as the prohibition of torture. Some governments, such as that of China, sought to undermine the UDHR because they wanted to assert the priority of state sovereignty over any form of international accountability for human rights practices.

Just as with the 1966 events, very little of this information will be found in the official histories, and the lesson we must derive, yet again, is that we can't take anything for granted. Indeed, that is the essential lesson represented by the UDHR—that human rights are inherent, not granted. The UDHR came into existence in 1948 and survived intact in 1993 only because concerned people from around the world came together, educated themselves, mobilized their neighbors, and exposed and confronted the efforts of many governments to undermine the UDHR. They raised their voices and shamed governments into recognizing that the UDHR and the rights it proclaims are not theirs to bestow or to cancel. In what may come to be recognized as one of the first of the globalization confrontations, a broad popular movement of NGOs demonstrated that human rights belong to "we the people," and that we are determined to hold onto them.

One of the things we have learned from our experience of human rights violations during the past three generations is that persons who have suffered and survived severe trauma, such as torture, tend to experience and express specific behavioral dysfunctions. We also know that if they are not effectively addressed, these behaviors are transferred within family and community systems for at least four generations, and that this is the case even in situations where there has been no direct contact between the ones who experienced the torture and the latter generations. We know it is at least four generations because that is the current extent of the research base, but the effects are probably, in fact, much longer.

The period of massive change continues, and the international community is faced with some major challenges if human rights are to become a meaningful reality in this decade. In the historical sense, we are at the threshold of the fourth generation of the human rights movement. We are presented with the challenge of breaking the cycle of human rights violations, of the behavioral dysfunctions that mark our human family—and that are increasingly extending their devastating effects on all political, social, and natural systems. In the thematic sense, in a world characterized by mass terror—state sponsored or otherwise—it is vital and urgent that we learn how to break the cycle of perceived mutual victimization.

Human rights is a commitment and a vision that is in constant development—both in theory and in practice. Despite serious threats, the core principles originally set out in the UDHR in 1948 have survived; despite obstacles and setbacks, the trend over the decades has consistently been to seek to achieve greater universality—extension of the scope and application of rights. There are at least four concrete priorities that need to comprise a human rights agenda for this generation.

1. We must come to terms seriously and definitively with the issue of impunity, that is, that we break the cycle by which those who commit violations continue to do so because, fundamentally, they know they can get away with it. The International Criminal Court must become a fully operational agency enjoying universal cooperation and application.

2. We must begin seriously to address the issue of responsibility for human rights in an inclusive manner. While recognizing the fundamental responsibility of government authorities for the promoting and protecting human rights, at the same time we must begin to frame as legal obligations the responsibilities and accountabilities of the various nonstate agencies that increasingly, whether legitimately or not, exercise quasi-state powers, such as corporations, commercial cartels, armed opposition groups, regional warlords, religious authorities, and the like.

3. We must come to terms with the need to define, set standards, and agree upon measures of accountability for social, economic, and cultural rights—including environmental sustainability—in a manner similar to that by which previous generations engaged the challenge of individual, civil, and political rights.

4. We must make education on human rights, including fundamental principles as well as actual entitlements, a persistent concern and perennial commitment. We should renew the understanding and vision of the pioneers of the first generation that human rights are a fundamental prerequisite for peace by placing an emphasis on learning the practice of recon-

ciliation. That is, we need to adopt as an urgent priority for education the development of skills for building peace—not simply by pulling conflicted peoples apart and separating contending entities, but by learning how to practice respect and tolerance because we recognize that we share the planet and that—whether we like it or not—we are in each other's future.[8]

The challenge facing the fourth generation is to make the coming decade the era of implementation, the era of making rights real—for ourselves, and for each other. The good news is that most of these things are within our grasp, if we have the will and the determination to address them.

NOTES

Derek Evans teaches and consults on strategic evaluation, conflict transformation, and human rights. He is a former Executive Director of Naramata Centre, one of Canada's foremost retreat and experiential learning centers (1999–2004). During the 1990s, he served as Deputy Secretary General of Amnesty International, with responsibility for research, policy, and strategic direction of the global human rights organization. Evans is a Fellow of the Canadian Academy of Independent Scholars and an Institute Associate of the Wosk Centre for Dialogue at Simon Fraser University. His most recent book is *Before the War: Reflections in a New Millennium* (Northstone, 2004). He lives in the Okanagan valley of British Columbia, Canada.

Material for this essay was drawn from two keynote addresses: "Making Rights Real" at *Seeking Justice: Human Rights in Our Communities*, a public symposium held at Simon Fraser University (Vancouver, November 2003); "The Principle of Universality," *Human Rights for All*, an international law conference convened by Amnesty International (Sana'a, Yemen, April 2004).

1. For an insightful and accessible treatment of the period see, for example, Eric Hobsbawm's four volume study of the period from the French Revolution in 1789 to the collapse of the Soviet Union in 1991: *The Age of Revolution: 1789–1848* (London: Weidenfeld & Nicholson, 1975); *The Age of Capital: 1848–1875* (London: Weidenfeld & Nicholson, 1962); *The Age of Empire: 1875–1914* (London: Weidenfeld & Nicholson, 1987); *The Age of Extremes: the Short Twentieth Century 1914–1991* (London: Penguin Group, 1994).

2. Some of the first organizations with an explicit understanding of themselves as "human rights" campaigning agencies operating with a global consciousness were formed during the early part this era. Typically, they were motivated by broad humanitarian concerns, though usually focused on a particular issue or mandate. Some of these first human rights organizations continue to function today, such as the Anti-Slavery Society (formed in 1823) and the International Committee of the Red Cross (founded in 1863). Nongovernmental Organizations dedicated to working on the promotion and protection of human rights as a defined field of concern emerged only during the latter part of the period, notably the International League for Human Rights (1941), Amnesty International (launched as a campaigning movement in 1961), and Human Rights Watch (formally established in 1988).

3. Canadian philosopher and historian Michael Ignatieff used the term *rights revolution* in his 2000 Massey Lectures to describe the way human rights have become, since the late 1940s, "the dominant language of the public good around the globe"— the surviving and defining ideological formulation of our time. Michael Ignatieff, *The Rights Revolution* (Toronto: Anansi, 2000).

4. Most key UN Documents concerning human rights, including the UN Charter and the Universal Declaration on Human Rights, are easily available at: http://www.un.org/aboutun/index.html.

5. Because of the initial focus on individual civil and political rights, and the subsequent tendency to restrict or identify the definition of human rights to this aspect during the cold war, many over the years have expressed the criticism that the UDHR lacks "universality" in that it predominantly represents Western cultural values and fails to adequately reflect Asian, Islamic, or other perspectives. It is clearly the case that the modern language of human rights derives largely from the political experience and legal traditions of America and Europe, and that these were the primary influences guiding the principal drafters of the UDHR. Context, of course, needs to be taken into consideration but, even given the limitations of thinking and the composition of the UN at the time, the UDHR is remarkable for the extent to which its contents were shaped by the representatives of small nations from all regions of the world. Although Eleanor Roosevelt of the United States and Rene Cassin of France were recognized as the prime movers behind the UDHR, the actual text was largely drafted by Canada's John Humphrey. Peng-chen Chang of China, Hernan Santa Cruz of Chile, and Charles Malik of Lebanon were recognized, among many others, as significant contributors. See Susan Waltz, "Universalizing Human Rights: The Role of Small States in the Construction of the UDHR," *Human Rights Quarterly, 23(1)* (February 2001).

6. The awarding of the Nobel Prize for peace to Amnesty International in 1977 may be seen as a recognition of the significance of this new dynamic—the significant and legitimate role of NGOs in mobilizing public opinion to shape public policy. Similarly, the awarding of the prize in 1999 to Medicins Sans Frontieres may be seen as recognition of the importance of renewing efforts to promote the integration for human rights and social and economic development.

7. The historian John Lukacs has observed: "The world is governed, especially in the democratic age, not by the accumulation of money, or even of goods, but by the accumulation of opinions. History is formed by, and politics dependent upon, how and what large masses of people are thinking and desiring, fearing and hating." Lukacs, *Democracy and Populism* (New Haven: Yale University Press, 2005). A key element in being a "superpower" rests in whether the opinions of the people of a country matter on the international level. The campaigns of the antiglobalization movement, and the challenge of human rights education more generally, may be understood as efforts to engage and influence public opinion to support peace, justice, sustainability, and the other positive values.

8. The issue of humanitarian intervention offers a clear example of both the evolutionary nature of human rights and the integral relation between peace and human rights—and one that is particularly relevant to Canadians. It also demonstrates the

contextual interweaving of theory and practice in human rights development. Although not originally conceived as a method of human rights protection, Lester Pearson basically invented UN military intervention as an application of the principles reflected in the UN Charter and practical component of international relations in 1958, and in so doing made it a defining element of our national identity for the past two generations. It played a growing role in maintaining peace and protecting human rights until the strategic shifts of the early 1990s. Romeo Dallaire has rubbed our collective noses in the conspiracy of duplicity, double standards, and dereliction of duty that led to the abandonment of humanitarian intervention as an active component of the international human rights system, and that arguably resulted in the betrayal and extrajudicial killing of almost one hundred thousand people a week in Rwanda in the late spring and early summer of 1994. One of the more important developments signaling the emergence of the "fourth generation" has been the work of the International Commission on Intervention and State Sovereignty, in which Lloyd Axworthy has played a leading and instrumental role. Since 2001, the commission has laid a groundwork for reviving humanitarian intervention by rejecting the notion of national sovereignty as an absolute and recasting it as constrained by the obligation to actively protect human rights—an obligation creating responsibilities on both national governments and the international community.

REFERENCES

Evans, D. (2004). *Before the war: Reflections in a new millennium*. Kelowna, CAN: Northstone.

Hobsbawm, E. (1962). *The age of capital: 1848–1875*. London: Weidenfeld & Nicholson.

Hobsbawm, E. (1975). *The age of revolution: 1789–1848*. London: Weidenfeld & Nicholson.

Hobsbawm, E. (1987). *The age of empire: 1875–1914*. London: Weidenfeld & Nicholson.

Hobsbawm, E (1994). *The age of extremes: the short twentieth century 1914–1991*. London: Penguin Group.

Huntington, S. (1993). The clash of civilizations? *Foreign Affairs, 72(2)*.

Ignatieff, M. (2000). *The rights revolution*. Toronto: Anansi.

Lukacs, J. (2005). *Democracy and populism*. New Haven: Yale University Press.

Waltz, S. (2001). Universalizing human rights: The role of small states in the construction of the UDHR. *Human Rights Quarterly, 23(1)*.

FOUR

Are We All Global Citizens or Are Only Some of Us Global Citizens?

The Relevance of This Question to Education

Nigel Dower

INTRODUCTION

ARE WE ALL GLOBAL CITIZENS or are only some of us global citizens? If we accept the latter claim, does that make global citizenship elitist? That is, is its advocacy a new form of cultural imperialism? A new manifestation of the division between haves and have-nots, global citizens having a certain status/privilege/power/obligations of "noblesse oblige"? My argument will be twofold. First, that in some respects we are all global citizens, for instance because of a certain moral or legal status, but in other respects only some people are global citizens by virtue of their self-descriptions and/or active engagement with the world. But in the latter sense, there is nothing essentially or inevitably elitist about this, though of course there are dangers of elitism as well.

The relevance of this to education is as follows. Insofar as we are all global citizens anyway, we are not educating people to *become* global citizens but rather educating them to become aware of themselves as having this status and of a set of opportunities that go along with this status. But insofar as being a global citizen is a matter of adopting a mode of self-conception and/or a manner of active engagement with the world, then the encouragement of this is an important aim of citizenship education and related programs such as development education. The latter moral judgment is of course premised on the assumption that the more people come to accept global responsibility, the better for the world.

I shall argue that both levels of being a global citizen are important to citizenship education. It may be thought that I am ducking two important questions here: first, if both levels are important, which is more important—that we produce a lot of educated young adults who at least have a basic knowledge of the world and an openness to it but who, apart from having certain a general attitude of tolerance of diversity and sympathy for those who suffer elsewhere in the world, do not actually *do* very much? Or that we produce a rather smaller number of educated people who become active global citizens and the future "movers and shakers" of the world? Second, does all this emphasis on global citizenship education (at either level) conflict with the normal agenda of ordinary citizenship education, either in competing for time and resources devoted to each, or in presenting conflicting sets of values? I shall argue later in the chapter, that the three goals—basic global citizen education, education for active global citizenship, and citizenship education itself—are largely (or rather can be, if properly conceived) complementary to one other. Generally, the same processes of education will lead to "the many" becoming globally aware and "the few" taking it farther to active engagement, and generally any form of citizenship education worthy of the name must be globally oriented. There is of course a further question: What exactly are the values that should inform global citizenship or our global orientation? Since the values accepted may vary considerably, does that undermine the project of global citizenship education? I shall argue that this poses no more serious a problem than does the fact that citizens qua active citizens promote a wide range of goals. The latter is consistent with there being a central core of values internal to citizenship (as this is ordinarily understood). Even if it is claimed that the core values of citizenship are contested, but that this does not prevent the acceptance of citizenship education, then it should no more do so for global citizenship education. I shall elaborate on all these points toward the end of the chapter, but see my first and main task to be the elucidation of the idea of global citizenship itself, using the "all or some?" question as the frame on which to set my conception out.

IN WHAT SENSE(S) ARE WE ALL GLOBAL CITIZENS?

It is customary to distinguish between an ethical component and an institutional component of global citizenship, or of its close equivalent cosmopolitanism.

THE ETHICAL

If someone says, "I am a global/world citizen," then at the very least she is saying something like: I accept that all human beings matter and that among other duties I have as an individual I have responsibilities that are transnational. Such a person could merely be making such a claim about herself, but in all probability she is really making a general claim not just about herself but about human beings generally. That is, there are universal norms and values that either ought to be recognized by others generally or in fact are so recognized, and that all people have in principle global responsibility toward one another.

Someone, then, who accepts global citizenship is generally making a claim that all human beings have a certain moral status, and that we have moral responsibility toward one another in this global moral domain/ sphere or notional community. That is, there are two components to a global ethic—a claim about universal values and norms and a claim about transboundary obligations (see, e.g., Dower, 1998).

Examples of this way of thinking may be given. Nussbaum, famously, in her case for cosmopolitan education suggested four aspects of our being global citizens, whether we realize it or not (Nussbaum, 1996):

First, "Through cosmopolitan education, we learn more about ourselves," since if we really know about the world, we and our children distinguish what is central to human life and what is accidental to their way of life;
Second, "We make headway solving problems that require international cooperation," such as population problems and environmental problems;
Third, "We recognize moral obligations to the rest of the world that are real and that otherwise would go unrecognized," especially our duties to tackle world poverty;
Fourth, "We make a consistent and coherent argument based on distinctions we are prepared to defend," in that it is only on the basis of genuinely global values that we can find a principled basis for genuine respect in a multicultural society.

Similarly, Piet Hein the Danish poet, some forty years ago, pronounced at an international conference, "We are global citizens with tribal souls" (quoted in Barnaby, 1988, 192). He did not expand on the reasons but in the context one can surmise that he was reflecting the fact that we share a common humanity, that we are collectively responsible for global problems such as environmental degradation and ought to take collective action, and that we do have transboundary obligations toward those who suffer in the world. But our lack of global souls means we are not aware of or at least sufficiently aware of these facts and dwell too much in more localized identities and concerns.

THE INSTITUTIONAL

If we turn to the "institutional" side of global citizenship, the side that captures what the "citizenship" bit might mean, we can identify various factors. Actually, the word *institutional* is a little restrictive. It is shorthand for something

entailed by citizenship that goes beyond a claim about moral values. It is generally taken to be some form of institution, but it could be something else,
such as *membership* in a community of some kind.

Before looking at various positive claims, let me put on one side a move
that stops this part of the discussion in its tracks. This is to say that, whatever
we may make of the ethical side of global citizenship, that is, moral claims
about global responsibility and belonging to a single moral domain, we simply aren't global citizens in an institutional or political sense. For that we
would need a world government or world state to be citizens of (see, e.g.,
Walzer, 1996). This is to take an overly robust view about what the idea of
"citizen" needs to convey. The idea of citizenship is contestable and we can
in effect extract from it whatever strands we feel to be appropriate. At least,
I hope to show that it is plausible to see global citizenship having, as things
are now, an institutional strand and indeed as part of this a political strand.

First, the idea of citizenship in its most general usage is the idea of membership in a community. This is actually broader than what is caught by the
word *institution* because it covers the idea of membership of a real social group
whose bonds and connections are more informal than suggested by the word
institution. I can illustrate this with an example from Aldo Leopold, the ecol-
ogist, who urged us to think of human beings not as masters of nature but as
"plain members and citizens of the land community" (Leopold, 1949, 204).
This idea of a biotic community includes several elements, not simply that of
actual ecological interdependence but also the idea of obligations toward
other members of this community. This, of course, goes beyond the sphere of
all humans, but the point I want to extract from it is that for Leopold this
community was a real moral community. Similarly even if we do not go that
far and remain within an anthropocentric perspective, we can make sense of
there being a real community of all human beings that reflects not just global
interdependence, but is also made up of myriads of smaller social bonds and
shared moral practices and values. This membership in a global community
goes beyond the merely ethical. A claim that we have responsibility toward
one another is just that—an ethical claim—not a claim about actual community, which is what the "citizenship" bit minimally captures.

Of great significance to our enquiry is the emergence of global civil society—one of the more encouraging manifestations of globalization. Now, as I
shall go on to indicate in a moment, much of global civil society has to do
with politics and with governance, but a lot of it does not—informal networks of shared concerns and interests, churches and so on. A lot of it is simply a manifestation of what Scholte calls the globalization of community
(Scholte, 2000).

Second, if we turn to the more obviously *institutional* aspects of citizenship we can see three aspects of this—the legal, the political, and the non-
legal/nonpolitical. As T. H. Marshall made very clear is his citizenship stud-

ies, one part of citizenship is the bearing of legal rights (Marshall, 1973). Whether these are political rights, civil rights, or social rights, these rights are constitutive of citizenship. Transferred to the global sphere, we can see that international human rights law produces the international analogue of citizenship rights within the state. We all now have the status of being citizens under an international legal system. This may not be a lot, but it is actually quite significant.

Even if we are not formally citizens of a world state, there is still a sense in which we are world citizens in a political sense. If the active part of citizenship is about participation in the public decision-making processes that affect our lives, then there are various ways in which people can engage in what is generally called global governance. In between the old internationalist model of Westphalian governance and a radically new form of governance in the form of world federalism lie various possibilities of governance. Tony McGrew (McGrew, 2000, 407) has suggested, for instance, three models of global democracy—first, the internationalist model in which global civil society in the form of NGOs acts in a cooperative but also critically supportive role in relation to states in the international community (what may be called a neo-Westphalian model); second, NGOs and more informal networks operating in a more communitarian mode, almost bypassing the international system, in what Linklater has called a post-Westphalian world (Linklater, 1998); and, third, the cosmopolitan democracy model of Held and Archibugi, which advocates more formal representation of people at the global level (Archibugi & Held, 1995).

While the latter—cosmopolitan democracy—is, like world government, an idea not yet realized, there are grounds for seeing the other two models as currently emerging. Either way, global civil society, certainly as manifested in the formal institutions of NGOs, constitutes an important factor in global governance. Indeed, Mary Robinson recently said: "There are two superpowers in the world today—the USA and Global Civil Society." Not everyone, I should note, is convinced about the significance or value of global civil society or NGOs in thinking about global citizenship—NGOs, for instance, may be seen as neither democratic nor part of global governance, nor the right vehicle of citizenship. Nevertheless, for many who advocate global citizenship, it is immersion in NGOs and the like which contributes an important part of political global citizenship in the world now.

Another part of the political aspects of global citizenship is operating through the political channels of one's own state—i.e., exercising one's ordinary citizenship with a view to global issues—campaigning to get UK foreign aid increased, for instance, or trying to stop the war in Iraq. This is how Bhikhu Parekh has characterized global citizenship, namely, globally oriented citizenship (Parekh, 2003, 44). Certainly being a global citizen need not be in conflict with being a citizen at all. They can complement one another and global citizenship can be expressed through citizenship. (This is not to deny that in other contexts, global citizenship moral priorities may sometimes clash with citizenship priorities.)

It will no doubt have occurred to some readers that the two aspects of political citizenship I have just identified are hardly evidence of everyone being citizens—unlike, for instance, the idea that we are all global citizens because we all bear human rights. So we are moving toward the second way of thinking about global citizenship, namely the idea that only some people are global citizens. Nevertheless, I want to insist on the point that although only some people actually get involved in NGOs for global concerns or press their MPs about global issues, the fact that the NGO network has developed bears witness to the fact that it is now possible for people generally to engage in such activities. Even people who live in countries with few NGOs and countries that are not democratic, are discovering increasing possibilities through the Internet and global communication networks to take up global issues (including the defense of their own rights, addressed to the world and not just their own country). There's much more to be said about this issue— and I return to it later on—but merely note now that the fact that within a state not all people do engage in active politics and not all people have the same access or ready resources for so doing does not prevent us from saying that they are still citizens of their country.

ARE ONLY SOME OF US GLOBAL CITIZENS?

It might be felt there is an air of unreality about the various claims made above—the world described is one of aspiration for those global citizens who see the world now as they would like it to be—a world of universal values, generally shared moral concerns, a real international human rights culture, widespread institutions so related to each other as to form a coherent form of global governance, and so on. But the reality is otherwise.

Now, the idea that the reality is otherwise may come from two rather different quarters—from those who thinks that none of us are really global citizens (even those who think they are) and those who think that some of us are global citizens and some of us—perhaps most of us—are not. And these two positions can both be motivated by two rather different normative agendas. The two positions might be put forward from the point of view of someone who is sympathetic to global citizenship—for instance, to the view that it would be good if we did become global citizens or that it is good that some people are now global citizens and, hopefully, more or all will one day become so. On the other hand, the two positions might spring from the opposite normative perspective—that it would be bad thing if we became global citizens, or that it is bad thing that some people now act as global citizens, because it is, in their analysis, elitist, culturally imperialist, and so on.

For the purposes of the current exposition I shall focus on the claim, made by both sympathizers and critics, that some of us are global citizens and others not. The other claim, that none of us are global citizens, I leave for the moment—I have discussed it elsewhere, in any case (Dower, 2002: see also Dower & William, 2003 for a wide range of perspective on the idea of global citizenship; and Heater, 2002 for detailed background analysis of the idea).

THE SYMPATHETIC ANALYSIS

Why might someone sympathetic to global citizenship want to make the claim that only some people are global citizens? Again, we can distinguish between the ethical element and the institutional element, though they are here less clearly distinct.

A global citizen on this view is someone who accepts and acts on a global ethic. If someone does not accept let alone act on a global ethic, then he or she is a global citizen. Whether or not the person who accepts a global ethic claims that his or her values are applicable to all others (some may, but some may not make this universal claim), the fact is that many people, probably most people, do not accept it. It may be that most people when pressed would say their ethic is implicitly universal in the sense that, if asked, they would say, "Yes, all people have a moral status," and, "Yes, one should sometimes feel obliged to help the starving overseas." But such an implicit "back of one's consciousness" ethic isn't the same as an active ethical concern about the world—and it is this active global ethic that is needed for someone to be a global citizen.

In short, what makes someone a global citizen is a certain form of con-sciousnesses. It may be centrally a self-description. Someone who says he's a global citizen and means it is a global citizen. (If he doesn't do very much except say this and mean it, he may be a rather poor global citizen!) But it may equally be a description used by a third party to describe others because of what they are, believe, or do. Someone who cares about world poverty, or joins Amnesty International, or advocates an ethic of global responsibility might not describe herself as a world citizen, but in effect she is doing and thinking the things that constitute global citizenship. Someone working for a UN agency might or might not describe himself as a global citizen, but if what he did was motivated by a genuine concern to improve the world, then others might so describe him anyway. Rather more controversial maybe would be the case of a businessman jetting across the world. A Danish busi-nessman once described himself as a global citizen to Richard Falk because he saw himself as part of global economic community of business (Falk, 1994).

Whether the description "global citizens" is a self-description or a description by another in virtue of his or her attitudes or activities, it will partly be in terms of the moral commitments involved, but it will also be, as the examples above show, partly in terms of the various kinds of social reality or institutional arrangements involved. Suppose I am part of what Scholte calls a "cosmopolitan solidarity" (Scholte, 2000), say, part of Greenpeace campaigning to save whales; then I am really part of a global community—along with others all over the world who share my values and recognize each other as a community of concern. This is a global community of which I may be a member, but it is not a universal community of all human beings. On this reading there are lots of different global or transnational communities—some formal, some informal—and many people, but not all, may be members of several of them. They do not have the same values and norms, and quite emphatically they do not constitute one big moral community. It is in virtue of these communities that some people are not just morally but also really global citizens and others not. On this reasoning, the Danish businessman is really a global citizen by virtue of his role in the global economy, the UN agency official a global citizen as part of another global community, and supporters of NGOs global citizens as part of myriads of other global communities, and so on.

Before I turn to the rival interpretation of these facts, it is worth noting that while supporters of global citizenship may stress that only some people are global citizens now and it is an aspiration that more should become so, generally those who are sympathetic are more likely to adopt a two-tier approach. That is, one can claim—and it is the position I have developed in my own writings—that in some respects we are all global citizens and in other respects only some of us are (Dower, 2003). In other words, we can combine the main elements of both approaches as I have outlined them so far. Although some of what I would say will emerge as we proceed, this is not my task here.

CRITICAL ASSESSMENT

The critic can, of course, home in on many different aspects of global citizenship, but I shall focus on the claim that it is ethically inappropriate and that in particular the fact that some people are global citizens and other are not is itself grounds for moral concern. The heart of much criticism is the assumption of universal values. Many critics are relativists, communitarians, or postmodernists who for various reasons deny that there are universal values—either in the sense that there aren't any universally or even generally shared values or in the sense that we can talk coherently of values that are universally valid or applicable, that is, that ought to be accepted by all reasonable people. On this basis, global citizenship as a universal category is actually incoherent, but more to the point, the fact that some people are global citizens in the sense that they espouse global values is a matter for concern, particularly if those people believe that these values are universal values. Those who accept a global ethic and work toward realizing it are in effect attempting to impose their values on others. They may or may not realize that they are doing this but that is what they are doing. If, for instance, one believes in global community, one may act as if there is a far greater degree of harmony in the world than there really is, and this may mask real power conflicts in which those with the dominant discourse (as reflected in the universal values of self-styled global citizens) usually have the upper hand.

As someone in the self-styled global citizenship camp I do not, of course, agree. This may be an instance of false consciousness, but at root there is the issue of whether we can forge or discern a basic morality that does indeed transcend cultural differences. What we need is a global ethic that somehow combines transnational responsibility with sensitivity toward different cultures without tolerating everything done in the name of culture—an ethic I have called "solidarist pluralism" (Dower, 1998). There is much more to be said about this issue in fundamental ethics. Sufficient to say here that if a global citizen is someone who affirms universal values and transnational responsibility, then it is bound to be the case that from the point of view of the nonglobal citizen, a global citizen who says that we are all global citizen whether we like it or not, is imposing a definition on someone who does not accept it. That is inevitable. But by the same token the skeptic is denying a description to the global citizen (at least in the sense intended by the global citizen) which the global citizen accepts for himself, and thus imposing his nondescription.

But there is another strand of criticism that also homes in on another aspect of elitism—namely the privileged status of the global citizen. Those who are active global citizens either by self-description or because of what others recognize in their style of life are simply privileged people—mainly in the rich North, who have sufficient wealth, leisure, opportunity, access to organizations, and so on. Most people even in richer countries, let alone poorer countries, simply lack these things. They lack resources, knowledge, access to political power, technology, and indeed the self-confidence that they can make a difference. Often the challenge is merely a matter of survival. Even if we consider rights that are supposed to be enjoyed by all, in fact there are great variations in the world. In many parts of the world human rights are not even incorporated in domestic law, let alone protected. To say we all enjoy rights is a mockery, given the realities of the world. Thus, those who are global citizens belong to a global elite and reflect the power imbalances of the world.

FURTHER DEFENSE

While I am sympathetic to some of the worries about potential elitism and potential cultural imperialism, much of this line of thought I cannot accept, especially the implication that somehow global citizenship is a bad thing or that it is bad thing that those of us who call ourselves global citizens do so.

At the heart of this lies the issue: Are those of us who are privileged in various ways—in terms of wealth, resources, abilities, opportunities—genuinely able to so act as to make things better for others? At the heart of much cynicism about altruism is a kind of pessimism about the possibility of change for the better, at least as brought about by those who are already better off. Global citizenship is, I believe, profoundly grounded in a kind of optimism, that things can get better and can get better through the voluntary efforts of those who are in a position to act.

To take an example: many self-styled global citizens will be well-off middle-class people who are part of a consumer culture and beneficiaries of the global economy. As such they are part of the problem, we may say. But does that mean we cannot genuinely and effectively work for better trade relations, ethical consuming, and the like? If little changes, is that because we are necessarily expressing bad faith? Of is it perhaps because actually not enough people have adopted this ethical perspective anyway?

Of course, vast numbers of people, especially in poorer countries, simply lack the resources and knowledge to become active self-styled global citizens. But that does not entail that those of us who are are somehow unfairly enjoying a state unfairly denied others. Others in the world will not come to enjoy the full status of being a world citizen unless those of us who are in a position to enjoy it do what we can to change the world. That some of us are at one level self-conscious global citizens represents not an elitist impediment to a more equal world, but rather the vanguard in the move toward a more equal world.

GLOBAL CITIZENSHIP EDUCATION

In the light of the above account I can now explore a little more fully the implications of all this for education.

WHICH EMPHASIS?

First, there is the question whether the emphasis of global citizenship education (the question whether it is done as part of citizenship education or not I come to later) should be on getting children to accept the universal status of global citizenship—to accept that all human beings are global citizens in a basic sense and to accept that they are themselves global citizens in this sense. Or should the emphasis be on making children aware of the idea of being active engaged global citizens and encouraging them to see themselves as becoming such engaged activists in some chosen field of interest?

While there may be a case for having more advanced classes/courses relating to active global citizenship either at the top end of high school level or at college level, my primary concern is with the nature of the more basic education that might be given to all children either at primary school level or at lower secondary school level. At this level it seems to me that the kind of education appropriate would actually serve both purposes. That is, the kind of education that gets children to see themselves as having a certain status in the world—as accepting that certain core values are universal (whether expressed as human rights or in other ways) and accepting that in some basic moral sense we belong to a single community of humankind—*is* the kind of education that will lead those who are naturally activist or have leadership qualities combined with a strong moral sense of responsibility, to become global citizens in the activist sense later on (or even within the school contest—such as trying to get their school shop to get fair-traded goods).

It is, I think, a mistake to present global citizenship in such a way that children are made to feel that they should later feel guilty or inadequate if they do not become active global citizens. The strains of psychological commitment are such that it is unrealistic to suppose that everyone could become the latter. Nor indeed do I think that the creation of seriously better world requires this. What we do need is a combination. Those who are active in campaigning, advocacy, and leadership for the right global values need to be combined with and backed by a general populace that has the right global attitudes and a willingness to play their part in the smaller ways that make for responsible moral agency generally. As I have indicated earlier, although the active/passive distinction is useful for analysis, we are really talking of a continuum, from very active through the completely passive-but-with-the-right-attitude to, beyond that, the status of being a global citizen without even being aware of it.

It is worth noting in passing that a child could be taught about universal moral status and global responsibilities without the terminology of global citizenship being used. But even here what is important is that the child accepts a global perspective, and this is a sufficient condition of our saying that someone else is being taught to be a global citizen in the basic sense (though in some respects she is a global citizen, whatever her values and whatever she is taught). This basic moral orientation includes playing one's part in collective efforts such as recycling practices, being willing to participate in the political process to the extent of voting in elections, being willing to be charitable in the face of human suffering, and being prepared to take part in ethical consuming (where this has become an available standard option, since it is the activist who does so *before* it becomes standard). You may say that even all this goes a long way beyond how most people behave. This is true. But I still think that it is within the realms of the possible to try and get this achieved in global citizenship education (in a way in which getting everyone to be *activist* global citizens is not).

RELATIONSHIP TO CITIZENSHIP EDUCATION

What about the relationship to citizenship education? There's a practical question here and a more theoretical one: First, should global citizenship education be part of citizenship education and seen as something that happens on a separate track? In fact, there is a further question here: Should global citizenship education be part of, as an explicit section of, other possible subjects (such as modern studies; environmental studies; religious studies), or should it be, rather, infused in courses generally, not as a separate section but as a lens, so to speak, through which many issues are discussed? While I think that there is a case for seeing all education increasingly informed by the global approach, and that we need to be pragmatic about where exactly global citizenship might fit inside other courses (in some schools, modern studies might be the place; in others, religious studies, etc.), I do think there is a case for seeing the topic of global citizenship as being an integral part of citizenship education, for the following three kinds of reasons:

1. If they are taught in separate parts of the school curriculum, the impression may be given that they are quite different subjects, which compete for resources and attention and may have conflicting agendas. Since none of these impressions is to be accepted, it would be better to have a frame that suggests the contrary.

   Now, this of course raises the more theoretical question: Do citizenship and global citizenship have the same or at least complementary agendas? If the values of citizenship are taken to be either (1) the celebration of patriotism in such a form that posits one's country's superiority or rallying round the flag, so that responding to need in one's own country takes priority as a matter of principle because of strong communitarian arguments, etc., or (2) the promotion of one's citizenship in such a way as to imply that these were right/superior to those either of minorities within one's own country or of other countries and cultures, then the values of citizenship would indeed clash with the values of global citizenship, as least as these are normally understood.

   It is true that a global citizen could have a very doctrinaire, proselytizing vision of the universal values he wishes to see universally accepted and this might parallel an intolerance of other cultures within a society in the publicly endorsed values of citizenship (take the recent line taken in France to the wearing of the *hijab* [veil] by Muslim women). But the mainstream emphasis within global citizenship discourse is on trying to create a multicultural basis (within limits) of mutual respect. Indeed, Nussbaum's fourth argument for multicultural citizenship we noted earlier was precisely premised on the claim that the acceptance of a tolerant global ethics was the best and most principled basis for genuine multicultural citizenship within a country.

2. Global citizenship helps to inform the character of citizenship is several ways. Since much of the emphasis in global citizenship education is on ethical values and the idea of moral responsibility, this helps to strengthen

the perception that citizenship education is not just about civics, political institutions, and democracy, but is also about the core values and virtues of human beings. Much of the current interest in citizenship focuses on issues such as aid, the environment, immigration, and international security. This is not surprising, since we increasingly suffer from what is called a "democratic deficit." Citizenship needs to be oriented, as I said before, in a global way. Citizenship in the modern world has to be globalized and thus informed by the very concerns I am identifying as global citizenship concerns. Someone once challenged me that it was hopeless trying to get people to become global citizens because it was difficult enough getting people to be citizens (as active responsible agents of change in their one society)! This challenge supposes that global citizenship somehow lies *beyond* responsible citizenship. My reply was that in fact one of the best ways to revitalize citizenship was via the global citizenship agenda. They lie side by side and interconnected, not one inaccessibly beyond the other until the other had been passed.

3. Citizenship in its turn helps to create a more sophisticated understanding of global citizenship as not being merely an ethical conception, but as having an institutional or political dimension, and there is replicated in the world elements of citizenship itself, in the form of global governance, NGOs, global civil society, and human rights regimes as international parallels to citizenship.

DIVERSITY OF VALUES

Finally, I need to consider the question: Since there may be a great variety of opinions about global values, is there a danger that in trying to include global citizenship education in the school curriculum teachers may promote various unacceptable moral positions? By contrast, it may be said, there is a resilient, settled, and agreed set of norms and values internal to citizenship education. Now, it has to be admitted that not all cosmopolitanisms are the same, and that some global ethics may be unacceptable. As Barber remarks, cosmopolitanism has its pathologies just as patriotism has its healthy forms (Barber, 1996). Nevertheless, I would submit that, other things being equal, it is better that people accept a global framework and the idea of global citizenship than that they do not, just as, other things being equal, it is better that people think of themselves as citizens qua active responsible members of their society, even if the particular values they promote may be unacceptable to most of us, than remain privatized couch potatoes in front of their TVs.

In any case, while what citizens may actually believe and pursue may be very diverse, those values may lie outside those that are central to citizenship education which are more limited and constitute a core of generally accepted values. In a sense, what citizenship is about is determined by an overlapping consensus (Rawls, 1993), even if what citizens promote within this framework may be very diverse. The same applies to global citizenship: while global citizens might (from a particular thinker's point of view) have the wrong values or goals, or might advocate means that a thinker might regard as either irrelevant, ineffective, or actually immoral (such as acts of civil disobedience), that is not part of the core values that would be in the curriculum (though constructive critical discussion of such issues might be a feature). These core values are those of openness to and interest in the world as a whole and commitment to the process values of dialogic and nonviolent communication, coupled with the acceptance of the universal status of all human beings and a sense of trans-society responsibility for what happens in the world. These may be as widely accepted as the core values of citizenship itself, and thus be appropriately part of the publicly justified education of those who are to take on the management of the world from ourselves.

REFERENCES

Archibugi, D., & Held, D. (Eds.). (1995). *Cosmopolitan democracy—An agenda for a new world order*. Cambridge: Polity Press.

Barnaby, F. (Ed.). (1988). *The Gaia peace atlas*. London: Pan Books.

Barber. B. R. (1996). Constitutional faith. In J. Cohen (Ed.), *For love of country: Debating the limits of patriotism*. Boston: Beacon.

Dower, N. (1998). *World ethics—The new agenda*. Edinburgh: Edinburgh University Press.

Dower, N., & Williams, J. (Eds.). (2002). *Global citizenship—A critical reader*. Edinburgh: Edinburgh University Press.

Dower, N. (2003). *Introduction to global citizenship*. Edinburgh: Edinburgh University Press.

Falk, R. (1994). The making of global citizenship. In B. van Steenbergen (Ed.), *The condition of citizenship*. London: Sage.

Heater, D. (2002). *World citizenship*. London: Continuum.

Leopold, A. (1949). *A Sand County almanac and sketches here and there*. Oxford: Oxford University Press.

Linklater, A. (1998). *The transformation of political community*. Cambridge: Polity.

Marshall, T. H. (1973). *Class, citizenship, and social development*. Westport, CT: Greenwood Press.

McGrew, A. (2000). Democracy beyond borders? In D. Held & A. McGrew (Eds.), *The global transformations reader*. Cambridge: Polity Press.

Nussbaum, M. (1996). Cosmopolitanism and patriotism. In J. Cohen (Ed.), *For love of country: Debating the limits of patriotism*. Boston: Beacon.

Parehk, B. (2003). Cosmopolitanism and global citizenship. *Review of International Studies, 31(2)*.

Rawls, J. (1993). *Political liberalism*. New York: Columbia University Press.

Scholte, J-A. (2000). *Globalisation: A critical introduction*. Basingstoke: Palgrave.

Walzer, M. (1996). Spheres of affection. In J. Cohen (Ed.), *For love of country: Debating the limits of patriotism*. Boston: Beacon.

FIVE

Caught Between Imaginaries

Global Citizenship Education and the Persistence of the Nation

George Richardson

INTRODUCTION: THE PERSISTENCE
OF NATION IN A GLOBALIZED WORLD

SOME YEARS AGO I taught in western Ukraine as part of an international development project designed to introduce Western approaches to teaching history and citizenship to Ukrainian teachers. Up to its independence from the Soviet Union, history teaching and civics education in Ukraine had been dominated by direct instruction and had focused on students studying history and citizenship from the perspective of scientific socialism in order to develop the correct understanding of the material forces that would lead, inevitably, to the triumph of international socialism. However, in the post-Soviet period a dramatic change took place in education—not in the mode of instruction, unfortunately, which remained firmly and grimly authoritarian—it was the subject matter that changed. Nation replaced class as the focus of instruction, and when I arrived on the scene, students were diligently using the principles of scientific nationalism to demonstrate that the nation was the ultimate expression of the march of history and that citizenship education meant developing a sense of loyalty and duty to the existing national order.

I cite this episode because in an age of globalization it might seem odd and perhaps even perverse to speak of the persistence of nation. Certainly, academics as diverse as Francis Fukuyama (1992), Anthony Giddens (2000), and Jurgen Habermas (2001) have, in one way or another, been announcing the "death of the nation" for more than a decade. But, to borrow from Mark Twain, I think that news of the death of the nation has been greatly exaggerated at best. And at worst, suggestions of the demise of the nation and of its analogue, national citizenship education, deprive us of the vital historical memory of the close and continuing connection between national identity and citizenship while at the same time they produce a naive and unrealistic impression that the move to educating for global citizenship is a normal evolutionary process and one that is essentially unproblematic.

Building on the persistence of the nation in the face of what is an undeniable shift toward globalization, this chapter makes two main arguments. The first argument suggests that the concept of global citizenship education has, as yet, developed neither the political structures that typically ground citizenship in regularized and generally understood civic practices, nor has it, to date, provided a powerful emotive bond comparable to the "imagined community" (Anderson, 1991) upon which national citizenship is based (Richardson, 2004; Richardson, Blades, Kumano, & Karaki, 2003). The second argument advances the position that while the concept of global citizenship education is, effectively, in its infancy, it is nevertheless possible to detect in students the emergence of what many scholars (Pike, 2000; Dower & Williams, 2002; Gaudelli, 2003) generally term a "global perspective" on issues of citizenship and civic life.

EXPLORING THE PROBLEMATICS
OF GLOBAL CITIZENSHIP EDUCATION

David G. Smith has noted that globalization has what he terms an undeniable "facticity" (D. G. Smith, 1999). Put more directly, it is an already existing discourse with a tangible series of effects ranging from unregulated worldwide flows of capital to cultural homogenization, to the creation of consumerism on a global scale. However, if there are few questions about the "fact" of globalization, there are significant questions about whether a parallel global civic discourse has emerged that provides us with what Dewey (1916/1966) termed the "democratic dispositions" to act as world citizens.

Reflecting on this issue, political philosopher Will Kymlicka has concluded, "Globalization is undoubtedly producing a new civil society, but it has not yet produced anything we can recognize as transnational democratic citizenship" (Kymlicka, 2001, p. 326). Echoing Kymlicka, Graham Pike notes that one of the central problems of globalization education is its failure to acknowledge the continuing "influence of national culture—the prevailing culture at the macro level of society—on both [global education's] proponents and practitioners" (Pike, 2000, p. 67).

In part, this failure to understand the pivotal role national culture plays in globalization education is the product of the deep structures of Western education. As John Willinsky has noted, these deep structures are specifically and intentionally imperial and organized around "learning to divide the world" in such a way that Western privilege is reinforced and reproduced in schools:

> We are schooled in differences great and small, in borderlines and boundaries, in historical struggles and exotic practices, all of which extend the meaning of difference. We are taught to discriminate in both the most innocent and fateful ways so that we can appreciate the differences between civilized and primitive, West and East, first and third worlds. (Willinsky, 1998, p. 1)

Yet despite the complexities associated with developing global citizenship education, it has become increasingly clear that in terms of educating the next generation of citizens, exclusive emphasis on national citizenship education "is no longer singularly sufficient for understanding our complex world" (Gaudelli, 2003, p. 157). In the face of what Anthony Giddens has termed the "democratic deficit" "between [nations] and the global forces that affect the lives of their citizens" (Giddens, 2000, p. 34), significant questions emerge about how and under what conditions it is possible for schools to take up the task of educating for global citizenship (Cogan, 1998; Kubow, Grossman, & Ninomiya, 1998). And these questions are made all the more complex given the persistence of the nation as both a disciplining structure of civic engagement and a symbolic force of affiliation.

Acknowledging that the nation remains a significant presence in civic education, in what follows I would like to suggest that there are four specific challenges schools face when educating for global citizenship. Despite these challenges, I would also like to suggest that there are emergent conceptions of global citizenship that offer students ways in which they might reimagine themselves as involved actors in a global civic society.

FOUR CHALLENGES TO
GLOBAL CITIZENSHIP EDUCATION

The first significant challenge has to do with the history of citizenship education itself and the close connection that civic education forged between citizenship and national identity formation. As it emerged in the late nineteenth century, citizenship education was bound to the interests of the nation state and realized in policy through national systems of public education (Hahn, 1998; Heater, 2001; Torney-Purta, Schwiller, & Amadeo, 1999; Jusdanis, 2001). Many scholars see this close link between national identity, citizenship, and schooling as a product of a modernist nation-building ethos in which education plays the central role (Reisner, 1925; Anderson, 1991;

Chatterjee, 1993; Richardson, 2002; A. Smith, 2001). For example, historian Eugen Weber (1976, p. 332) notes that the production of civic pride and national sentiment has been the "greatest function of the modern school" and, more directly, social studies educator Walter Feinberg (2001) notes that

> [c]itizenship education is a way to stabilize a normative conception of a nation and its instrument of governing, the state. It does this by developing appropriate interpretations, competencies, and loyalties, that is, those that encourage individuals to think of themselves as a people and that justify, enable, protect and defend their partiality toward one another. (p. 203)

As compared to the establishment of a close relationship between national and civic identity, which has been an integral part of public education and one of its chief intents for well over one hundred years, the link between global identity and global citizenship enjoys a far shorter history and suffers from having few intentional mechanisms to establish, develop, and maintain the connection at the conceptual level, let alone develop strategies for how the notion plays itself out in classroom practice. For example, Franck (1999, p. 138) notes that global citizenship has developed, as yet, only the "rudimentary institutional construction of arenas and allegiance" as compared with national citizenship, and Dower (2002), although a passionate advocate of global citizenship education, observes that the concept of active global citizenship requires the development of modern technologies such as the Internet that are, at present still in the developmental stages.

Thus, while scholars such as Alger (1986) can emphasize the "removal of the national border as a barrier in education" (p. 257) it seems more accurate to conclude, as does Gaudelli (2003, p. 156) that "we lack the vocabulary, categories and master images" that would make the link between world-mindedness and world citizenship. And even when regional or national curriculums do make the attempt to tie global identity and citizenship together, the relationship is typically framed as an extension of national self-interest and almost exclusively tied to the existing civic structures of the nation-state (Pike, 2000; Heater, 2004; Richardson, 2004).

If the close link between nation building and citizenship represents the first challenge to educating for global citizenship, the second is a problem of architecture. What I mean by this is that, in a national sense, both the foundations and superstructure of citizenship education are already in place. They have a tangible aspect that allows, for example, students in most Western nations to recognize both the Judeo-Christian foundations of citizenship as well as the liberal democratic superstructure of regular elections, representation by population, and parliamentary democracy through which it is maintained. In its most physical expression, the familiar architecture of national citizenship is made manifest by the Canadian Parliament buildings or, in the United States by the Capitol, or, in Britain, by the Houses of Parliament. In the case of global citizenship it is far more difficult for students to identify the roots of the concept much less recognize any kind superstructure that could be said to represent the visible aspect of global citizenship. As Benjamin Barber (1996, pp. 33–34) has noted, no one actually lives "in the world of which the cosmopolitan wishes us to be good citizens." This lack of intellectual or material presence has prompted William Gaudelli (2003, p. 175) to conclude, "Global civics is a challenging notion, one that we lack a sufficient vocabulary to adequately discuss."

A third challenge to global citizenship is the contemporary geopolitical context itself and the way in which the nation has reinscribed its presence global affairs. In his essay *The End of History and the Last Man*, Francis Fukuyama (1992) suggested that the post–cold war triumph of liberal democracy and its analogue free market capitalism would produce an ahistorical age in which national rivalry no longer existed and in which the pursuit of individual fulfillment would constitute the universalist ideology of a more enlightened era.

Events subsequent to the publication of the work certainly suggest that, if anything, nationalism and national rivalry have greatly intensified since the fall of the Soviet Union. For confirmation of this trend we need go no farther than the dangerous rise of unilateralism on the part of the United States and the different fundamentalisms that have emerged in response to "Pax Americana." In the context of global citizenship education, and more to the point here, those institutions such as the UN and the World Court at the Hague, which were optimistically regarded in the period after World War II as nascent structures of world government, have lost a great deal of their legitimacy in the current context. At this point whether or not this legitimacy can be recovered seems very much moot.

A final challenge to global citizenship education has to do with the problematics of developing a global imagination that is capable of providing students with a deep structure of identification with the world as a geopolitical whole. David G. Smith (1999) notes that such abstract concepts as "nation" or "global community" are best seen as what he terms "imaginaries." For Smith, the power of an imaginary "pertains less to any characteristic of the world in its ordinary condition than to what certain people imagine that condition to be" (p. 3). In this regard, historian Benedict Anderson (1991) has suggested that nations are very much imagined communities in which what he terms "deep horizontal comradeships" develop among people who have never and will never see one another. As Anderson and others have noted, the realization of this sense of national communion was the product of the emergence of national print media in the nineteenth century and of conscious, sustained efforts on the part of the state to cultivate a sense of national uniqueness and superiority to other nations through emergent systems of public education (Gellner, 1983; Hobsbawm, 1983; Greenfield, 1992; Anderson, 1991).

But as cultural artefacts of specific and often violent historical forces, what is typically unsaid about the production of national identity and citizenship is the degree to which both are characterized by a discourse of exclusion and threat. That is, the nation and its loyal citizens are at once different from and at the same time menaced by other nations who threaten its way of life and civic culture. For example, Julia Kristeva (1993) comments on the imagined "cult of origins" that underlies modern nationalism, noting that recourse to originary roots as the source of national identity involves a process by which its devotees "anxiously shelter among their own [roots], hoping to suppress the conflicts they have with them by projecting them on others—the strangers" (pp. 3–4).

Among its proponents, global citizenship education has typically been represented as a kind of moral imperative (Pike & Selby, 1995; Nussbaum, 1997; Gower & Williams, 2002; Gaudelli, 2003) that would address the ills of a world beset by the ugly consequences of national rivalries. But this emphasis on "the good" however desirable and laudable has consistently failed to take the seductions of the dark side of the nation into account.

The challenge global citizenship education faces, then, is how to reorient the civic imagination away from xenophobic language that promotes the construction of a menacing foreign Other as the chief locus of civic and national identity (Volkan, 1988; Baker, 1997; Triandafyllidou, 1998; Richardson, 2004).

POSSIBILITIES FOR GLOBAL CITIZENSHIP EDUCATION

Having identified some challenges that complicate the mission of educating for global citizenship, I would like to suggest some hopeful signs that indicate that the task is one to which we can productively focus our energies.

The first, surprisingly, is the notion that citizenship education, whether it be oriented toward national or global citizenship, has typically failed to achieve its ends and that many young people have rejected civics as taught in schools. One of the "gifts" of this failure has been the creation of spaces for suggesting that there are alternate understandings of what citizenship can be and what a civic community might look like. A case in point is the protests surrounding WTO meetings in Seattle, Montreal, and Genoa. These protests, organized outside the context of traditional politics, suggest the emergence of a politics of global involvement that has moved beyond the constraints of national citizenship. It is certainly a politics that bears little resemblance to notions of "responsible citizenship" that have characterized much of civic education in the last twenty years (D. G. Smith, 2001; Richardson & Blades, 2005).

And, as a counterpoint to the perceived difficulty of cultivating a global civic imaginary is recent research (Richardson, Blades, Kumano, & Karaki, 2003) that suggests that students may well already be thinking of themselves as global citizens. The first part of that research involved engaging 194 secondary school students in Japan and Canada in conversation, through questionnaires, written responses to statements, and special forums, about how they understand and imagine their responsibilities as active world citizens. Our meetings with these high school students revealed that despite cultural and linguistic differences, they share very common attitudes and concerns about global issues and their responsibilities as citizens of the world. For example, more than 90 percent of the students in each country agree with the statement, "During this century it will be more important to understand the responsibilities of being an active and responsible member of the world community than being a member of a particular country" (Richardson, Blades, Kumano, & Karaki, 2003, pp. 411–412). Students were also in agreement that the most important issues facing humankind are related to environmental degradation, and the exact same percentage of students in both countries identified global warming as the single most important environmental issue facing humankind.

While students in both countries acknowledged that the nation-state system remained the dominant political paradigm and that national self-interest complicated such notions as global citizenship, my colleagues and I were very much heartened by their willingness to look beyond the nation when they thought of how they should act as global citizens. As Jenna, a tenth grade student in Canada reminded us, "Yes it's a really big jump to think of ourselves as just a citizen of a city to a citizen of the world, but in reality we're all born of the same thing . . . the countries don't own us. We created them. . . . We're just ourselves. That's what we are in the end. We have to take responsibilities for our actions in the long run; otherwise we deal with the consequences" (Richardson, Blades, Kumano, & Karaki, 2003, p. 414). Jenna's emergent sense of the way in which the civic ideal can play itself out on a global stage appears to go some distance toward the realization of Kenneth Boulding's assertion voiced almost two decades ago that "the concept of global civic culture requires the acceptance at some level of a shared identity with other human beings" (1988, p. 56).

This acknowledgment of the other, and particularly of the other who lies outside the confining and comfortable boundaries of the nation, seems a tentative move in the direction of what Martha Nussbaum (1996) has termed "cosmopolitan education." As Nussbaum notes,

> The emphasis on patriotic pride is both morally dangerous and ultimately, subversive of some of the worthy goals patriotism sets out to serve—for example, the goal of national unity in devotion to worthy moral ideals of justice and equality, These goals, I shall argue, would be better served by an ideal that is in any case more adequate to our situation in the contemporary world, namely the very old ideal of the cosmopolitan, the person whose allegiance is to the worldwide community of human beings. (p. 4)

In some senses, the notion of cosmopolitanism that Nussbaum and others (Held, 1995; Gower & Williams, 2002) propose as a substitute for national citizenship can be traced back to Dewey's understanding of the school as an agent of social reconstruction. As he noted in 1916, "As a society becomes more enlightened, it realizes that it is responsible not to transmit and conserve the whole of its existing achievements, but only such as make for a better future society. The school is the chief agency for the accomplishment of this end" (1916: p. 20). But, at the same time as we acknowledge the intriguing possibilities that global citizenship education might hold for creating Dewey's "public" on worldwide scale, it is important to keep in mind that citizenship education remains tied to and rooted in national affiliations and that even Nussbaum herself considers cosmopolitanism "less a political idea than a moral idea that constrains and regulates political life" (Nussbaum, 1997, p. 59).

To conclude, then, when we think of educating for global citizenship, we need to see the complexity of the task but also keep in mind its hopeful possibilities. We need to see how citizenship has been continually read through the nation, but we also need to see the emergence of a global civic imagination of the part of young people. In the context of educating for global citizenship, the persistence of nation is much more than a problem to be overcome; it is a presence to be acknowledged. If we make this acknowledgment, and, at the same time, begin to look for other imaginative possibilities, Jenna's hopeful vision of global citizenship becomes much more achievable.

REFERENCES

Alger, C. F. (1986). Implications of microelectronically transmitted information for global education. In A. Cuthbertson & L. L. Cunningham (Eds.), *Microcomputers and education* (85th yearbook for the National Society for the Study of Education, Part 1) (pp. 254–273). Chicago: University of Chicago Press.

Anderson, B. (1991). *Imagined communities: Reflections on the origins and spread of nationalism*. London: Verso.

Baker, H. D. (1997). Obsessional and hysterical modes of national identity. *Journal for the Psychoanalysis of Culture and Society, 2(2)*, 129–145.

Barber, B. (1996). Constitutional faith. In J. Cohen (Ed.), *For love of country: Debating the limits of patriotism* (pp. 30–27). Boston: Beacon Press.

Boulding, K. (1988). *The meaning of the 20th century: The great transition*. New York: Harper Collins.

Chatterjee, P. (1993). *The nation and its fragments: Colonial and postcolonial histories*. Princeton: Princeton University Press

Cogan, J. J. (1998). The challenge of multidimensional citizenship for the 21st century. In J. J. Cogan & R. Derricot (Eds.), *Citizenship for the 21st century: An international perspective on education* (pp. 155–167). London: Kogan Page.

Dewey, J. (1916/1966). *Education and democracy*. New York: Free Press.

Dower, N. (2002). *Does global citizenship require modern technology?* Aberdeen: University of Aberdeen School of Philosophy and Cultural History. http://www.abdn.ac.uk/philosophy/cpts/dower.hti.

Dower, N., & Williams, J. (2002). *Global citizenship: A critical reader*. Edinburgh: Edinburgh University Press

Feinberg, W. (1998). *Common schools, uncommon identities: National unity and cultural difference*. New Haven: Yale University Press.

Franck, T. M. (1999). *The empowered self: Law and society in an age of individualism*. London: Oxford University Press.

Fukuyama, F. (1992). *The end of history and the last man*. London: Hamish Hamilton.

Gaudelli, W. (2003). *World class: Teaching and learning in global times*. London: Lawrence Erlbaum.

Gellner, E. (1983). *Nations and nationalism*. Oxford: Blackwell.

Giddens, A. (2000). *Runaway world: How globalization is reshaping our lives*. London: Routledge.

Gower, N., & Williams, J. (2002). *Global citizenship: A critical reader*. Edinburgh: Edinburgh University Press.

Greenfield, L. (1992). *Nationalism: Five roads to modernity*. Cambridge: Harvard University Press.

Habermas, J. (2001). *The postnational constellation: Political essays*. Cambridge: MIT Press.

Hahn, C. (1998). *Comparative perspectives on citizenship education*. Albany: State University of New York Press.

Heater, D. (2001). The history of citizenship education in England. *The Curriculum Journal, 12(1)*, 103–124.

Held, D. (1995). *Democracy and the global order: From the modern state to cosmopolitan governance*. Cambridge: Polity Press

Hobsbawm, E., & Ranger, T. (1983). *The invention of tradition*. Cambridge: Cambridge University Press.

Jusdanis, G. (2001). *The necessary nation*. Princeton: Princeton University Press.

Kymlicka, W. (2001) *Politics in the vernacular: Nationalism, multiculturalism, and citizenship*. London: Oxford University Press.

Kristeva, J. (1993). Nations without nationalism. (Trans.), L. S. Roudiez. New York: Columbia University Press.

Kubow, P., Grossman, D., & Ninomiya, A. (1998). Multidimensional citizenship: Educational policy for the 21st century. In J. J. Cogan and R. Derricot (Eds.), *Citizenship for the 21st century: An international perspective on education* (pp. 115–133). London: Kogan Page.

Nussbaum, M. C. (1997). *Cultivating humanity: A classical defense of reform in liberal education*. Cambridge: Harvard University Press.

Nussbaum, M. C. (1996). Patriotism and cosmopolitanism. In J. Cohen (Ed.), *For love of country: Debating the limits of patriotism* (pp. 3–20). Boston: Beacon Press.

Pike, G. (2000). Global education and national identity: In pursuit of meaning. *Theory into Practice, 39(2)*, 64–74.

Pike, G., & Selby, D. (1995). *Reconnecting. From national to global curriculum*. Godalming: Worldwide Fund for Nature (UK).

Reisner, E. (1925). *Nationalism and education since 1789*. New York: Macmillan.

Richardson, G., and Blades, D. (Eds.). (2005). *Troubling the canon of citizenship education*. New York: Peter Lang.

Richardson, G. (2004). Global education and the challenge of globalization. In A. Sears & I. Wright (Eds.), *New trends and issues in Canadian social studies* (3rd Ed.) (pp. 138–149). Vancouver: Pacific Educational Press.

Richardson, G., Blades, D., Kumano, Y., & Karaki, K. (2003). Fostering a Global Imaginary: The Possibilities and Paradoxes of Japanese and Canadian Students' Perceptions of the Responsibilities of World Citizenship. *Policy Futures in Education, 1(2)*, 402–420.

Richardson, G. (2002). *The death of the good Canadian: Teachers, national identities, and the social studies curriculum*. New York: Peter Lang.

Smith, A. (2001). *Nationalism and modernism*. New York: Routledge.

Smith, D. G. (1999). Globalization and education: prospects for postcolonial pedagogy in a hermeneutic mode. *Interchange, 30*, pp. 1–9.

Smith, D. G. (2000). A few modest prophecies: The WTO, globalization, and the future of public education. *Canadian Social Studies, 35(1)*, retrieved at http://www.quasar.ualberta.ca/css.

Torney-Purta, J., Schwiller, J., & Amadeo, J. A. (Eds.). (1999). *Civic education across countries: Twenty-four national case studies from the IEA civic education project*. Amsterdam: The International Association for the Evaluation of Educational Achievement.

Triandafyllidou, A. (1998). National identity and the "other." *Ethnic and Racial Studies, 21(4)*, 593–612.

Volkan, V. (1988). *The need to have enemies and allies*. Northvale, NJ: Jason Aronson.

Weber, E. (1976). *Peasants into Frenchmen: The modernization of rural France 1870–1914*. Stanford: Stanford University Press.

Willinsky, J. (1998). *Learning to divide the world: Education at empire's end*. Minneapolis: University of Minnesota Press.

SIX

De-subjecting Subject Populations

Historico-actual Problems
and Educational Possibilities

Ali A. Abdi

In his third intercontinental voyage in 1498, Columbus sailed south to Sierra Leone, where the native inhabitants were black, then sailed due west to Trinidad and the top of South America, where he encountered native inhabitants who were "white." This completely destroyed the traditional explanation for human diversity, leading to the rise of racist theories about radical biological differences between peoples and the superiority of the "white race" to all others.

—Gary Taylor, *Buying Whiteness*

INTRODUCTION

WHILE THE RISE of "race"-based categorization of peoples of different skin colors is generally known to have started with the proliferation of European maritime traveling in the fifteenth century, the specific date used by Gary Taylor (in the above quotation) is indeed interesting. For those who have been on the wrong side of the "race-ing" project, the subjectively infantile nostalgia for what could have been if Columbus and his ilk had not gotten it wrong, may be permissible, especially in the context of the across-the-centuries regimes of oppression and marginalization that have since been inscribed at birth. Here also, one should discern the power of moments and ideas where one simple encounter with one uninvited guest (Columbus) shapes the destiny of billions of people via the time and space-wise progressive programs of slavery, colonization, and their products of multilayered marginalization, which continuously affirm the perforce "permanentization" (as opposed to voluntary or nature-induced permanence) of so many children and their forefathers in the so-called third world. We also know that there were textual glimmers, actually finely recorded capsules of Eurocentric arrogance that was exercised before Columbus.

A case in point can be found in the exhortations of the Roman historian, Pliny, who in his *Historia Naturalis* (see Davies et al., 1993) spoke about the monstrosity of non-European peoples. But those sayings and others like them in the pre-Columbus temporalities did not advance their observations on the basis of naturally subject peoples who were to be subjugated on the basis of their skin color or the henceforward invented platitudes of race-based differences. But looking back at the world in the last five hundred or so years, one can see how, in the life platforms we are describing here, nothing stayed the same. Before I proceed, though, let me clearly state that one main objective of this chapter is to provide a personal understanding of the pivotal beginning of a subjugation process that was mainly justified on the basis of skin pigmentation, and how that has created and sustained the subjecting of the world's non-white majority whose global citizenship is not still at par (not even close) with Europeans and Euro-Americans. As should be expected, the point is not to engage a blanket generalization of every facet of people's lives since 1493 (or one year before that), for there were cases where non-Europeans subjugated others. There is also the current case where Asian countries such as Japan and some of the so-called Newly Industrialized Countries (NICs) in Southeast Asia, may not be doing that badly. Needless to add that the expected emergence (some of it already happening) of China and, selectively, India as a global economic and military powers, could also modify some elements of the global power relations. But all of that does not and should not minimize our analyses here, which should also include how centuries (indeed, millennia) of community development and human dignity programs that were achieved and thrived before 1492 were rescinded by the benighted contact. As I describe these issues below, therefore, I will also discuss the negative role colonial education (or miseducation) has played in the process of disenfranchisement, and will complete my disquisition with some suggestions for reeducating people for inclusive citizenship and social development. After all, this book project should not abandon its forward-looking perspective, but more corrective possibilities of the historical project is essential if we have to achieve full citizenship and dignified human progress. As I continue writing in the following pages, I will aim for a line of analysis that has a global resonance, but my focus should have, especially in the latter stages of the discussion, a more direct link with African experiences and actualities.

THE SUBJECTING OF GLOBAL CITIZENS:
BEGINNINGS AND PROCESSES

To continue from the introduction, therefore, the Columbus project, which is extensively celebrated in the United Sates of America, acquainted itself (we should know by now: it did not discover anything) with the Americas in 1492. While many of us may focus more on the residential upheavals and changes it has achieved, the results have been, indeed, catastrophic for the indigenous populations who had already developed what should be characterized as civilizational qualities that might have been at par, if not superior, to anything that was accomplished in Europe. In his 2002 article in the Atlantic Monthly, "1491," which has now been turned into a book, Charles Mann, while fully cognizant of what he terms the most destructive demographic upheavals in the history of humanity, also relates the following about superior life systems in the pre-Columbus Americas:

> The Aztec capital of Tenochtitlán dazzled Henán Cortés (one of the Spanish Commanders) in 1519. It was bigger than Paris, Europe's greatest Metropolis. The Spaniards gawped like hayseeds at the wide streets, ornately carved buildings, and markets bright with goods from hundreds of miles away. They had never before seen a city with botanical gardens, for the excellent reason that none existed in Europe. The same novelty attended the force of a thousand men that kept the crowded streets immaculate. (Streets that weren't ankle-deep in sewage. The conquistadores had never heard of such a thing.) [And] Central was not the only locus of prosperity. Thousands of miles north, John Smith of Pocahontas fame, visited Massachusetts in 1614, before it was emptied by disease and declared that the land was planted with "gardens and corn fields and so well-inhabited with a goodly, strong and well proportioned people . . . [that] I would rather live here than any where."

But with the European psyche already corrupted by the widespread pathology of racial superiority, these facts on the ground did not diminish the level of contempt and destruction that were meted out against the native populations of the Americas. Sometime between Cortes's city life experiences and Smith's admiration of the land, it was also clear that as we will see also in the African case influential Europeans were furnishing sweeping generalizations about the native population that mainly aimed to dehumanize the latter, which expectedly increased the atrocities that were committed against them. In that vein, the Catholic Knight Villegagnon described the Indian population as "beasts with a human face," and the medical doctor Laurent Joubert, after examining five Brazilian women, concluded that since these women did not have periods, they cannot belong to the human race (de Botton, 2001). These temporally powerful, but otherwise nonsensical descriptions should not surprise us, especially when we realize that in the fifty years between 1531 and 1581, the indigenous population in the Americas was so decimated that it went from about eighty million to ten million (de Botton, 2002). In some places such as present-day Argentina, for example, there are estimates of up to twenty million indigenous inhabitants killed, which apparently "cleared" all the land for the advancing Spanish settlers and profiteers.

The mass scale of European colonialism in the Americas was, therefore, one of the most destructive practices of human cruelty that led, not only to the subjugation of millions of people, but to the complete erasing of whole cultures and systems of life. So much so that today, indigenous populations are so marginalized in this part of the world that we could run the risk of assuming an expansive historical amnesia as to what has happened to the millions of people who once populated the plains, the mountain chains, and the forested streams and rivers of what we now know as the Western hemisphere. But the project of European colonialism, whether in the Americas, Africa, the South Pacific, or elsewhere, was mostly similar and even where the quantitative aspects of the overall destruction of human and natural resources was relatively less extensive, the main objective of subjugating non-Europeans was always the main agenda on the table. As Mark Cocker, in his excellent work, *Rivers of Blood, Rivers of Gold* (2000), analytically shows, Europe's conquest of indigenous peoples all over the world was bent on a unilinear but multidimensional project of achieving riches via creating extensive streams of blood, which eventually created and sustained the world order we have today.

In the context of Africa, the two-tier project of slavery and colonialism have established complex processes of subjugation that are still functional (at least at the psychocultural levels) in both continental Africa and in the Americas. Again, the project here was purely based on the need for resources and riches to be achieved at dehumanized platforms that were to reduce Africans into a commodity to be used as occasioned by the needs of the new propertied class. As far as the program of colonizing continental Africa is concerned, once again, as Mazrui (1990) and Cesaire (1972) noted, the case was purely based on subjugating Africans so they submit both themselves and their resources to the colonizing entity. In his small magnum opus, *Discourse on Colonialism* (1972), Cesaire laments the temporal configurations of the program of colonialism. As profit seekers and marketers became a part of the dominant European class, so it also was the time (from late fifteenth century to early sixteenth century) when the continental contacts started in earnest and continually intensified in the following five hundred or so years, and into the current stage where a combination of American military force, and Western European financial power are joining forces to, perforce, socialize the nonconforming so-called radical or renegade political and geographical entities into submission. As should be known, though, colonialism, was not limited to the exploitation of the physio-social and natural resources of the colonized, it was also bent on achieving a globally miseducated and, by extension, decultured world population that looks for protection and psychological sustenance from the European metropolis, and these two dimensions (i.e., the processes of miseducation and deculturation) were the most potent weapons in achieving the sociopolitically deconscientized and economically detached majority of our world. Indeed, as Albert Memmi (1991) so effectively noted, the project of creating subjects (not citizens) eventually leads to the psychosocially disenfranchised becoming complicit in the project of their oppression. That is, as the wretched of the earth (as Frantz Fanon would call them) internalize heavy doses of their decommissioned existentialities and are ontologically dehistoricized, they seek some comfort in "naturalizing" their forlorn, peripheral beingness (with an apparent notification of Hegelian dialectics). And it gets worse: as the benighted space is inherited by the children and the grandchildren of the perennially subjugated, it becomes intergenerational, thus demanding, in this tragically interwoven trajectory of human life, less European or Euro-American effort to maintain the status quo.

In terms of the tactical changes European imperialism has employed to perpetuate the subjugation of others, it is interesting how, with the near exhaustion or lack of enough viable resources, either in the hitherto colonized Americas or in European soil, the expansion of the colonial project intensified from the eighteenth century into the twentieth century. In the African case, the falsity of the so-called *mission civilsatrice* (for more analysis on this, see Said, 1993), which colonial powers used as a disguise to conquer foreign lands, was exposed, among many others, by none other than one of the greatest beneficiaries of the program, the Englishman Cecil Rhodes. Rhodes, who among many other "accomplishments" named two African countries after himself (Northern Rhodesia and Southern Rhodesia, now Zambia and Zimbabwe respectively), was too practical not to see the economic need to colonize Africa and other zones of the world (Luchembe, 1995). But again, even economic-based conquests could not be simply mechanically located. In all the projects of colonial expansion, therefore, it seems that a campaign of lowering the ontologies and the general life systems of the people to be conquered was to happen (recall the "beasts with human face" point above). And by and large, the results of the contact and the subsequent projects of colonization have been so destructive that I am apt to repeat Van Sertima's Holocaust analogy to describe the situation (van Sertima, 1991).

Once again, though, and as should be explicated more diametrically, this campaign of the destruction of the collective African environment was preceded by the denying of people's situational or global contributions before their contact with the invading groups from Europe. In the African scene, for example, this included prominent social scientists and writers such the Oxford University historian Hugh Trevor-Roper describing this ancient continent as ahistorical, which also means people without agency and, therefore, in need of being saved from themselves. Indeed, as Eric Wolfe, in his magisterial work *Europe and the People Without History* (1997), says, colonialism and its accompanying projects did not only deny the historical viability of the non-European societies, these also rewrote anything that should have been said about the present as well as the past life systems of these societies. A very interesting point in this regard is how even some thinkers and philosophers who should have known better also jumped on the bandwagon of demeaning the life situations and the mental capacities of the people that were to be subjugated. Among these are, for example, the well-known and so-called philosophers of freedom and liberty such as Voltaire (1822) and Montesquieu (1949) and many others. In a nutshell, therefore, the general colonial project apparently started with the free-for-all philosophizing about the subjugated populations, followed by the willful dehistoricization of whole continents, and eventually leading to what we have today: Europeans and Euro-Americans as the first-class citizens of the world, and the rest of societies placing themselves, not only in categories that are fundamentally less endowed, but locating themselves in specific platforms that are, by and large, defined and validated by the former. Beyond the African and the Americas case, quasi-similar colonial experiences have also taken place in Asia where beyond the replacement of ancient life systems and civilizations, which were trumped by the European onslaught, the systems of domination that were put into place were so complex that they seem to have achieved an unbroken and continuing chain of cultural supremacy for colonizing entities (Guha, 1997). From a Fanonian perspective (see Fanon, 1968, 1967), subjecting citizens, especially when they are either psychologically or physically (or both) subjugated, leads to whole project where people are objectified, and to de-objectify them would need as significant a quantity of doses, if not more, of psychocultural rehabilitation that might reconstitute some form of mental and somatic enfranchisement for them. But this requires some balance in the power relations plateau, which does not seem to be on the horizon at this point in time. Power, as Walter Rodney (1982) noted some years ago, could be the most important variable in human relations, and it is through the continuing appropriation and expropriation of power contexts that those whose peoples have been subjugated have inherited and are still living with actual subjugation in its many manifestations.

The story described here and the current realities of globalization are indeed interesting, not in their temporal and transgeographical dimensions, but as well, in their not-so-spoken about role in continuing the regimes of superior and inferior livelihood plateaus. These cases of existence have been apparently and selectively in place since the dawn of European hegemony, which judging from historical data provided in Janet Abu-Lughod's well-known work, *Before European Hegemony* (1991), should have also been trans-actional starting from about the time seafaring captains such as Columbus assured the sustainability of European maritime supremacy. And with global-ization literally sustaining the current unequal realities of the world, one wonders what educational possibilities there are. Indeed, as Hardt and Negri (2002), in their book *Empire*, noted, the project of globalization is nothing more than an imperial hubris and practice without the physical colonies. Indeed, others would go so far as to call current global arrangements as real colonization (Saul, 1993), but the common point of those who are less ideo-logical and in the pragmatic know (Stiglitz, 2002; Brawley, 2000) is that glob-alization is a pathology for the subjected populations of the world, and as Bello (2002) notes, novel trends of deglobalization are needed. As such, even the current programs of globalization, which may be selectively compre-hended as a continuation of the colonial project has, according to Ankie Hoogvelt (2001), created concentric circles that endow the elite of the world wherever they may be geographically located vis-à-vis the rest of the subju-gated populations. And education, whether in colonial times or in its current mechanistic trends, did not and does not really liberate people from either colonialism or its affiliated practices such as globalization. In the next sec-tion, I discuss the role colonial education has played in subjugating citizens.

EDUCATION AS A COLONIAL PROJECT
OF SUBJECTING FORMER CITIZENS

One area where people's lives should be enhanced but that has not yet hap-pened, especially during colonialism, is education and educational programs. Ironically, education, which should be, in "normal" human relations, a platform for individual and community development (Abdi, 1998; Mandela, 1994; Fagerlind & Saha, 1985), was used in this context to psychologically oppress and thus deform the identities of people, instigating, in the process, the colo-nized people internalizing heavy doses of their imposed dehumanization, and eventually collaborating with the colonizer (see Memmi, 1991) in the mainte-nance and realization of the colonial scheme. As Nyerere (1968) noted in post-colonial Tanzania, one way that colonialism destroyed African programs of development and, by extension, the citizenship of people, was inherent in the demeaning and outright decommissioning of indigenous African education. As should be known to many, the cultural, educational, and linguistic priorities of colonialism were all designed to impose new life systems that were antithetical to all things that were native. One excellent example of this took place in the Indian subcontinent. In the mid-nineteenth century, the British governor in India, Thomas Macaulay, put out his famous "Minute on Indian Education." There, Macaulay lamented the educational and linguistic problems that were facing Indians in India, and spoke about what was needed to Anglicize (presumably for the benefit of both groups) the native population. Clearly, Macaulay (1994) could not physically transform Indians into Englishmen and women, and therefore "cleverly" suggested the psychocultural transformation of full blooded Indians into English men and women.

Indeed, historically situated and culturally inclusive education should be, at all times and in all places, the type of learning that encourages full human development. This does not mean, of course, that different peoples in different parts of the world should not borrow knowledge from elsewhere, but as I have written previously (Abdi, 2002), the need and the action of borrowing must still be identified by local peoples who should know what they desire and how to use it. In his book *How Europe Underdeveloped Africa*, Walter Rodney (1982) discussed the importance of traditional African education, especially as it relates directly to the lives of the people that are using it. It is, therefore, the case that colonial education and linguistic imposition did not advance any viable citizenship possibilities for people. To the contrary, they have advanced the subjugation of peoples, thus leading, as Ngugi wa Thiongo (1993) stated, to decontextualizing the natives' worldview via, among other media, colonial languages whose perceptive implications and intra/interpersonal nuances were foreign to them. As such, colonial education has taken away from the African people their cultures, the center of their lives, and may have even de-patterned their mental dispositions.

The de-patterning of people's mental dispositions, situational judgments, and overall valuing of specific life systems, also advances what I have warned against at the beginning: internalized regimes of ontological inferiortization that inscribe in the minds of people a feeling, indeed, an acceptance of lower expectations and possibilities in their lives vis-à-vis others. For me, this is what, among others, Ashis Nandy (1997) and Ngugi wa Thiongo (1986) would call mental colonization. In this sphere of affairs, Nandy (1997, p. 170) observes:

> This colonialism colonizes minds in addition to bodies and it releases forces within the colonized societies to alter their cultural priorities once and for all. In the process, it helps generalize the concept of the modern West from a geographical and temporal entity to a psychological category. The West is now everywhere, within the West and outside the West; in structures and in *minds with the most potent weapon that collectively and gloriously achieved these for the West having been and still remaining to be colonial languages and colonial and postcolonial systems of education.* (emphasis mine)

Indeed, as Abdi (2002, 1998) and Bassey (1999), have pointed out, among the most potent weapons of subjugating colonized populations were the regimes of educational and related cultural impositions that have, as much as other elements of the conquest, wreaked havoc on the lives of people. As Abdi (2002) notes, though, there may have been certain points where the colonial project of education miscalculated the critical effects it could have induced in the minds of the small elite that was chosen from the native population for advanced learning possibilities. As such, when one looks at the African context, for example, one should not miss the reality that most of those who led the struggle against colonialism were, proportionally speaking, from this minute group of elites who were educated at some of the most distinguished higher education institutions in the West. So does this imply some goodness in colonial education? The contents as well as the conjectural value of the answer to this important question may depend on who the respondent is. Colonial powers and their contemporary apologists would most probably respond in the positive; after all, did not Europe call its destructive imperial programs (including all their educational dimensions) civilizing missions that would dilute the savagery of the natives (see Pells, 1970). In pragmatic terms, though, a much shorter but more relevant answer should be situated like this and should include at least one important counterquestion: What were the main objectives of giving advanced education to chosen natives? The answer to this last inquiry would be effectively located in Thomas Macaulay's educational directive (see above), but to repeat his points, this tiny elite was being trained to effectively and, indeed, loyally represent the colonial project in all its spheres, but especially in its spatial and geographical endurance. It was never educated to liberate people from colonialism.

DECOLONIZING THE IMAGINATION AND EDUCATING FOR CITIZENSHIP

If education and its cultural attachments were responsible for the subjugation of colonized populations, who are the current majority of the world's inhabitants, then the role of education, whether formal or informal, in decolonizing people's psychosomatic existences and existentialities should be highlighted. As we have seen, the subjecting of peoples involved more than conquering them on the battlefield. This was actually an organized program of imposed identity deformations (Abdi, 1999) that, in Charles Taylor's characterization (at least partially) (see Taylor, 1995), deliberately or otherwise misrecognized people's realities and in the process, imposed false identities on them. The counteridentity deformations of education that are needed to de-subject people would be responsive to the harnessing, in learning and social development terms, of what Freire (2000 [1970]) would characterize as a multicentric liberating praxis that tears centuries of oppressive practices asunder. In that vein, possible schemes of the de-subjecting education will aim for an expansive project of freeing the majority of the world's population so they seek and achieve viable and dignified livable contexts that could constitute the opposite of what they have been hitherto exposed to. Here, it should be important to note that while a number of educational discussions, at least at the theoretical level (see, inter alia, Dei, 1996; Dei et al., 2000; Greene, 1995, 1993; Freire, 1970 [2000]; selectively Dewey, 1926), present the possibility of liberating education ideals, one needs to seek the real pragmatics of learning possibilities that lead to real life changes in, especially, current international contexts of life such as globalization and its continuities (as mentioned above), which may might be correctly termed as "the subjecting process by the other means."

In all events and aspects of current life situations that have to be de-subjected, two important and parallel schemes of educational development might be required. These two are aimed generally for an inclusive social development, which should seek to give people skills that empower them vis-à-vis powerful multinational corporations and, many times, their own oppressive governments, which have become, more often than otherwise, a post-colonial curse, especially in the actual African landscape (Davidson, 1992). The second type of learning program that enfranchises the lives of the twenty-first-century disenfranchised is citizenship education, which inculcates, indeed, instills in the minds of people, not only their inalienable rights *contra* the powers that be, but also, gives them the moral ground to demand accountability and wider social inclusion in the management of their lives and their resources. It is the case that in today's global arrangements, the gap between the haves and have-nots, which are still distinguished by skin color considerations, is bigger than ever. The point to be made here, therefore, is to de-subject populations not only on the basis of economic liquidity, but also and equally important, on achieving basic human rights via specially designed programs of decolonizing education that aim to free the imagination as well as the psychological dispositions in the manner Ngugi wa Thiongo (1986) spoke about. In terms of which should come first, education for economic emancipation or citizenship education, I would say that the two can go together, but referencing that well-known debate between Amartya Sen (1993) and Samuel Huntington (1993), I would agree with the former that the preservation of basic human rights tenets should always take priority over everything else, thus concurring again with Sen's (2000) characterization of human development as freedom.

To be more inclusive in my observations and analyses here, though, let me suggest that the educational project to "re-citizenize" the historically, culturally, socioeconomically, and psychologically "de-citizenized" has to be one collective project that aims for the multiperspective humanization of the billions who are, in a world where billionaires (in U.S. currency) are being created on daily basis, forced to survive on less than one dollar a day or, in many cases, starve to death. These practices, which are not, by the way, natural happenstances of the natural order, have a lot to do with the highly eschewed and historically located hegemonic structure of the world. Indeed, as Steven Klees (2002, p. 467) so cogently observes, the North, *and its international predatory agencies,* generally seem to believe collectively . . . that the wealth of the North has been earned, not gained (and, *perforce,* maintained) through a history of piracy and exploitation, and that if two billion are on the *new global* Titanic, all that can be done is to throw a few life preservers. (emphases added)

On the same page, and still on the obscene realities of how so many would-have-been full citizens of our world have been pushed, again via all or some of the history and current realities discussed here, to decrepit corners of low untenable lives by the North, Klees (2002, p. 467) adds a very important footnote that is also worth (indeed, demands) quoting:

Today we look in astonishment and disgust at social beliefs of superiority and worthiness that gave rise to slavery or eugenics. I believe that in the future, people will look back at us in astonishment and disgust and ask what possible values and beliefs of superiority and worthiness could give rise to a society where someone gets billions of dollars each year and someone else gets one dollar a day.

Indeed, the tasks that await us in achieving the greatly needed programs of liberating education are huge, and interesting in all the analyses on the topic is what we might call the corrupted spirit of postcolonial educational programs in the world. One of the failures of these programs lies in their continuing adherence to the philosophical, ideological, and understandings of Western global division. Among these ideologies is the quasi-religious belief system that some of the world's people (mainly the ones Huntington [1971] described as traditional and backward) have to have lower levels of living standard that should and cannot be compared to those enjoyed by Europeans and to some few other countries that are managing their capitalist-based economies more effectively. But where is the human or natural justification for such a thing? What such ideologies are actually affirming and maintaining is nothing more than the continuing subjugation of billions of people who may be categorized as lesser beings than those in the more endowed zones of the globe. As such, any educational programs designed for the de-subjecting of citizens have to start with and be undertaken on a platform that aims for the achievement of people's full humanity, not only in the specific contexts in which they reside, but also in the global configurations of life in which they have been forced to participate.

So, cultivating and achieving our humanity, in more categories than those implicated in Nussbaum (1998), would call for learning possibilities that advance the holistic being of the group and the individual (Nyerere, 1968) so they interactively harness viable and selectively "pragmatizable" existentialities for the whole community. Here, one could even aim for a world where life trajectories do not have to be measured in the amount of dollars one carries in his or her pocket (or purse) or expects to be in the bank account. My point has something in its kernel that might not have been discussed as much as it deserves. In a world where neoliberal monetarist policies reign supreme, one should ask the question why so many in Africa, for example, are ineptly situated in the monetary categories of life. Was it because these people never had any money, or that they were, before the current hegemony of monetarism, from circa early 1980s, in premonetary societies that had no use for money. Both accounts are, for all pragmatic undertakings, wrong. Here is what I think has happened, at least in the past twenty years or so. With the introduction of Structural Adjustment Programs (SAPs), which were touted (before their dismal failure) as the blueprint for African development by the International Monetary Fund (IMF) and the World Bank, many people in the African continent and elsewhere were money-wise, situationally endowed, if in no other way, due to the fact that the small amounts of money they had were enough to satisfy their daily expenses. But with the introduction of SAPs, one of the main conditions from the Bretton Woods institutions was that all countries would adjust the values of their currency relative to the American dollar. As should have been expected, and with most of these currencies very weak vis-à-vis the globally transferable dollar, the hyperinflation that became the norm in most of Africa, Asia, and Latin America led to the immediate pauperization of hundreds of millions who now had sacks of paper money that could buy few items in the marketplace and had almost no transactional value outside these areas. Worse, even if two neighboring African countries had the audacity to trade between themselves, they usually had to conduct their business in the dollar, which again marginalized their finances and economies while continually elevating the already undisputable supremacy of the American currency.

In sum, therefore, people's money has been demonetarized, rendering whole populations, in the process, destitute figures in the shadow of globalization, where based on the dollar value, all the notes they are carrying would be categorized as living on one or two dollars per day. Here, even the type of currency that is being used across the board and without any concerns from anyone around, is interesting. Would it have helped, for example, if local currency figures were used to estimate people's liquidity characterizations; would that have lessened the possible psychological affects that the visually absent dollar would induce in how individuals and groups understand and define their situations? These question may sound simple, and one may even question their educational positioning, but as far as I am concerned they are exceptionally important, for as should be clear by now, the project of decolonizing ontologies, cultures, and learning platforms and giving people their primordial citizenship, should involve, as much as anything else, the right to redefine issues, attach meanings to both past and actual events, and use local resources, including money, not relative to other more powerful, foreign institutions, but with respect to indigenous needs and expectations. Hence, the need to also educate people about how they define and use economic resources in their daily lives, which may not be easy, as most, if not all of the cards are still in the hands of International Financial Institutions (IFIs) and their Northern governments.

As the former chancellor of the University of Ghana Alexander Kwapong (1994), noted, societies can only use education for meaningful socioeconomic and political enfranchisement when it contains certain aspects of their culture and when it can be extrapolated to some meaning-making categories that directly describe their lives. What Kwapong is talking about falls vertically on using education to achieve meaningful citizenship that restores, above all other things, people's confidence and believe in managing their lives with respect to issues that are relevant to both the historiographies and current tempo-spatial realities of their situations And that would immediately attach meanings and values to daily transactions of life and related expectations, anxieties, and relationships. If and when that is not achieved, what Mahmood Mamdani (1996) would call the world of subject populations will continue to grow, and the effects of that fateful maritime journey of 1492 will continue to overwhelm us.

CONCLUSION

I began this chapter with the objective of historically locating the beginnings of subjecting whole populations and continents based primarily on their skin color. That has led to a cluster of other marginalizations, which included several hundred years of slavery (employing both indigenous peoples in the Americas and those imported as a commodity from Africa and elsewhere), complemented by almost as many years of colonialism, all of which continually affirmed the, perforce, achieved superiority of Europeans and the justifiable subjugation of the rest. In both these schemes of subjecting former citizens, education (whether formal or informal) was used to justify the viability, even the natural variability of oppression and subsequent genocides (the latter mainly in the Americas). With the formulation as well as the implementation of these across-the-centuries regimes of subjugation, it seems that a quasi-permanentized world system of the perennially enfranchised and the perennially disenfranchised has been formed, and the case has apparently continued to perpetuate the current, savagely unequal distribution of resources and intersubjective recognitions. With global problems in place, and with the majority of the world's population still subject to the combined forces of globalization, corrupt local elites, and selectively exclusionist Western advanced monetary policies, the chapter calls for some way to reeducate the world's populations to consider the possibility of reharnessing some aspects of their long lost citizenship, which, even if it had different characteristics and shapes, should still be theirs. Here, a simple principle should be welcomed, that is, the radical equity, precisely the full sanctity of all people, regardless of who they are and where they reside, as full human beings. By achieving that, indeed, a project that awaits all of us, we can achieve, regardless of the tragedies as well as the numerous accidents of history and current intersections of deprivation and attempts at dehumanization, an expansively attractive global platform that is both humanistically and humanely desubjected, "re-citizenized," and might even fit what the Negritude poet Aime Cesaire had in mind: "No [group or region] possesses the monopoly of beauty, intelligence and force, and there is room for all of us at the rendezvous of victory."

REFERENCES

Abdi, A. A. (2002). *Culture, education, and development in South Africa: Historical and contemporary perspectives*. Westport, CT, & London: Bergin & Garvey.

Abdi, A. A. (1999). Identity formations and deformations in South Africa: A historical and contemporary overview. *Journal of Black Studies, 30(2)*, 147–163.

Abdi, A. A. (1998). Education in Somalia: History, destruction, and calls for reconstruction. *Comparative Education, 34(3)*, 327–340.

Abu-Lughod, J. (1991). *Before European hegemony: The world system A.D. 1250–1350*. Oxford: Oxford University Press.

Bassey, M. (1999). *Western education and political domination in Africa: A study in critical and dialogical pedagogy*. Westport, CT: Bergin & Garvey.

Bello, W. (2003). *De-globalization: Ideas for a new world economy*. London: Zed Books.

Brawley, M. (2003). *The politics of globalization*. Don Mills, Ontario: The Broadview Press.

Cesaire, A. (1972). *Discourse on colonialism*. New York: Monthly Review Press.

Cocker, M. (2000). *Rivers of blood, rivers of gold*. New York: Grove Press.

Davidson, B. (1992). *The black man's burden: Africa and the curse of the nation-state*. New York: Times Books.

Davies et al. (1993). *Barbaric others: A manifesto on Western racism*. London: Pluto Press.

de Botton, A. (2001). *Consolations of philosophy*. New York: Vintage.

Dei, G. (1996). *Anti-racism education: Theory and practice*. Halifax: Fernwood Publishing.

Dei et al. (2000). *Indigenous knowledges in global contexts: Multiple readings of our world*. Toronto: University of Toronto Press.

Dewey, J. (1926). *Democracy and education*. New York: Macmillan.

Eze, E. (1997). *Race and the enlightenment*. Cambridge, MA: Blackwell.

Fagerlind, I., & Saha, L. (1989). *Education and national development: A comparative perspective*. Pergamon Press.

Fanon, F. (1968). *The wretched of the earth*. New York: Grove Press.

Fanon, F. (1967). *Black skin, white masks*. New York: Grove Press.

Freire, P. (2000 [1970]). *Pedagogy of the oppressed*. New York: Continuum.

Greene, M. (1995). *Releasing the imagination: Essays on education, the arts, and social change*. San Francisico: Jossey-Bass.

Greene, M. (1993). The passions of pluralism: Multiculturalism and the expanding community. *Educational Researcher, 22(1)*, 13–18.

Guha, R. (1997). *A subaltern studies reader, 1986–1995*. Minneapolis: University of Minnesota Press.

Hardt, M., & Negri, A. (2000). *Empire*. Cambridge: Harvard University Press.

Hoogvelt, A. (2001). *Globalization and the postcolonial world: The new political economy of development*. Baltimore: Johns Hopkins University Press.

Huntington, S. (1993). Economic development must precede democracy. In J. Petrikin (Ed.), *The third world: Opposing viewpoints*. San Diego: Greenhaven Press.

Huntington, S. (1971). The change to change: Modernization, development, and politics. *Comparative Politics, 3(3)*, 283–322.

Klees, S. (2002). World Bank education policy: New rhetoric, old ideology. *International Journal of Educational Development, 22*, 451–474.

Kwapong, A. (1994). Culture, development, and democracy: Role of intellectuals in Africa. In S. Soermadjan and K. Thompson (Eds.), *Culture, democracy, and development: The role of the intellectual*. New York: The United Nations University Press.

Luchembe, C. (1995). Legacy of late nineteenth capitalism: The cases of W. R. Grace and C. J. Rhodes. *UFAHAMU: Journal of the African Activist Association, XXIII(2)*, 4–28.

Macaulay, T. (1994). Minute on Indian education. In B. Ashcroft, G. Griffiths, & H. Tiffin (Eds.), *The post-colonial studies reader*. New York: Routledge.

Mamdani, M. (1996). *Citizen and subject: Contemporary Africa and the legacy of late colonialism*. Princeton: Princeton University Press.

Mandela, N. (1994). *Long walk to freedom: The autobiography of Nelson Mandela*. Toronto: Little, Brown.

Mann, C. (2002, March). 1491. *The Atlantic Monthly*, pp. 41–53.

Mazrui, A. (1990). *Cultural forces in world politics*. London: James Curry.

Memmi, A. (1991). *The colonizer and the colonized*. Boston: Continuum.

Montesquieu, Baron de (1949). *The spirit of the laws*. New York: Hafner Press.

Nandy, A. (1997). Colonization of the mind. In M. Rahnema & V. Bowtree (Eds.), *The post-development reader*. London: Zed Books.

Ngugi wa Thiongo (1993). *Moving the centre: The struggle for cultural freedoms*. London: James Curry.

Ngugi wa Thiongo (1986). *Decolonising the mind: The politics of language in African literature*. London: James Curry.

Nussbaum, M. (1998). *Cultivating humanity: A classical defense of reform in liberal education*. Cambridge: Harvard University Press.

Nyerere, J. (1968). *Freedom and socialism: A selection from writing and speeches, 1965–67*. London: Oxford University Press.

Pells, E. G. (1970). *300 years of South African education*. Westport, CT: Greenwood Press.

Rodney, W. (1982). *How Europe underdeveloped Africa*. Washington, DC: Howard University Press.

Said, E. (1993). *Culture and imperialism*. New York: Vintage.

Saul, J. (1993). *Recolonization and resistance: Southern Africa in the 1990s*. Trenton, NJ: African World Press.

Sen, A. (2000). *Development as freedom*. New York: Anchor Books.

Sen, A. (1993). Economic development need not precede democracy. In J. Petrikin (Ed.), *The third world: Opposing viewpoints*. San Diego: Greenhaven Press.

Stiglitz, J. (2002). *Globalization and its discontents*. New York: Penguin.

Taylor, C. (1995). *Philosophical arguments*. Cambridge: Harvard University Press.

Taylor, G. (2004). *Buying whiteness: Race, culture, and identity from Columbus to hip-hop*. New York: Palgrave Macmillan

Van Sertima, I. (1991). *The lost sciences of Africa*. In I. Van Sertima (Ed.), *Blacks in science: Ancient and modern*. New Brunswick, NJ: Transaction Books.

Voltaire (1826). Essai sur les moeurs. Paris: SN.

Wolfe, E. (1997). *Europe and the people without history*. Berkeley: University of California Press.

SEVEN

The Short History of Women, Human Rights, and Global Citizenship

Ratna Ghosh

All human beings are born free and equal in dignity and rights.
—Article 1, Universal Declaration of Human Rights

ALTHOUGH WOMEN AND MEN are different, they are equal in dignity and rights. In recent years there has been global recognition of the rights of women. Globalization has tremendous implications for women, human rights, and citizenship. The globalization process poses both threats and opportunities for citizenship. On the one hand, economic liberalization and restructuring, and market driven forces, have eroded the economic and social rights of citizens in many countries (especially in countries of the South). On the other hand, elimination of barriers in communications has increased international awareness of rights and the creation of civil society networks, institutions, and legislation on a global scale. Technological convergence, the blurring of national borders, and the complex changes that diffuse values and restructure cultural practices (Petras & Veltmeyer, 2001) have led to the homogenization of certain patterns of behavior and values. This homogenization is influencing the globalization of human rights, especially women's rights and other democratic values.

The Universal Declaration of Human Rights was proclaimed by the United Nations in 1948. The United Nations Human Rights Center defines human rights as those basic standards without which people cannot live in dignity. To violate someone's human rights is to treat that person as though she or he were not a human being. To advocate human rights is to demand that the human dignity of all people be respected. Most states attempt to observe the basic human rights of their citizens. These rights exist by virtue of the fact that one is human, and is therefore entitled to be treated in a way befitting that status. Although states disagree about the precise content of this body of rights and some states deny that these rights are governed by international law, there has been a dramatic change in the last forty years. This change toward recognition of human rights as inalienable rights of any citizen has been spurred by three major precedents: the Nuremberg Trials, genocide of groups of people, and the development of the Universal Declaration of Human Rights. Despite some differences among countries' equality legislation, the globalization of women's inferior status has been taken up by the world community. This has resulted in the United Nations conventions against discrimination and violence toward women.

Human rights legislation and women's movements in modern democratic societies demand that all citizens as human beings have equal rights and opportunities. Equality legislation implies that while men and women are different, they are equal. This idea has been accepted by most countries of the world barring a few Islamic countries where religious *Sharia* laws prevail and do not give women equal rights. But even most Muslim countries are gradually granting women more rights, such as the right to vote—Kuwaiti women were given the right to vote as recently as 2005.

The focus on legislation and protection of the individual through documents and constitutional guarantees has moved international law away from its traditional, exclusive focus on the state. While the enforcement of the rights depends on the states, and the state's role in enforcing rights differs from country to country, the focus is now on citizens of the state as key stakeholders in constructing practical foundations of human rights practices.

Given the existence of global legislation for more than half a century, how can we explain the persistence of inequalities between men and women within and among nations? This chapter will briefly consider the very concept of rights and the need for agency if rights are to be secured and taken advantage of. The capabilities approach (Sen,1992; Nussbaum, 1997) will provide the conceptual framework for discussing the rights of women and their role as global citizens. After looking at the question of whether human rights are universally acceptable I point to the wide variety of legislation by the United Nations on human rights and especially on women's rights and human rights education. Are women as citizens of the globe able to benefit from the rights and privileges citizenship bestows upon them? While progress has been made for women in some areas, do women benefit from legislation equally in all societies and at all levels? Evidence of the inequalities that still persist between women and men indicate that the legislative approach to human rights and the rights of women as citizens is a necessary but not sufficient condition for protecting the human rights of women. Women need to develop capabilities to function and to act and make choices for themselves as well as for others. Given its important role in the socialization process I discuss the role of formal education in perpetuating the inequalities faced by women, which act as barriers to the development of their capabilities and in their ability to act.

WHAT IS A RIGHT?

"The idea of human rights is by no means a crystal-clear idea" (Nussbaum, 2006). Not only are rights understood in many different ways but the question arises: What are they rights *to*? Are they rights to resources, or to opportunities and capacities for one's life choices? A human right is a claim on society that makes others responsible for promoting, protecting, and respecting that right (United Nations Development Programme 2000). One way to think of rights is to see that they can be secured or obtained. The capabilities approach suggested by Amartya Sen (1992) and Martha Nussbaum (1997)[1] links human rights[2] to capabilities[3] and to agency[4] (Sen,1995) in securing the rights granted to a person. Both Sen and Nussbaum connect the capabilities approach closely to the idea of human rights. Nussbaum analyzes the relationship of human rights particularly to women's capabilities. The need for agency is stressed by Sen. For example, women might have the political right to vote but their social circumstances may forbid them to leave the house thus preventing them from voting. They do not then have the capability to vote and this right is meaningless. Women, in this case, must have the capability to function as a citizen. Capability to do so involves more than the knowledge of the right and knowledge of how to vote: it also implies the power or ability and choice to act. Human agency—both individual and collective—is crucial for participation in personal, cultural, economic, social, and political life. Agency is the ability to set and pursue one's own goals, interests, and a variety of values as well as the *freedom* to do so (Sen, 1977). Freedom and motive for choice are important concepts in agency. For example, one's motive for not voting could be that a woman wants to earn praise for being a devoted wife who stays home. Education as a significant socialization agent has the potential for developing both capabilities and human agency.

The concept of capabilities is explicitly linked to political principles that form the foundations for human rights legislation to underlying ideas of human dignity and John Rawls's conception of justice (Nussbaum, 2000). In her influential book *Women and Human Development*, Nussbaum (2000) provides the philosophical underpinning for the basic constitutional principles that should be respected and implemented by all governments as a "bare minimum of what respect for human dignity requires" (p. 5). She relates the list of central human capabilities[5] and the threshold level of each capability to fundamental human rights. What each person is capable of doing depends on basic capabilities as well as combined and internal capabilities, which are in turn dependent on external conditions that can be improved by the state (through human rights legislation). While Sen's focus links capabilities to the quality of life, Nussbaum's is on rights. And although *functioning*, not simply *capabilities*, is what makes a life fully human, she would leave the *choice* to function to the citizen. However, the citizen must have that choice and have the ability (agency) to make that choice. In the case of a woman who does not exercise her right to vote, the question is not whether she votes but has she, in fact, the choice? In other words, is she prevented (for example) from doing so by her husband who does not want her to go out of the house, or does she feel that there is no candidate she wants to vote for?

UNIVERSALITY OF HUMAN RIGHTS

Is the human rights discourse universal? Does granting universality to a strong set of human rights undermine the particular framework of a society? The development of the United Nations Universal Declaration of Human Rights has presupposed the universality of the concept of rights. Yet, the question of universal applicability of the United Nations document has been fiercely challenged in many parts of the world. The basic question is that since there is no universal culture, can there be a universal code of human rights? Specifically, how can women's rights be universal when women's roles, responsibility, and desirable behavior are defined by different societies very differently? The economic question, that given economic disparities among countries and people of the world, can there be anything universal, is an important one too. Allman and Wallis (1995) note that postmodernists today focus on the pluralistic aspirations derived from difference. They deny the legitimacy, or even the possibility, of universal morals and values. They call for individual fulfillment instead of shared collectivity. They state that the desire to create a more just world is at the heart of consciousness in all the objective and subjective dimensions. Therefore, universality of rights is a concept of "humanized social relations" (pp. 25–26). Despite these and several other objections, the universality of human rights is supported by the majority of countries globally. Although in some ancient cultures such as the Vedic, Confucian, and some African traditions the emphasis is on duties rather than rights there are very few societies where the concepts of justice, law, and human dignity are not important (see Sen, 1997 for a discussion of this point with reference to India and China). The cultural relativism argument—that human values vary according to different cultural perspectives—is a weak one because cultures are dynamic and always changing. What was cultural practice at one time—for example, slavery—may not be acceptable by societies with time and as they evolve. This argument is often used to keep power by force.

Thinkers in countries of the South, for example, Ashis Nandy (1980) and Veena Das (1995), have shown how indigenous concepts and processes involving injustice and violence resonate with human rights discourse in the everyday lives of people in their societies. Although the idea of rights is linked to the European Enlightenment, the wide range of ideas in the Universal Declaration has been brought together from a variety of sources. The drafting of the Universal Declaration and the Covenants was influenced by the intervention of several countries with very different cultures; these countries were India and China, Chile and Panama, Cuba, Lebanon, and later Ghana and Nigeria. As Nussbaum (2000) points out, it is one thing to say that local knowledge is necessary to understand the problems of women in different societies and quite another to say that the norms of personal dignity and integrity of the body (for example) are not relevant to non-Western societies.

From the gender perspective, feminists have challenged human rights for being male centered because in their quest for equality they do not include some abilities and opportunities that are fundamental to women, for example, bodily integrity, freedom from domestic violence and sexual harassment. Nussbaum proposes a list of ten capabilities while emphasizing the need to modify them according to context (sociocultural and economic) and explicitly incorporates female specific rights (such as choice in matters of reproduction; security against sexual assault and violence) for which she claims a degree of universal relevance (Nussbaum, 2006, p. 48).

Historically, the idea of a universal set of human rights came about after the atrocities of World War II. To quote the preamble to the Universal Declaration, the "barbarous acts which have outraged the conscience" of humankind, and the common discourse against brutality and violence has gained universal spirit. The Universal Declaration is for every human being and "represents a broader consensus on human dignity than does any single culture or tradition" (Charles Norchi quoted in Ayton-Shenker, 1995). The declaration describes the minimum standards required for human dignity. The moral principle underlying this idea is that human beings should not fall below a certain level of living and the international community should be able to protect that minimum threshold for everybody. Individual rights are especially important for women because women have been historically treated as "supporters of the ends of others, rather than as ends in their own right" (Nussbaum, 2000, pp. 5–6). The declaration does not impose one cultural standard. Finally, as Shashi Tharoor points out, universality does not presuppose uniformity. Rather, human rights reflect our common universal humanity from which no human being must be excluded (1999/2000).

WOMEN'S RIGHTS AS HUMAN RIGHTS.

When the Universal Declaration of Human Rights was proclaimed by the United Nations in 1948, equality was not interpreted to include equality for the sexes. It was not until 1967 that one of the most far-reaching resolutions on equality for the sexes was adopted: The Declaration of the Elimination of Discrimination Against Women (CEDAW). Although the declaration was only a statement of moral and political intent, without the contractual force of a treaty, it nonetheless focused on international standards articulating the equal rights of men and women. With women's movements gaining momentum, the need to frame women's equality and empowerment in political terms gave the impetus for internationally acceptable norms. "In terms of political values like the concept of democracy, it is an important step forward for all human beings and all cultures" (Coomaraswamy, 1997). International legislation has attempted to extend rights to all women on the principle that men and women are different but equal. However, it was not until the 1980s that international lawmakers paid attention to women whose work was relegated to the private domestic sphere. This attention challenged the patriarchal system that maintained a rigid separation between public and private spheres and assured that both the formulation and implementation of legislation were done by males who were insensitive to the demands or needs of women.

Articles 213 and 215 of the CEDAW reaffirmed that all human rights—civil, cultural, economic, political, and social, including the right to development—are universal, indivisible, interdependent, and interrelated. It also affirmed that the human rights of women and girl children are an inalienable, integral, and indivisible part of universal human rights. The full and equal enjoyment of all human rights and fundamental freedoms by women and girls is a priority for governments and the United Nations and is essential for the advancement of women. Governments were called upon not only to refrain from violating the human rights of all women, but to work actively to promote and protect these rights.

The 1995 United Nations World Conference on Women, held in Beijing, identified the reasons for the continuing lack of women's rights in countries around the globe. It was noted that women's full enjoyment of equal rights is sometimes undermined by the discrepancies between national legislation and international law and international instruments on human rights. A few other reasons were overly complex administrative procedures, lack of awareness within the judicial process, inadequate monitoring of the violation of the human rights of all women, the underrepresentation of women in justice systems, insufficient information on existing rights, and persistent attitudes and practices that perpetuate women's de facto inequality. The de facto inequality is also perpetuated by the lack of enforcement of family, civil, penal, labor, and commercial laws or codes, or administrative rules and regulations intended to ensure women's full enjoyment of human rights and fundamental freedoms. It is important to note that the explicit prohibition of violence against women is singularly absent from CEDAW. Not until the 1990s was violence against women (public and private spheres) on the international agenda. The turning point in public attitude toward violence against women was the United Nations Vienna Conference on Human Rights in 1993. The Vienna Declaration on Violence Against Women, 1993, and the Programme of Action state that any act of gender-based violence that results in, or is likely to result in, physical, sexual, or psychological harm or suffering to women, including threats of such acts, coercion, or arbitrary deprivation of liberty, whether occurring in public or private life (Article 18) are priority objectives of the international community. The Vienna Declaration and Programme of Action also focused on human rights education as a fundamental tool in guaranteeing and maintaining respect for all rights of citizens, stating that human rights education was essential for the promotion and achievement of peace in the world and for the development of knowledge and respect for human rights and fundamental freedoms of citizens.

HUMAN RIGHTS EDUCATION AND WOMEN'S RIGHTS

In proclaiming the United Nations Decade for Human Rights Education (1995–2004), in December 1994, the General Assembly defined human rights education as: "a life-long process by which people at all levels of development and in all strata of society learn respect for the dignity of others and the means and methods of ensuring that respect in all societies." The General Assembly resolution particularly linked human rights education to women's rights. According to the resolution, education for the purpose of the decade shall be conceived to include the equal participation of women and men of all age groups, all sectors of society, both in formal learning through schools as well as vocational and professional training and in nonformal learning through institutions of civil society, the family, and the mass media.

The concepts of "citizen" and "citizenship" have historically referred to national identity. Global citizenship refers to universal values and common problems. All societies need to educate their young people for the many facets of global citizenship (Noddings, 2005). Human rights education involves empowerment through development of capabilities and agency through confidence to act. Women's participation in social and political transformation must eventually lead to change. De Lourdes (1996) calls for change, which will come about only if women at all levels are fully aware of their rights and responsibilities. Citizenship and human rights education are closely linked concepts as both serve to elevate the level of awareness in moral values and participation in the political, social, and economic process. The coming together to learn as citizens and as moral subjects will undoubtedly develop a universal respect for the dignity of human beings and their fundamental rights. The UN definition of human rights education is an ideal that can be compromised within societal contexts. While its approach largely rests on the administration of legal rights based on a view of human rights in which the legal and constitutional rights accorded to citizens (therefore, women) are taken as the guarantee that all citizens have and will enjoy the same rights, in fact, local customs and traditions can, and do, have more power to execute judgment where the law is contradictory.

THE ROLE OF THE STATE: WOMEN AS CITIZENS

The UN documents place the responsibility for upholding rights on the governments of the countries around the world. Citizenship is one of the most important ways in which individuals and collectivities engage with the state. Citizenship is status attained (either won through struggle or bestowed by the constitution) by those who are full members of a community—the nation-state. All those who possess that status are presumed to be equal with respect to the rights and duties with which the status is endowed.

According to the eighteenth-century philosopher Immanuel Kant (1991), the characteristics of an active citizen are freedom, equality, and independence. Active citizenship includes both process (active participation) as well as outcome (possession of rights). It involves agency and structural constraints and the interplay between the two (Giddens, 1996). The modern concept of citizenship implies the existence of a civic and political community, a set of rights and obligations, and an ethic of participation. Important thinkers such as H. T. Marshall (1950) and Ralph Dahrendorf (1959) have written extensively on civil society and the meaning of citizenship. Although Marshall questioned the relevance of categories (such as class) in a period when citizenship has conferred one universal equality of status on all citizens, nonetheless, women as a category, have had to fight to have equal rights with men (e.g., the franchise), and in many countries still do not have all the rights of citizenship.

Traditionally, women, as citizens, were consigned to the passive category, together with children, because they lacked "civil independence" (such as the right to vote). In Canada, the Persons' Cases during the late nineteenth century graphically illustrate how sex constituted a disabling factor for women. Women were not "persons" under British law for, among other things, the purposes of holding office and gaining entry to the universities or professions. A ruling in British common law in 1876 emphasized the problem for Canadian women by saying, "Women are persons in matters of pains and penalties, but are not persons in matters of rights and privileges" (canadaonline.about.com). A range of cases was heard in the United Kingdom and Canada, as well as Australia, regarding the statutory interpretation of the word *person*. It was not until Emily Murphy led a group of Canadian women in the legal and political battle to have women recognized as persons under the British North America Act that women won that right in 1929. The landmark decision by the British Privy Council, the highest level for legal appeals in Canada at the time, was a milestone victory for the rights of women in Canada. The United States still has not succeeded in passing an equal rights amendment.

In addition to the attempt to masculinize the universal, for example, by taking the word *person* to mean *male*, which serves to exclude women, there are cultural (including religious) factors that are used to withhold privileges from women. In many countries poverty and economic crisis, political instability, and civil war make "rights" a distant dream. Unfortunately, in these countries several sectors, which largely escape accountability and control but have considerable power, have a negative effect on citizenship—especially for women who lack labor protection and health benefits. These include transnational corporations from industrialized countries, international financial institutions, and the military of individual countries as well as of foreign powers. Government institutions in disadvantaged countries are often powerless to protect their citizens.

World citizenship today is not what it was twenty or thirty years ago. Economic globalization has by far overtaken other aspects of globalization. Citizenship is a "multi-dimensional construct and practice"(Abdi, Ellis, & Shizha, 2005, p. 460) and is associated with the globalization process. Yet, the discussion on citizenship usually occurs within national boundaries and asserts the basic civil, political, and socioeconomic rights of individuals. However, the link between citizenship, equality, and territory is now challenged by globalization. It is no longer sufficient to understand the phenomenon of citizenship by concentrating almost exclusively on the relation between the individual and the state. Factors that affect citizenship exist at many levels of society, from the most local through the most global; and it is increasingly necessary to examine how different forces of identity and experience are related. Citizenship has multiple layers and world citizenship is one layer added to local and national citizenship, not replacing them.

One positive impact of globalization is that it encourages international solidarity in terms of standards and institutions that uphold universal rights and related issues affecting every human being as an inhabitant of the planet. People are creating transnational alliances and demanding new rights within supranational arenas. For example, women have been able to forge a strong international association demanding recognition of reproductive rights.

The principle of equality between women and men is not a fundamental value of all societies. The dilemma is that there are issues such as female genital mutilation and *Shari'a* law that violate basic tenets of the Women's Convention. Many multiethnic states fail to end practices that dictate different standards for marriage, divorce, custody of children, inheritance, and maintenance as well as the type of punishment that should be given to women. This reluctance by governments is in order to avoid antagonizing their minorities (or, in some case, majorities). Because they are social practices, societal institutions (such as schools) may be giving out messages that contradict equality legislation. In addition, countries are at different stages of development with regard to women's rights, and political will depends on that. For example, the United Arab Emirates ratified the CEDAW only in 2004.

What are the facts regarding women around the globe? What has been achieved?

Has acceptance of the principle that women are different but equal changed the status of women globally? Yes, women's status has improved considerably in most countries in the past quarter century. Over the past two decades school enrollment for girls in countries of the South increased from 38 percent to78 percent. Women have made significant gains in higher education enrollment in most regions of the world. As a matter of fact, in some regions (both industrialized and nonindustrialized countries) women's enrollment equals or surpasses that of men. There has been a significant change in the quality of women's lives. Women are marrying later and there has been decline in early marriage and childbearing so that birth rates continue to decline in all regions of the world. Women's economic activity has increased in most regions and women are engaged in organized as well as unorganized sectors of work.

Has legislation made a difference? Most countries of the world have been inspired by human rights legislation at the international level and have adopted legislation regarding women's rights in their constitutions. However, evidence shows that while women have made advances, they are far behind men in achieving equal rights and dignity in countries of both the South and the North (where marginalized minority group women are at a particular disadvantage), despite legislation granting constitutional rights to all citizens. In no country have women achieved equality with men in all spheres, legal, social, and economic, although Scandinavian countries are closest to equality between men and women. It is not that gaining the right to work gives equality to women because often by doing so they forfeit the right to leisure. Women's multiple roles and responsibilities make men's and women's lives qualitatively different. In general, women have fewer resources and economic opportunities than men and they participate less in the political sphere.

Of the world's 1.3 billion people living in poverty, 70 percent are women. Two-thirds of the world's nearly one billion illiterates are women and two-thirds of the 130 million children worldwide who are not in school are girls. In general, although more women are earning, they get about three-fourths of the pay of males for the same work (outside agriculture) in countries of both the South and North. In agriculture, rural women produce more than 55 percent of all food grown in countries of the South though they get very little money. Healthwise, women are worse off than males not only because they eat less in quantity and quality (although one in every four households in the world is headed by a woman) but also because they are more at risk for diseases. They account for one-half of all HIV/AIDS cases, and young women are at higher risk than young men of contracting the disease. Annually, women undergo fifty million abortions, twenty million of which are unsafe. While women comprise one-third of the world's labor force and they have made inroads into many fields, the majority of women still work in lower status, lower paid jobs than men. They continue to remain at the lower end of a segregated labor market and are concentrated in a few occupations with little or no decision-making power. They continue to struggle to reconcile paid work with childbearing/childrearing and domestic responsibilities. Millions of girls and women worldwide are physically and sexually abused and two million girls between the ages of five and fifteen are introduced to the commercial sex market annually.

Inequalities in power around the world mean violation of the human rights of citizens globally. Inequalities in men and women's situation is a violation of women's rights. Despite the tremendous changes of the last century and progress in science and technology discrimination and violence against women remain. Gender inequalities persist because they are supported by social norms (often by legal institutions) and are firmly rooted in cultures globally. Many cultures either condone or ignore violence against women, and equality legislation (if it exists) is not always respected. Moreover, religious fundamentalism, which is on the rise, institutionalizes male domination and even erases some of the rights that women have achieved. Religious fundamentalism, chauvinistic tendencies, and nondemocratic regimes always suppress women's rights in multiple ways. Women's NGO groups have lobbied strongly to include the violation of women's rights resulting from religious extremism as a major area of concern. Because of their lobbying efforts, the mandate of the United Nations Special Rapporteur on Violence Against Women identifies religious extremism as one of the causes of violence against women. In addition, rampant capitalism unchecked by an enlightened social agenda also leads to abridgment of women's rights because ruthless global market competition annihilates the fundamental rights of women and all marginalized groups

Evidence suggests that despite higher levels of women's education, gender inequalities still persist. What is the reason? An important reason may be found in the context of schooling. Educational content (as distinct from educational ideals) is embedded in the sociocultural matrix of every society. Educational practice inculcates the prevalent ideologies, and educational curricula are designed to reflect the values and biases of the ruling elites who propagate the norms of the dominant group. When the dominant group norms are either feudal, religious, or militaristic-chauvinistic then the educational discourse constructs citizenship identities that are determined by these ideologies. For example, an analysis of texts and curricula in a South Asian country (Naseem, 2004) shows that women are depicted by the educational discourse to exist and operate exclusively in the private domain and totally outside the "practical" domains of politics and economics, which are constructed as male domains. Citizenship is linked by the educational texts to religious fundamentalism, nationalism, militarism, and patriotism. These qualities are then constructed as masculine attributes, thus excluding women from citizenship identities. The identities are then inculcated into the cognitions of pupil-citizens from a very young age. As these pupil-citizens advance in educational systems these identities are further strengthened by texts and course content that normalize authority, knowledge, and civic and democratic values as exclusively male attributes. Women are thus constituted as the "other" of the male "self" and their status and rights thus also suffer. When education is a template of either feudalistic and undemocratic, religious fundamentalist, militaristic-chauvinistic societies, education will be framed in the male mold and disempower women. Worldwide educational discourses, in their current form and state, work largely to exclude women (and other marginalized groups) from their rightful place in citizenship and human rights discourses. Despite the efforts of the United Nations and especially CEDAW, "rights" and "citizenship" continue to be molded in the male and masculine image and thus are not inclusive enough. Socialization through education and other agents prevents the development of what a female could do or be (capabilities) and emphasizes her *inability* to act.

CONCLUSION

As long ago as 1795 Immanuel Kant, the eighteenth-century philosopher, wrote in his book *Perpetual Peace* (Reiss, 1991) that it is less essential to achieve peace in itself than to create a world system of laws that can in turn create peace. He identified three levels of law rule in our societies: *jus civitatis*, or national law; *jus gentium*, international law including the rights of national minorities; and *jus cosmopoliticum*, the law of world citizens. One and one-half centuries later the United Nations has created a world system of laws. The question is, How effective is the world system?

The capability approach suggests that we look at capabilities when making normative evaluations of human rights and social justice issues. "The capabilities" refers to people's situations of being and doing—to their functionings. Together, all capabilities lead to the kind of life people have reason to value (they make the choice), which is based on a rights approach rather than a utilitarian point of view. Human rights legislation proposes a moral and substantial set of goals for the good life of all citizens in any society (and globally). Capabilities give concrete form to rights. Nussbaum argues that the "language of capabilities gives important precision and supplementation to the language of rights" (Nussbaum, 2006, p. 46). For example, the right to education is made more concrete by expressing it in the language of capability: "being able to be educated and to use and produce knowledge" (Robeyns,

2006, p. 82). Robeyns points out that lists of capabilities (based on Sen's work) that have been drawn up by people from diverse backgrounds not only overlap but are all in some way included in the Universal Declaration of Human Rights (p. 86). This suggests that both the UN Declaration of Rights and the categories of capabilities are universally important. The attempt must now be to make women more capable of exercising their rights.

So far as women are concerned, despite the efforts of the United Nations and especially CEDAW, rights and citizenship continue to be molded in the masculine image and thus are not empowering for females. Women, by and large, continue to be underrepresented in the definitions and constitutions of citizenship discourse and identities. Greater access to education is a significant starting point for women's empowerment but the *message* of education is most important in the attainment of gender equality. Educational messages are filtered through the lenses of prevalent prejudices of all societies. This is especially true in countries that have not moved to the postreligious stage, so that religious and traditional ideas of women continue to permeate the curriculum and condition the minds of boys as well as girls. Early socialization develops their identities in favor of traditional male-dominated thoughts and practices.

Human rights as well as citizenship education have been disseminated through the existing educational frameworks, which reflect societal norms. Human rights education has attempted to *improve* the curricula by adding to the existing educational discourses rather than *changing* the curricula and questioning the framework and basis of traditional assumptions of power. Global citizenship is about understanding and living human rights and tackling injustice and inequality, not merely teaching about them while maintaining the social structure. Globalization has brought focus to the different but equal status of women and has put women's status on the international agenda. This is a tremendous achievement and both women and some liberal men should be given credit for it. However, as mentioned above, legislation is a necessary but not a sufficient condition for women's rights. In the words of Martin Luther King Jr.: Legislation cannot change the heart, but it can restrain the heartless. Legislation will not only help protect women but also guide societies. Women must develop capabilities and continue to fight for voice and agency in making decisions affecting their families, communities, and societies. Education should lead to empowerment but women have to extract equality from society. In Nehru's words: No people, no group, no community, no country, has ever got rid of its disabilities by the generosity of the oppressor . . . [women] will have to fight for their rights.

NOTES

Thanks to Charlotte Baltodano for her help with revisions.

1. Amartya Sen pioneered the capabilities approach based on functioning and capability in welfare economics. Martha Nussbaum collaborated with him on this pro-

ject for social justice and gender justice and while there are differences in their perspectives the main ideas are similar. The framework has been widely applied to several fields such as gender inequality (Nussbaum, 2000; Robeyns, 2002). It has gradually developed into a paradigm. Applied to gender inequality, the core argument of this concept is the generation of capabilities. The concept moves beyond and between fields and has a normative base.

2. Both first generation rights (political rights and civil liberties) and second generation rights (economic and social rights).

3. What a person is able to do or be.

4. Ability to act or bring about change.

5. Sen does not provide a list of capabilities in order to avoid a fixed canonical list. Nussbaum and Robeyns both propose a list of capabilities (which are sensitive to context) in order to offer valuable normative guidance on social justice issues (Agarwal et al., 2006).

REFERENCES

Abdi, A., Ellis, L., & Shizha, E. (2005). Democratic development and the role of citizenship education in sub-Saharan Africa with a case focus on Zambia. *International Education Journal, 6(4)*, 454–466.

Allman, P., & Wallis, J. (1995). Challenging the Postmodern condition: Radical adult education for critical intelligence. In M. Mayo & J. Thompson (Eds.), *Adult learning, critical intelligence, and social change*. London: NIACE.

Ayton-Shenker, D. (1995). *The challenge of human rights and cultural diversity*. United Nations Department of Public Information DPI/1627.

Coomaraswamy, R. (1997). Reinventing international law: Women's rights as human rights in the international community. The Edward A. Smith Visiting Lecture, Human Rights Program, Harvard Law School, Cambridge, Massachusetts.

Dahrendorf, R. (1959). *Class and class conflict in industrial society*. London: Routledge.

Das, V. (1995). *Critical events: An anthropological perspective on contemporary India*. Oxford: Oxford University Press.

De Lourdes, P. M. (1996). *Caring for the future: Report of the independent commission on population and quality of life*. Oxford: Oxford University Press.

Giddens, A. (1996). T. H. Marshall, the state, and democracy. In M. Bulmer & A. M. Rees (Eds.), *Citizenship today*. London: UCL Press.

Kant, I. (1991). *The metaphysics of morals* (M. Gregor, Trans.). Cambridge: Cambridge University Press.

Kant, I. [1795] (1991). Toward perpetual peace: A philosophical sketch. In Reiss, *Kant's Political Writings* (2nd ed., pp. 93–130). Cambridge: Cambridge University Press.

Marshall, T. H. (1950). *Citizenship and social class and other essays*. Cambridge: Cambridge University Press.

Marshall, T. H. (1964). *Class, citizenship, and social development*. New York: Double-day.

Nandy, A. (1980). *At the edge of psychology*. New Delhi: Oxford University Press.

Naseem, A. (2004). *Education, the state and subject: Constitution of gendered subjectivities in/through school curricula in Pakistan. A post-structuralist analysis of social studies and Urdu textbooks for grades 1–8*. PhD dissertation, Faculty of Education, McGill University.

Niezen, R. (2004). *A world beyond difference: Cultural identity in the age of globalization*. Blackwell.

Noddings, N. (Ed.). (2005). *Educating citizens for global awareness*. New York: Teachers' College Press and the Boston Research Center for the 21st Century.

Nussbaum, M. (2006). Capabilities as fundamental entitlements: Sen and social justice. In B. Agarwal, J. Humphries, & I. Robeyns (Eds.). *Capabilities, freedom, and equality: Amartya Sen's work from a gender perspective*. New Delhi: Oxford University Press.

Nussbaum, M. (1997). Capabilities and human rights. *Fordham Law Review, 66*, 273–300.

Nussbaum, M. (2000). *Women and human development: The capabilities approach*. Cambridge: Cambridge University Press.

Petras, J., & Veltmeyer, H. (2001). *Globalization unmasked: Imperialism in the 21st century*. London: Zed Books.

Robeyns, I. (2002). *Gender inequality. A capability perspective*. Doctoral Dissertation. Cambridge, UK.

Robeyns, I. (2006). Sen's capability approach and gender inequality: Selecting relevant capabilities. In B. Agarwal, J. Humphries, and I. Robeyns (Eds.), *Capabilities, freedom, and equality: Amartya Sen's work from a gender prespective*. New Delhi: Oxford University Press.

Sen, A. (1995). Agency and well-being: The development agenda. In N. Heyzer, S. Kapoor, & J. Sandler (Eds.), *A commitment to the world's women* (pp. 103–112). Washington, DC: UNIFEM.

Sen, A. (1992). *Inequality re-examined*. Oxford: Clarendon Press.

Sen, A. (1997, July 14/21). Human rights and Asian values. *The New Republic*, pp. 33–41.

Sen, A. (1977). Rational foods. *Philosophy and Public Affairs, 6*, 317–344.

Tharoor, S. W. (1999/2000). Are human rights universal? *World Policy Journal, XVI*, 4.

United Nations Development Programme. (2000). Human Development Report 2000. New York: Oxford University Press.

EIGHT

Re/presentation of Race and Racism in the Multicultural Discourse of Canada

Carl E. James

EACH YEAR on March 21, Canadians, like others around the world, commemorate the International Day for the Elimination of Racial Discrimination as established by the United Nations in 1966 after the 1960 Sharpville Massacre, when more than sixty-nine black South Africans were killed and 180 wounded. In schools, colleges, and universities, special activities such as lectures and seminars are held when we discuss the injuries of racial discrimination. On such occasions, we are be reminded that Canada was one of the first countries to support this United Nations declaration, and that in 1989, the Department of Canadian Heritage launched its annual March 21 Campaign. That campaign, the Canadian Heritage Web site (2005) states,

> was initiated in response to the need to heighten awareness of the harmful effects of racism on a national scale and to demonstrate clearly the commitment and leadership of the federal government to foster respect, equality and diversity. For more than ten years, the March 21 Campaign has mobilized youth across Canada to rise up and to take a stand against racism. Through their participation in the campaign, Canadian youth have spoken loudly and eloquently: there is no place for racism in their lives!
> Every year, to mark the International Day for the Elimination of Racial Discrimination, numerous activities aiming to raise public awareness on the issue of racism take place across Canada. *The Racism. Stop It* National Video Competition is one of the means by which the federal government leads the fight against racism and mobilizes thousands of youth across Canada to rise up and take a stand against racism. (http://www.pch.gc.ca/march-21–mars/ why-pourquoi/index_e.cfm)

But the public "awareness" of racism that is being promoted is more about the racism that is evident in individuals' attitudes, ideas, and actions, and not that which exists in the policies and regulations of institutions and the society as a whole. Racism at these levels is often more difficult to identify, but its existence is apparent and recognizable in the regulations, rules, and resulting norms that shape and govern individuals' values, attitudes, and practices. Hence, in our commemoration of March 21, and as we pride ourselves on the fact that Canada played a major role in the fight against apartheid in South Africa, we need to critically examine the structural reality of racism in Canada and our connection to the system of apartheid in South Africa. For as Michele DuCharme (1986) reminds us in her article "The Canadian Origins of South African Apartheid," public archive documents indicate that "South African government officials visited Canada at different times . . . [between] 1948 and 1963 in order to tour Indian reserves and industrial schools in the West. For example, as late as July 1962, the South African High Commissioner W. Dirke-van-Schalkwyk visited selected Indian reserves in Western Canada" (p. 1). DuCharme goes on to say that the establishment of the apartheid policies of South Africa in the 1960s was "around the same time that the South African High Commissioner was touring our Canadian reserves" (p. 2). Hence, much as the apartheid laws of South Africa regulated the lives of blacks with the pass laws which they protested, so too the Indian Act of Canada regulated the lives of Aboriginal Canadians.

So why the inattention to the structural realities of racism in Canada? It is, in part, because Canadians, typically white Canadians, tend to hold on to the "truth" that, unlike South Africa, as a society, and by extension its institutions, Canada does not differentiate people by race or skin color; rather, any differentiation that is made among people is seen to be related to culture. Racism and racial discrimination, then, insofar as they exist, are perceived to be a product of individuals' ignorance of (due primarily to lack of exposure to) each other's cultural differences—an ignorance that, as the March 21 activities indicate, can be remedied through individuals becoming aware of each other's culture, and in doing so address "the harmful effects of racism." As such, racism and racial discrimination are conceptualized as mainly about individuals' attitudes and not about structures or ideologies. In this chapter, I argue that if awareness of racism among Canadians is indeed to be heightened, and respect, equity, and diversity are to be fostered, then the education of young people, and Canadians in general, must not only be about bringing them to an awareness of the individual racism that we witness in our everyday lives, but necessarily helping them to develop an understanding of individual racism as informed by and connected to institutional and structural racism. In other words, young people must come to understand the interrelationship among individual, institutional, and structural racism, and how these racisms have operated and continue to operate in Canada to influence and shape individuals' participation and achievements in the society.

In what follows, I discuss: (1) the concept of culture, and then go on to show how within the Canadian multicultural discourse culture is used to signal race and difference, (2) individual, institutional, and structural racism and the interlocking relationship between them, (3) the ways in which, historically, "cultural differences" has been used as a code for race to mask the racism that is inherent in the Canadian state and as such rationalize the treatment of racial minority people, and (4) the idea that "celebrating" the "culture" of racial minority Canadians through events is considered to be a recognition of their differences and presence in Canadian society. I conclude with the argument that racism cannot be addressed, much less eliminated, until race is acknowledged as a social and political construct of our society, and that racism structures and maintains that construct. Therefore, if equity and respect for differences among Canadians is to be fostered, there must be education that brings awareness to the historical and structural realities and consequences of race and racisms.

CULTURE AND THE MULTICULTURAL DISCOURSE

Culture refers to the ways in which a group of people or a given society organizes and conducts itself in response to the environment in which it exists. The beliefs, values, and behaviors of a group of people provide them with a degree of personal and social meaning that lends significance to their human experience (Ghosh & Abdi, 2004; James, 2003). Culture also denotes "the forms through which people make sense of their lives . . . [and] is all pervasive" (Rosaldo, 1993, p. 26). The most important part of culture, writes Kallen (1995, p. 20), "is that it is a learned phenomenon; it is acquired, for the most part, through the ordinary processes of growing up and participating in the daily life of a particular ethnic collective." However, distinctions must be made between the ethno-racial group that holds the dominant position in society because of its numbers, early settlement, or its significant influence on the main political and economic institutions, and minority or subordinate groups that have much less influence on legislations, policy making, and limited access to resources (Smolicz, 1981, p. 17).[1]

Therefore, culture cannot be conceptualized in terms of unified systems of meanings, but rather as conflicting, contradictory, ambiguous, and full of contending discourses, all of which are mediated by power. Power difference informs individuals' struggle over meanings and the ways in which they conceive of being in the world (Spivey, 1998). And as Kondo (1990) argues, some in the world were and are more legitimate, more rewarded, more recognized than others—as anyone in a marginalized position will attest. How groups and individuals construct culture and participate in it will be fragmented, highly problematic, and puzzling because they do so based on "contending personalities" (Spivey, 1998, p. 48). Culture, then, is much more than costume, food, music, and dance. As Jackson and Meadows (1991) explain, "Culture must not be treated as a loose amalgam of customs, as a leap of anthropological curiosities" or seen merely in terms of artifacts such as language, specific knowledge of customs and rituals (p. 70). Observable aspects of culture are merely surface and, in some ways, tangible reflections of a complex, interconnected set of elements that fulfills specific functions in the lives of the members of society (James, 2003).

In the context of Canadian society the official multicultural policy/act structures a discourse of the nation as "multicultural," promoting the myth that cultural freedom and equality of opportunity exist for everyone; and culture is used as the basis for defining diversity and difference, as related to the racial, ethnic, immigrant, language, and religious backgrounds of Canadians. As such, there is a reliance on the observable and ascribed characteristics of culture, particularly of minority Canadians, in terms of constructing and understanding their differences. And while race or skin color, specifically, being nonwhite, is employed in the identification of individuals as different (à la the term *visible minority*), the multicultural discourse holds that it is not race per se—that is, the physical characteristics of the body—that is used as identification, but the culture of the individuals or group members.[2] To not "see" race or color means not having "race problems" like our southern neighbor against which Canada defines itself. In this way, Canada's emphasis on the "mosaic" of peoples being permitted to maintain their ethnic cultural particularisms and differences constitutes a fundamental difference between the two countries (Clarke, 1998, p. 100). This idea of color blindness, and framing culture in terms of difference (and vice versa), has the effect of rendering invisible or immaterial the ways in which race, and related discriminatory experiences, operates to inform the cultural values, attitudes, and expressions of racialized Canadians.[3]

Furthermore, as Benhabib (2002) argues in his book *The Claims of Culture: Equity and Diversity in the Global Era*, cultures are not "unified, harmonious, seamless wholes that speak with one narrative voice" (p. 102). And while "community leaders" (specifically, those representing minority ethnoracial groups) may try to represent the culture of "their community" to other Canadians as a unified whole, they often do so, not simply because of their need to control, but in their bid to obtain whatever benefits they can. But more critical are outside observers such as politicians, policymakers, educators, and community workers, particularly those representing the dominant ethno-racial group, who characterize the culture of ethno-racial minority groups as a unified whole because of their need "to comprehend, search for the truth, and maintain social control" (Benhabib, 2002). The power that these outsiders hold enables them to put into practice the idea of homogeneity of ethno-racial minority groups and their culture, and in so doing silence "dissenting opinions and contradictory perspective" and produce a "dominant master narrative of what the cultural tradition is, who is in, and who is out" (Benhabib, 2002, p. 194). And in Canadian cultural discourse, the cultural traditions—sometimes ascribed—are used to rationalize the beliefs that are held about, and related treatment toward, those considered different. In other words, racism—individual, institutional, and structural—helps to instruct and shape the beliefs and resulting interactions.

HIDDEN/MISSING IN THE CULTURAL TRANSLATION: THE STRUCTURAL REALITIES OF RACISM

Fleras and Elliott (2000) define racism as "a doctrine that unjustifiably asserts the superiority of one group over another on the basis of arbitrary selected characteristics pertaining to appearance, intelligence and temperament" (p. 52; see also Li, 2000; Henry & Tator, 2005). In other words, racism is an ideology that considers race as immutable and directly linked to the biological, intellectual, emotional, and behavioral characteristics of racial groups. However, salient in the way in which racism is conceptualized are not the biological or physical differences between groups, but "the public recognition of these differences as being significant for assessment, explanation, and interaction" (Fleras & Elliott, 2000, p. 55), which is held in place by the power based on ideological, economic, political, and social factors that is exerted by one racial group over another. This power, evident in the unequal distribution of scarce resources, is sustained by established laws, regulations, policies, conventions, and customs and consequently becomes normalized and, to quote Ng (1993), "taken-for-granted." It is important to give attention to the different levels and forms of racism—the "different racisms," as Hall (1978, p. 26) says, "each historically specific and articulated in a different way." Individual racism, the negative attitudes that individuals hold regarding others, is structured by an ideology or set of ideas and beliefs that are reflected in the willful, conscious or unconscious, indirect, and reflexive conjectures of individuals (James, 2003; Dobbins & Skillings, 1991). And that individuals are able to cultivate and act on their racism (i.e., discriminate) is related to the fact that institutions (institutional racism) and the society generally (structural racism) through their rules, policies, regulations, and laws instill the ideology in the first place. Institutional racism exists in organizations and/or institutions where the established rules, policies, and regulations systemically reflect and produce differential treatment of various groups based on race. In such cases, it is individuals who, because of their training and allegiance to the organization, put in place and implement the racist policies and regulations, thus helping to maintain a system of social control, as well as the status quo that favors the dominant group in society (Fleras & Elliott, 2000;

James, 2003). Further, the ideology, including the norms and values, upon which individuals and institutions operate, is premised on and sustained by the rooted inequities of society, which also serve to justify the allocation of racial groups to particular categories and class sites—structural racism (James, 2003). This explains how the ideas of inferiority and superiority, based on socially selected physical characteristics, function to exclude racial minority group members from accessing and participating in major economic, political, social and cultural institutions of society.

Scholars agree that it is fundamental in any examination of racism to give particular attention to structural racism (Henry & Tator, 2005; Hughes & Kallen, 1974; Satzewich, 1998). In doing so, we come to terms with the complex, interlocking, and multilayered characteristics of racisms at all three levels and the reciprocal relationship between them. It also means recognizing that racism is about power and that expressions of racism vary in relation to historical and social contexts and specificity, taking into account factors such as ethnicity, class, religion, gender, and immigrant status. As Stuart Hall reminds us, "Racism is not a static ideology or set of social practices, but takes on specific meaning in different circumstances. The forms, expressions and meanings of racism vary on the basis of those who articulate and put into practice racist ideas, as well as on the basis of those who are the particular targets of those ideas and practices" (cited in Satzewich, 1998, p. 22). And within the context of majority/minority power relations based on race, as Kallen, (2003) writes, "racist ideologies are transposed into potent political instruments wielded by dominant ethnic [or racial] authorities to oppress (deny political rights), neglect (deny economic rights), diminish (deny social rights), and deculturate (deny cultural rights) members of ethnic [racial] minorities" (Kallen, 2003, p. 89).

But in the everyday life, as already mentioned, racism, if at all acknowledged, is commonly thought to be an individual's shortcoming based predominantly on cultural differences and lack of exposure to those considered different. This multicultural reading of the existence of racism negates the power differentials based on race and the normalized white cultural identity, which helps to maintain the notion of color blindness, as well as cultural neutrality and freedom of the society and institutions. In this regard, then, private and governmental institutions are absolved of any responsibility for the systemic inequities and the resulting privileges that have accrued to some members of the society. As well, privileges and disadvantages based on social class are perceived to have no relationship to race. So, in the recent debates in Toronto over the idea of setting up "black focused schools" to address the poor performance and underachievement of black students in the existing school environment, newspaper columns and editorial pages continuously declare that the problem with black youth is not race, but class—that is, the "poverty" situation in which blacks live and are educated (see for instance,

Jim Coyle, *Toronto Star*, September 27, 2005, pp. B1&2).[4] This tendency in the popular discourse to separate class and race is likely related to attempts to uphold the notion that democracy and meritocracy exist in the society whereby individuals can work hard, apply themselves, and succeed. The thinking is that individuals can gain upward social mobility on the basis of merit, hence overcome the limitations of their working-class position (or poverty situation), for there is no escaping the casualties of race. In a color-blind context, then, class, as opposed to race, is considered to be the main determinant of success or failure.

But according to Forcese (1997), people of European backgrounds are more often allowed to meet the meritocratic ideals and expectations particularly through education, while working class and racialized individuals do not have the same chances. As Forcese puts it, "As a means to meritocratic egalitarianism, the educational organization has acted to secure meritocracy for the meritocrats, or middle-class status for the middle-class" (p. 133). And as Fleras and Elliott (2000) remark, "All the deeply engrained myths in the country cannot disguise the obvious: Canada remains a stratified society where differences in pigmentation and ethnic background continue to make a difference" (p. 137). The authors further point out that the inequities that exist in the society do not result from psychology, culture, or some sense of human nature, but from social and public policy, the social structure, human behaviors, and the broad racialized and stratified structure of society (Fleras & Elliott, 2000). As such, the social situation of individuals and their access to opportunities are not random, but rooted in structural racism and its reciprocal relationship with individual and institutional racism, as well as their intersecting link to sexism, classism, and ethnocentrism. The following section places structural and institutional racism in a historical context showing how racism operated in the early years to maintain a racially and culturally "white" Canada.

CONSTRUCTION OF "RACE DIFFERENCE" IN HISTORICAL AND STRUCTURAL TERMS: SOME REFERENCES

In the introduction, I indicated that there are similarities between the 1876 Indian Act of Canada and the apartheid laws of South Africa against which the blacks there fought. The Indian Act, a form of structural racism, served, and still serves, as a mechanism to maintain a culturally "white" Canada. To this end, Aboriginal people were placed on reserves with a Western governance structure that was imposed by the federal government. They were required to carry permits, were watched over by Indian agents who enforced the laws, were Christianized, and their children were sent to residential schools. The Indian Act also declared that all Indians who married non-Indians or who received an education in a Christian residential school would be recognized as "civilized" and "fit for white society." All of these "enfranchised" Indians and their families were required to leave the reserve. As Frideres (1993) points out, the assumption by many was that the longer native people reside in an urban area, the more likely they will integrate into the dominant white society (see also Adams, 1989; Buckley, 1993; Haig-Brown, 1993). And with reference to how the various forms and levels of racism operated in his life, Aboriginal scholar Adams (1989) writes:

> In a white-supremacist society, more opportunities and privileges exist for Indians and halfbreeds who "look white": those who "look Indian" are doomed to stay at the bottom of society. They are forced into the extreme of racism, and they suffer most as a result. It was no accident that I managed to get a good education and a good job, since my appearance is predominantly white. Throughout my school years I was favored, because I closely resembled white students. More privileges were extended to me than to other Métis children who looked more Indian. The white community responded to me in less racist manner than it did to other halfbreeds. . . . However, the question arises: What happens to the masses of Indians and halfbreeds who are forced into the deep crevices of the "caste" order because of their Indian appearance and life-style? There is no escape from such discrimination. (pp. 15–16)

With Aboriginal people consigned to reserves, the early colonialists sought to establish a population of citizens who would help to build the political, economic, social, and cultural structures of a Canada that represented their vision. As such, racist immigration policies were constructed with the specific aim of keeping Canada "white."[5] As a result, most of the immigrants to Canada came from Britain and British and other Western European communities in the United States. Kalbach and McVey (1971) state that "the only persons to enter Canada with a minimum of red tape were those who belonged to the preferred groups, i.e., United States citizens and British subjects by reason of birth or nationalization" (p. 37).[6] In this regard, well into the twentieth century, factors such as race, ethnicity, nationality, and social class were used to control the quality and character of immigration and ensure the "assimilability" of those who immigrated (Kubat et al., 1979; Porter, 1965). In other words, structural racism, operationalized through immigration policies and practices, not only determined who was permitted into the country, but also controlled the economic, political, social, and cultural lives of those who managed to get in.

In the case of Africans, the immigration polices reflected a disregard for their presence and their contributions to the building of the country through their labor as slaves beginning in the early 1620s.[7] There were also former enslaved Africans who migrated from the United States, some via the Underground Railroad; black Loyalists who came to the Maritimes in 1783, some as refugees from the War of 1812; and still others, Jamaican Maroons, who were resettled in Nova Scotia by the British in 1796. In fact, the Census of 1901 indicates that some 17,437 "Negroes" were residing in Canada (cited in James 2003, p. 247). And when some thirteen hundred black American homesteaders from Oklahoma arrived at the Alberta border in 1911 seeking to immigrate (Shepard, 1997), the liberal government at the time denied them entry. Of course, black Caribbean immigrants did not fare any better, in fact, during the late 1800s and early 1900s, the small number of mostly men who came, settled in Nova Scotia, and worked in the coal mines and the coke ovens of steel plants, "because of the myth" as Calliste (1994, p. 135) writes, "that blacks could withstand the heat better than whites."[8] These policies and practices were all part of the racist ideology and discourse of the government, which were represented in the comments of the then-deputy minister of immigration in January 14, 1955. He stated:

> It is from experience, generally speaking, that coloured people in the present state of the white man's thinking are not a tangible asset, and as a result are more or less ostracized. They do not assimilate readily and pretty much vegetate to a low standard of living . . . many cannot adapt themselves to our climatic conditions. To enter into an agreement which would have the effects of increasing coloured immigration to this country would be an act of misguided generosity since it would not have the effect of bringing about a worthwhile solution to the problems of coloured people and would quite likely intensify our own social and economic problems. (cited in James, 2003, p. 247)

In restricting Asian immigration, the Canadian government introduced policies in 1885 that required Chinese to pay a $50 "Head Tax." This tax was increased to $100 in 1900, and to $500 in 1903 (Bolaria & Li, 1988). The head taxes and other restrictive measures not only served to limit the number of Chinese, mostly men, who could afford to come to Canada to work on the railroad, it also hampered family unification. Japanese immigration to Canada was similarly restricted. For example, in 1920 only about 150 Japanese were allowed to immigrate (Kalbach & Mcvey, 1971). And it is well known that Japanese were disallowed from entering Canada during World War II, and those already residing in Canada, even as citizens (some having been born here), did not escape the "enemy alien" label, which meant that they were placed in internment camps in British Columbia. At the end of the war they dispersed all over the country to live. Interestingly, while the label *enemy alien* was lifted for Germans in 1950, it was not lifted for the Japanese until two years later. This treatment of Japanese reflects the fact that the Canadian government and Canadians generally were so concerned about people considered to be nonwhite that, as Jansen (1981) writes, Japanese-ascribed racial characteristics were "considered more 'threatening' to Canadian society than national characteristics" (p. 19).

In fact, on the question of Asians residing in Canada, Prime Minster Macken-zie King in 1947 stated in the House of Commons that "Canada is perfectly within her rights in selecting the persons whom we regard as desirable future citizens. It is not a 'fundamental human right' of any alien to enter Canada. It is a privilege. It is a matter of domestic policy. . . . The people of Canada do not wish, as a result of mass immigration, to make a fundamental alteration to the character of our population." He added that the "large-scale immigration from the Orient would not be permitted to change the fundamental composition of the Canadian population" (cited in James, 2003, p. 246).

South Asian immigrants were also required to pay $200 (up from the initial $25) to enter Canada (Bolaria & Li, 1988). But most telling was the 1908 "Continuous Voyage" legislation, which required people immigrating to Canada to come "by continuous voyage from the countries of which they were natives or citizens and upon through tickets purchased in that country" (cited in Bolaria & Li, 1988, p.170).[9] When some 376 passengers came by "continuous voyage" from India in 1914 on the ship *Kamagata Maru*, arriv-ing in Vancouver Harbor on May 23, with the exception of a few who were dependants of earlier immigrants, most of them were denied entry and remained on the ship for two months. During this time, the ship was guarded by police, and upon leaving, it was escorted out to sea by a naval ship (Bolaria & Li, 1988, p.171). The media referred to the ship's passengers as "Hindu invaders" and accused them of "preaching sedition and treason" (Kelly & Trebilcock, 1998, p.152). And in upholding the government's immigration policy, the British Columbia Court of Appeal ruled that "the laws of this country are unsuited to them, and their ways and ideas may be a menace to the well-being of the Canadian people" (cited in Kelly & Trebil-cock, 1998, p. 144).

The concerns that Canada's early settlers had about maintaining a "white" Canada, even to the point of consigning Aboriginal peoples to reserves and, in the case of the Beothuk, exterminating them from the Cana-dian landscape, as well as restricting the immigration of non-Europeans to Canada, reflect the pervasiveness of racism within the governmental and institutional structures of the society. The resulting racism that we witness among individuals (individual racism) is shaped by and reciprocally related to the structural and institutional racisms that have operated over the years, and are found in our laws, policies, programs, and practices. The immigration policies and practices, as "shameful" as they were (Burnet, 1984), not only account for the ethnic and racial diversity of the population, but also the use of race as a socially significant, legitimate, and convenient marker by which "nonwhite" Canadians are distinguished and considered culturally different (Li, 2000, p. 12).

But today, in our attempt to address this historical past and recognize the diversity of the population, governments and institutions sponsor and "celebrate" events that are intended to acknowledge the histories, heritages, and experiences of all Canadians, particularly those historically marginalized. For the most part, these "recognitions" are time-limited and time-bound events—as celebrations are—thus leaving intact the structures, information, and relations that have historically served to create and maintain the system of racism. In the following section, I discuss how one such "recognition" event gets taken up in schools—an important socializing institution.

CELEBRATING DIVERSITY, MODELLING INCLUSIVITY: THE EVENT APPROACH

Holding "multicultural" events is a typical approach to addressing issues of diversity. In schools there are "multicultural days," organized by educators to showcase the "cultural" heritages of students (James, 2001). This practice is premised on the idea that students' exposure to those considered "culturally different," including racial minorities, will help them to develop a positive attitude toward each other. Black or African History Month is one of the most common "recognition" events that is "celebrated" annually in schools and other institutions in February. It is a multicultural event that attempts, as one teacher-candidate said in our online conference (1997), "to make students, teachers, parents and the community aware of the great contributions and past sufferings of Black people." Another teacher-candidate agreed, saying that such celebration is "a very positive approach that would serve to raise consciousness of the long and diverse history of African people as well as their accomplishments." Yet another said Black History Month provides opportunities to invite "role models" into schools. These sentiments by teacher-candidates are in keeping with that of the Board of Education (Toronto), which in its declaration of the month in 1993 issued a statement that read in part: "The acknowledgement of African History Month gives schools an opportunity to respond to the goals of the Ontario Ministry of Education which includes the development of students' self worth and fostering of understanding of the culture and achievement of a wide variety of social groups."

Though usually unstated, the celebration of Black History Month could be seen as one of the ways in which some schools are addressing the issues of alienation, poor performance, high dropout rates, and low academic attainment among black students. The month's activities seem to support the idea that such recognition or "display of black culture" in school will communicate to black students the school's commitment to their well-being. This recognition is reflective of the race relations and/or antiracism policies and programs of some school boards that were developed during the 1980s and 1990s to supplement multicultural education and address racial tensions in schools (in Toronto and Halifax, for example), and the failure of the school system to meet the needs, interests, and aspirations of racial minority students and parents, especially black and Aboriginal peoples. But while "celebrating" Black History Month, National Aboriginal Day, Asian Heritage Month, Chinese New Year, Ramadaan, Eid ul Fitr, and other historical, religious, and/or significant events might appear to be a progressive step toward recognizing race and racialization as factors in students' schooling experiences and educational outcomes, the situation of racial minority students remains unchanged. This is because educators conceptualize race to be mainly skin color, racism to be a result of ignorance, and minority students' lack of success to be a result of cultural deficit, low self-concept, and the absence of positive role models (James, 2001). Such conceptualization of race and racism is informed by a cultural discourse that fails to take into account the systemic and structural inequalities and complexities of racism that must be acknowledged if the concerns and problems of racial minority people are to be addressed.

TOWARD AN EDUCATION OF RESPECT AND EQUITY: MOVING BEYOND THE CULTURAL SCRIPT

I started this chapter by making reference to the commemoration of the International Day for the Elimination of Racial Discrimination and the efforts that Canada puts into bringing awareness to the "harmful effects of racism" in this country. However, the "cultural script" of racial or color blindness and cultural neutrality of the state premised on the multicultural policy, leaves unacknowledged the historical, social, and political construction of race and the role played by institutional and structural racisms in structuring and maintaining that construct. Clearly, racism is not simply about individual attitudes, but is configured in the laws, regulations, and policies that over the years have operated to inform attitudes, behaviors, and practices. Therefore, the efforts to bring awareness to racism and discrimination must be based on an education that unsettles the notion of cultural democracy and meritocracy—that all members of our society are living comfortably, participating equally, and can achieve their aspirations on merit irrespective of their racial, ethnic, class, and religious backgrounds.

The fact is, Canada is not a color-blind society, and we are not neutral on questions of race. Since the coming of Europeans to this part of the world, known to Aboriginal people as Turtle Island, racism has served to maintain a system of inequity thereby affecting the emotional, social, political, educational, economic existence of all Canadians—not just racialized Canadians. I say all Canadians, for the economic, political, social, and psychological costs of maintaining racist structures, cultivating racist ideology, and committing racist acts are ultimately borne by all of us. Such costs could be addressed, if not eliminated, if only we understood this widespread cost and our relationship and responsibility to each other. In this regard, Susan Dion's (2005) comment about the relationship between majority Canadians and Aboriginal people is quite instructive. She asserts that majority Canadians often tend to plead innocence, ignorance, or lack of knowledge of Others when asked to acknowledge their own locations within positions of privilege and oppression. Using the metaphor "perfect stranger," she writes:

> There's a way in which this position as perfect stranger allows a kind of innocence and a kind of not being responsible, because that's out there. And I am a perfect stranger, therefore, I don't need to worry about it or I can't do it; therefore, I don't have a responsibility to do it. . . . But we're not perfect strangers to one another . . . because in fact we do have a relationship. If we want to contribute to a new and better relationship, we need to recognize ourselves in relationship to that history and in relationship to each other. (p. 2)

To conclude, in a society where race matters and racism operates to affect the life circumstances and outcomes of individuals, we need to have a program of education at all levels of schooling that brings awareness to and understanding of our history of racism and discrimination—a history that informs the economic, political, social, cultural, and educational realities of today's Canada. This education is necessary if we are to learn, work, play, and live together appreciating and accepting our diversity and differences in a context of social justice, equity, and democracy.

NOTES

1. Smolicz (1981) goes on to say: "It must be recognized, however, that ethnic minority cultures have their own independent historical continuity, and although they may interact with other cultures in a plural society, this does not make them a mere facet of the dominant group's tradition" (p. 18).

2. Using cultural background to account for, or contextualize, the actions of individuals, as Benhabib (2002) contends, "imprisons the individual in a cage of univocal cultural interpretations and psychological motivations; individuals' intentions are reduced to cultural stereotypes; moral agency is reduced to cultural puppetry" (p. 89).

3. The irony of color blindness is the pretension that the construction of racial minorities as "culturally different" is not based on their racial "visibility," but on their "observable" behaviors, values, and attitudes. These ascribed characteristics are perceived to be products of their "culture" from elsewhere rather than of the structural and institutional inequities connected to race, racism, and discrimination that are inherent in our society. I refer to this as *race culture discourse* (see James, 2005).

4. The same argument was made in the aftermath of the hurricane Katrina when it was mostly black faces we were seeing on television as those mostly affected by the hurricane. Many Americans were attributing this situation to social class—they were

poor people—and not race (see also Michael Ignatieff, *The New York Times Magazine*, September 25, 2005, pp. 15–17).

5. For instance, in 1908, Robert Boden, the Conservative minister responsible for immigration, bluntly stated that "the Conservative Party stands for a white Canada." This meant attracting to Canada Western Europeans, except Jews who were classified as a different race of people (see Abella & Toper, 1982). When these immigrants stopped coming, the Canadian governments turned to Eastern Europeans (see Porter, 1965).

6. As spelt out in the Immigrant Policy at that time, British subjects were those born in Britain, as well as people from Ireland, Newfoundland, Australia, New Zealand, and the Union of South Africa. Of note is the fact that people from other African countries, as well as India, Pakistan, Ceylon, the Caribbean and other so-called Commonwealth countries, were not included (see Kubat et al., 1971; Porter, 1965).

7. Recall slavery ended in the British colonies, including Canada, in 1834.

8. The reverse was also argued. Burnet (1984) writes that as late as the 1950s federal government ministers had to defend their claims, which they alleged were based on "scientific" grounds that "Blacks could not endure cold climates" (p. 19).

9. It is worth noting that at that time the only company able to offer a continuous journey from India to Canada was the Canadian Pacific Railroad, and the government of Canada issued a directive that they were not to sell any through tickets to Canada (Bolaria & Li, 1988, p. 170).

REFERENCES

Adams, H. (1989). *Prison of grass: Canada from a Native point of view*. Saskatoon: Fifth House.

Benhabib, S. (2002). *The claims of culture: Equity and diversity in the global era*. Princeton: Princeton University Press.

Boleria, B. S., & Li, P. (Eds.). (1988). *Racial oppression in Canada*. Toronto: Garamound Press.

Buckley, H. (1993). *From wooden ploughs to welfare: Why Indian policy failed in the Prairie Provinces*. Montreal: McGill-Queen's University Press.

Calliste, A. (1994). Race, gender, and Canadian immigration policy: Blacks from the Caribbean, 1900–1932. *Journal of Canadian Studies, 28(4)*, 131–147.

Coyle, J. (2005). Black school fails youth. *The Toronto Star*, Tuesday, September 27, pp. B1&2.

Clarke, G. E. (1998). White like Canada. *Transition (73)*, 98–109.

Department of Canadian Heritage. (2005). Racism, stop it: Why March 21. (http://www.pch.gc.ca/march-21–mars/why-pourquoi/index_e.cfm). Accessed September 23, 2005.

Dion, S. (2005). *Voices of diversity & equity*. Centre for the Support of Teaching, York University, February.

DuCharme, M. (1986). The Canadian origins of South Africa apartheid. *Perspectives*, pp. 2–3.

Fleras, A., & Elliott, J. L. (2000). *Unequal relations: An introduction to race, ethnic, and Aboriginal dynamics in Canada*. Scarborough, ON: Prentice-Hall.

Forcese, D. (1997). *The Canadian class structure*. Scarborough, ON: McGraw-Hill Ryerson.

Frideres, J. S. (1993). *Native peoples in Canada: Contemporary conflicts*. Scarborough, ON: Prentice-Hall.

Ghosh, R., & Abdi, A. (2004). *Education and the politics of difference: Canadian perspectives*. Toronto: Canadian Scholars Press.

Haig-Brown, C. (1993). *Resistance and renewal: Surviving the Indian residential school*. Vancouver: Arsenal Pulp Press.

Hall, S. (1978). Racism and reaction. In *Five views of multiracial Britain*. London: London Commission of Racial Equality.

Henry, F., & Tator, C. (2005). *The colour of democracy: Racism in Canadian society*. Toronto: Harcourt Brace.

Hughes, D. R., & Kallen, E. (1974). *The anatomy of racism: Canadian dimension*. Montreal: Harvest House.

Ignatieff, M. (2005). The broken contract. *The New York Times Magazine*, September 25, pp. 15–17.

Jackson, A. P., & Meadows, F. B. (1991). Getting to the bottom to understand the top. *Journal of Counseling and Development, 70(1)*, 72–76.

James, C. E. (2003). *Seeing ourselves: Exploring race, ethnicity, and culture*. Toronto: Thompson Educational Publishing.

James, C. E. (2001). Multiculturalism, diversity, and education in the Canadian context: The search for an inclusive pedagogy. In C. Grant & J. Lei (Eds.), *Global constructions of multicultural education: Theories and realities* (pp. 175–204). Mahwah, NJ: Lawrence Erbaum.

Jansen, C. J. (1981). Problems and issues in post-war immigration to Canada and their effects on origins and characteristics of immigrants. Paper presented at Meetings of the Canadian Population Society. Dalhousie University, Halifax.

Kalbach, W. E., and McVey, W. W. (1971). *The demographics bases of Canadian society*. Toronto: Mc Graw-Hill.

Kallen, E. (1995). *Ethnicity and human rights in Canada*. Toronto: Oxford University Press.

Kelly, N., & Trebilcock, M. (1998). *The making of the mosaic: A history of Canadian immigration*. Toronto: University of Toronto Press.

Kondo, D. K. (1990). *Crafting selves: Power, gender, and discourses of identity in a Japanese workplace*. Chicago: University of Chicago Press.

Kubat, D., Merhlander, U., & Gehmacher, E. (1979). *The politics of migration policies: The first world in the 1970's*. New York: Center Migration Studies.

Li, P. (2000). The racial subtext in Canada's immigration discourse. University of Saskatchewan & Prairie Centre of Excellent for Research on Immigration & Integration. http://www.riim.metropolis.net/events/Pa...r20Nov.202000/Li_text 20of20talk.hlml. Accessed November, 2002.

Ng, R. (1993). Racism, sexism, and nation building in Canada. In C. McCarthy & W. Crichlow (Eds.), *Race, identity, and representation in education* (pp. 50–59). New York: Routledge.

Porter, J. (1965). *The vertical mosaic: An analysis of social class and power in Canada.* Toronto: University of Toronto Press.

Rosaldo, R. (1993). *Culture and truth: The making of social analysis.* Boston: Beacon Press.

Satzewich, V. (1998). *Racism and social inequality in Canada.* Toronto: Thompson Educational Publishing.

Shepard, R. B. (1997). *Deemed unsuitable: Blacks from Oklahoma move to the Canadian Prairies in search of equality.* Toronto: Umbrella.

Smolicz, J. J. (1981). Culture, ethnicity, and education: Multiculturalism in a plural society. *World yearbook of education: Education of minorities.* London: Kegan Page.

Spivey, M. (1998). *Identity politics of a southern tribe: A critical ethnography.* Unpublished doctoral dissertation, Department of Sociology. York University, Toronto.

NINE

Popular Education and Human Rights

Prospects for Antihegemonic Adivasi (Original Dweller)
Movements and Counterhegemonic Struggle in India

Dip Kapoor

INTRODUCTION

WHEN INDIA'S FIRST prime minister, Pandit Jawaharlal Nehru, asked the
tribals and peasants of Orissa to make way for the Hirakud dam, exhorting
them to make a sacrifice in the interests of the nation, displacement was not
met with any apparent show of resistance as the Nehruvian state promised to
address tribal interests and recognize the need for tribals to progress in a manner consistent with their ways. Fifty years of postindependence development
has meant that 85 percent of those displaced by development by irrigation,
mines, thermal power plants, wildlife sanctuaries, and industry have been
tribals (Fernandes & Paranjpe, 1997). What has also become increasingly
apparent is the emergence of Adivasi struggles and resistance to such marginalization by development in the form of movements (Pimple & Sethi,
2005) such as the Narmada Bachao Andolan (NBA), the Adivasi Ekta
Parishad (AEP), and the National Alliance of People's Movements.

Adivasi-state/market relations are likely to continue down this path as the
Nehruvian socialist promise has rapidly unraveled into what some political
observers (Ray & Katzenstein, 2004) note as the rise of the twin forces of neoliberalism, with its attendant implications for accelerated capitalist penetration of
Adivasi Scheduled/Protected Areas, and a religious conservatism characterized
by the electoral success of the Hindu saffron brigade, with implications for the
subordinate sociocultural status of Adivasis. A case in point in relation to the

former is the IMF–World Bank adjustment package of 1991, which has prompted the Indian state to move aggressively in the direction of economic liberalization, a process that increasingly protects the rights of global and domestic capital while equivocating around the rights of social groups that are "in the way of development" (Blaser, Feit, & McRae, 2004,p.2) and global corporations.

Popular adult educators working with Adivasi communities and movements need to recognize the potential of rights and citizenship-based rhetoric in advancing and/or constraining these struggles and actively seek to address capitalist and colonialist intrusions as hegemonic forces (Gramsci, 1971) that will continue to marginalize Adivasis. The proposition being advanced here is that the discourse of rights and citizenship needs to be appropriated by popular struggle to address counter and antihegemonic possibilities in the interests of advancing Adivasi ethico-political commitments and the life chances of populations increasingly marginalized by development. Such a process would repoliticize a politically sanitized, individualized, decontextualized neoliberal conception of human rights and citizenship that advances the hegemonic interests of the state-corporate nexus in penetrating Adivasi space for economic exploitation and the subsequent enrichment of national and global elite-consumer classes. This chapter first introduces specific international and national human rights and legal commitments with import for Adivasi well-being. Second, brief examples of contradictions and active engagements to subvert these very rights and commitments are discussed to illustrate hegemonic aspirations, especially issues pertaining to access and control of land and forests given their spiritual and material significance for reproducing an Adivasi existence rationality. This is followed by a proposition for popular adult educator-outsiders to play a bridge-learning role between Adivasis and other movements and communities, harnessing human rights guarantees and rhetoric in a counter and antihegemonic politics. Finally, concluding reflections pertaining to Adivasi culture and the utility of a human rights–based approach to securing Adivasi space through popular education endeavors are considered briefly.

While some of the reflections and analysis in this chapter are informed by a decade-long experience as a popular educator-outsider working through an NGO with Kondh Adivasi struggles and movement building in the east coast state of Orissa, home to almost one-quarter of India's eighty-two million "Scheduled Tribes" (Shah, 2004, p. 92), others are developed from institutional and academic literature pertaining to Adivasis or indigenous people's and human rights.

HUMAN RIGHTS AND HEGEMONY:
RHETORICAL FLOURISHES AND CONTROLLING REALITIES

Human rights discourse needs to be understood in relation to the increasing penetration of an exploitative post/neo-colonial capitalist political economy and a historically rooted sociocultural attitude toward tribals that largely determines the material reality of rights-based implications for Adivasi communities and their potential location as citizens of national or global political entities. As Neil Stammers observes, "Ideas and practices concerning human rights are created by people in particular historical, social and economic circumstances" (1995, p. 488). The dominant liberal view of human or individual rights as empowering people in the fight against persecution and injustice leading to conclusions of optimism and hope, fails or refuses to recognize the social and political construction of rights or the possibility that rights could be construed "as power over people, expressed in exclusionary practices that deny the full participation of those who fail to support the interest of the dominant group" (Evans, 1998, p. 4), that is, rights can be concerned with establishing and maintaining the moral claims that legitimate particular interests, such as neoliberal and religious conservative interests in the current Indian context vis-à-vis Adivasis. Exclusions are often justified on the basis of alleged lack of rational or moral capacity of excluded groups to engage in decision-making processes or the simple prejudiced assertion that such groups are "mad" (Evans, 1998, p. 4).

In Gramscian (1971) terms, given the numerous contradictions between rhetoric and reality (discussed later in this paper), the human rights commitment of an increasingly corporatized Indian state can be convincingly construed as an instrument in the exercise of hegemonic control by the corporate state, as different and potentially resistant groups are encouraged to accept an order characterized by "a common social-moral language," namely, human rights and citizenship, that expresses a singular version of reality "informing with its spirit all forms of thought and behaviour" (Evans, 1998, p. 5). That is, in its bid to secure the right to exercise social and political control that binds the ruler and the ruled in a consensual order that legitimates power, the hegemon or corporate–Indian state nexus utilizes human rights rhetoric as part of a process of socialization to enhance control based on might with that based on right, in order to secure its "intellectual and moral leadership" (Gramsci, 1971, pp. 57–58).

Human rights discourse in India has been used by the state to advance neoliberal and dominant religious conservative interests in relation to the Adivasi place (or active exclusion) in the contemporary Indian polity. Indeed, as Blaser, Fiet, and McRae (2004, p. 6) observe in relation to an international human rights context, "In contrast to those organizations who specialize in Indigenous issues, the wider human rights network does not see development aimed at integrating indigenous peoples into the national society as a human rights violation." That is, the ability of indigenous organizations to call on human rights groups to further indigenous projects is limited since they tend to view the state's integrationist agenda as being legitimate, as long as the developing state follows the model of the developed countries and avoids the most flagrant violations of human rights in executing its projects. Such perspectives fail to problematize the cultural and political trajectory of the development project as it pertains to the agency and self-determined aspirations of sociocultural groups who live by onto-epistemic conceptions of social life that enjoy a historical maturity which eludes the grasp of myopic advocates of a self-absorbed rogue modernist project. If the modernist purpose of rights and related notions of citizenship are to create the conditions for individuals and peoples to lead a dignified and peaceful life, then the promise of human rights lies in its potential to stimulate political struggles that transgress the hegemonic hijacking of the construction, interpretation and mis/application of rights. Or as Paulo Freire (2004, p. 25) suggests, "Washing one's hands of the relationship between the powerful and those deprived of any power just because it has been said that 'all are equal in the eyes of the law' is to shore up the power of powerful. . . . What to me seems impossible to accept is a democracy founded in the ethics of the market, which is mean, solely aroused by profit, and makes democracy itself unviable."

Human Rights Commitments: International Conventions and Indian Constitutional Provisions Pertaining to Indigenous/Tribal Control over Their Own Development

India has ratified several international covenants and conventions having direct import for state-Adivasi relations, such as the International Covenant on Civil and Political Rights in 1979 and the Convention on the Elimination of all Forms of Racial Discrimination in 1968. However, it is the International Labor Organization (ILO) Convention 107 adopted by the ILO in 1957 and by India in 1958, that establishes a recognized international commitment toward indigenous peoples. The ILO Convention addresses the situation of "indigenous" and "tribal" peoples or those who would be referred to as "scheduled tribes" in India and Pakistan or "hill tribes" elsewhere in Asia (Hannum, 2003, p. 76).

Despite its "paternalistic and assimilationist" intent (Hannum, 2003, p. 88), this convention bound the Indian state (and other parties to the convention) to recognize collective and individual indigenous land ownership, to prohibit forced integration, to respect indigenous customary laws, and to honor the right to be compensated for land taken by the government. Subsequently replaced some thirty years later by a nonassimilationist and nonintegrationist text, Convention No.169, it now requires governments to adopt special measures to safeguard indigenous interests and to recognize and protect their "social, cultural, religious and spiritual values and practices," while "indigenous peoples shall have the right to decide their own priorities for the process of development as it affects their lives, beliefs, institutions and spiritual well-being and the lands they occupy or otherwise use, and to exercise control, to the extent possible, over their own economic, social and cultural development" (Hannum, 2003, p. 88).

With respect to the issue of land, governments are to recognize the "rights of ownership and possession . . . over the lands, which they traditionally occupy . . . and safeguard the right of the peoples concerned to use lands not exclusively occupied by them, but to which they have traditionally had access for their subsistence and traditional activities" (Hannum, 2003, p. 88). Hannum also notes that with a few exceptions, most indigenous groups have no desire to secede formally from the states within which they are located. What they do desire is a large degree of "self-government, including the right to veto or reject incompatible state laws, while remaining within the internationally recognized boundaries of the state" (p. 79).

Meanwhile, as per Constitutional Order of 1950 and Article 366(25) of the Constitution, the newly independent Indian state defined and recognized "Schedule Tribes" (Shah, 2004, p. 92) and various articles were included in the constitution pertaining to safeguarding tribal interests and well-being and prohibiting all forms of discrimination against tribals, such as the Prevention of Atrocities Act of 1989. Under the fifth and sixth Schedules of the Constitution and the more recent Provision of the Panchayats Extension to the Scheduled Areas Act in 1996, the state recognizes the ownership rights of the indigenous and tribal peoples to their traditional lands, which have been declared as Protected Areas under these constitutional provisions. The 1996 inclusion is a constitutional provision that extends a scheme of decentralization to Adivasis in the Scheduled Areas (a victory of sorts for the Adivasi bid for more political autonomy). Another significant legal development pertaining to legal interpretations and application of the fifth Schedule of the Constitution is the recent "Samatha v. the State of Andhra Pradesh (AP)" 1997 Supreme Court judgment pertaining to mining leases being provided by the state to corporate interests in Scheduled/Protected Areas in the state of AP. The Court's judgment (section 111) recognized the "policy of total prohibition on the transfer of the land in Scheduled Areas to non-tribals" (www.saanet.org/kashipur/intro.htm retrieved April 11, 2005).

Fifty-four years after the recognition of "tribes," the government of India has finally initiated a process for developing a National Policy on Tribals (Draft National Policy) that seeks to provide specific guidelines addressing implementation of the various constitutional provisions pertaining to Scheduled Tribes. While these are some examples of international and national human rights and legal commitments to Adivasis in India, contradictions in relation to these provisions, discussed in the following section, lend credence to the argument that human rights provisions are merely part of the state's arsenal in securing hegemonic control over a populace (by offering them rights in a bid to secure the moral right to govern) while all the while simultaneously usurping these rights in the service of securing the dominant interests of a global and national corporate-consumer elite.

SUBVERSION OF HUMAN RIGHTS COMMITMENTS: CONTROLLING REALITIES

Since the first notification to recognize Scheduled Tribes in India in 1950 and the Indian commitment to indigenous/tribal peoples expressed through the ILO and other international covenants and conventions, according to a report on the Draft National Policy on Tribals by the Asian Center for Human Rights (ACHR), "non-implementation of these laws and adoption of laws and procedures to negate these legal protections has had an adverse impact on indigenous people" (ACHR, 2005, p. 2). The report notes that contradictory legal provisions and failure to implement or translate constitutional provisions into reality" (p. 4) continue to undermine indigenous assertions as self-determined peoples. For instance, while the fifth Schedule of the Constitution and the Provisions of the Panchayats Act (Extension to the Scheduled Areas) (1996) "recognize the ownership rights of indigenous peoples to their traditional lands recognized as Protected Areas" (p. 4), such assertions are undermined by forest laws that confer "usufruct rights" to use minor forest products without a right to ownership and subject to a "whimsical no damage to the forest" determination by forest officials (p. 5).

The ACHR report points to several such similar contradictions between constitutional provisions under the fifth and sixth Schedules and specific acts such as the Forest Conservation Act of 1980, the Wild Life (Protection) Act of 1972, and the Land Acquisition Act of 1894. For instance, when it comes to the issue of forced or illegal evictions (euphemistically/officially referred to as "displacement"), several aspects of human rights recognized under the International Covenant on Civil and Political Rights and the Covenant on Economic, Social and Cultural Rights, not to mention national constitutional rights are invoked. But under the Forest Conservation Act, the Wild Life (Protection) Act, and the Land Acquisition Act, forced evictions take place "according to procedure established by law and not necessarily according to due process of law. The government has the sovereign right to evict people for undefined public interest or 'larger interest' but the affected people do not have the right to question the decision of the government on forcible evictions" (ACHR, 2005, p. 9). The Land Acquisition Act (1894), which has been instrumental in the eviction of indigenous and tribal peoples for more than a century, has no provision for resettlement and rehabilitation, not to mention right to free, prior, and informed consent. The National Human Rights Commission, in a hearing on the proposed Land Acquisition Act Amendment Bill on 13 February 2001 "expressed the view that it was desirable to incorporate the rehabilitation and resettlement package in the Land Acquisition Act itself as an ILO convention, to which India is party, since it provides for the protection of rights of indigenous and tribal peoples" (ACHR, 2005, p. 9). The Amendment Bill has since been shelved.

Meanwhile, while the symbiotic relationship between tribal peoples and forests is recognized and the same conventions and constitutional safeguards apply, large areas of cultivable lands of indigenous and tribal peoples are being categorized as encroachment areas under the Indian Forest Act of 1927 and the Forest Conservation Act of 1980—cultivable lands that existed prior to both acts. For instance, the National Commission on Scheduled Castes and Scheduled Tribes noted that as a result of the Forest Conservation Act, some 148,000 people (mainly tribals) occupying 184,000 hectares of land in forest areas in the state of Madhya Pradesh suddenly became encroachers on October 24, 1980, and thus liable to eviction (ACHR, 2005, p. 10). Similarly, the report notes that while there are a number of laws prohibiting transfer of lands from tribal to nontribal, "non-implementation of the 5th and 6th schedules of the Constitution of India has caused extensive land alienation, exploitation and pauperization of the indigenous and tribal peoples across India" (p. 12). Such examples of consistent and widespread legal contradiction in relation to forced/illegal evictions, and forest and land rights, lends credence to the argument that human rights commitments serve the hegemonic aspirations of the state and the dominant interests that inform state partiality to elite projects that contradict the well-being of Adivasis despite various protective provisions.

In their analysis of neoliberal impacts on land policies and processes of land alienation, Pimple and Sethi (2005, p. 239) conclude that "under the application of neo-liberal land policies . . . traditional occupiers of land under customary law confront the prospect and reality of becoming illegal encroachers on land they have cultivated and sustained for generations— they are vulnerable and subject to summary eviction." They describe several ways in which the current neoliberal state is contributing to land/forest-related alienation of tribals. First is the process of reservation (originally practiced by the British in the 1800s) of forests whereby large tracts of land are declared as reserved or protected forests and cultivable and wasteland areas in these demarcated territories are declared to be out of bounds, often leading to the eviction of village inhabitants in the area, unless a source of cheap/free tribal labor is needed by the forest department.

The second means is through the leasing of forest land to industrialists for timber felling, regeneration, agribusiness, mining, or tourism ventures and relatedly, a third means of land alienation is enabled by the land acquisition Amendment Act, which simplifies the procedures for the acquisition of land by state-controlled or state-owned enterprises on the grounds of serving a public purpose. Such processes themselves involve numerous legal and not so legal machinations, as state-corporate interests collude in a Machiavellian political economy of tribal dispossession, justified, ironically, in the developmental interests of the tribal and the broader public interest.

In the manner of a brief illustration from a region that is familiar to this author, the decade-long struggle of the Prakrutik Sampad Surakshya Parishad (PSSP), a movement of Kondh, Penga, Paraja, and Jhodia tribes against a billion dollar open-pit Bauxite mine in South Orissa being proposed by Utkal Alumina International Ltd. (a consortium of global and national companies, including ALCAN of Montreal, Canada, and Indal, subsidiary of Hindalco Industries, a filial of the Aditya Birla Indian conglomerate), is an attempt by these Adivasis to convince state-corporate interests that this mine project is not in their interests as Adivasis protected under the fifth Schedule of the Constitution and by the Samatha judgment. A protracted struggle over the issue is testimony to the state's refusal to back down from the project, despite concerns raised around potential displacement (thirty to sixty thousand Adivasis), ecological degradation (the mandatory environmental impact study conducted by Engineers India Ltd. is yet to be made public), and the spiritual significance of the Baplimali plateau to the Adivasis. According to Bhagawan Majhi, the convenor of the PSSP, the UAIL consortium and the state have resorted to several tactics which allegedly include: failure to abide by the right to information, as surveyors have simply entered the area under the pretext of conducting surveys to build a railway line; orchestrated public hearings after developmental activities were under way (PSSP supporters were obstructed from participating and project supporters—those offered potential employment from the project—were bussed in from out of state); the use of violence and intimidation including the death of three Adivasis in the 2001 police shooting at Maikanch village; the use of international NGOs to soften people into compliance through the promise of social development/charitable schemes; and sporadic/sudden increases in compensation offered for displacement, especially after strong shows of opposition to the project (www. saanet.org/kashipur/articles/majhi.htm, retrieved on April 11, 2005).

Given the increasing number of such struggles in the state, the government of Orissa has proposed an NGO Management and Control bill (tabled in the 2005, Monsoon session of Parliament) that seeks to curb anti-industry lobbying by Adivasi and peasant populist struggles (who are often exercising their rights under the fifth Schedule) and social action NGOs found to be supportive of such agitations. According to Mines, Minerals, and People (mm&P), an alliance of tribal groups and organizations working in mining areas in Scheduled Areas, the fifth Schedule itself is currently under threat of being amended to effect transfer of tribal lands to nontribals and corporate bodies (see www.mmpindia.org). When it comes to the detribalization of tribal land through leasing for industrial purposes, Pimple and Sethi (2005,

p. 242) note that "more of such instances are now coming to light as the overall economic trend towards privatization is tempting state governments."

The Wild Life (Protection) Act of 1972 (a fourth means of land/forest alienation) has been used to redefine the "tribal as the enemy of ecology and the outsider/environmentalist as protector" (Pimple & Sethi, 2005, p. 242), as tribals are displaced from lands and forests demarcated as national parks and sanctuaries and even grudging concessions such as licences that permit limited access are challenged by some environmentalists. The authors conclude, "The overall result of state alienation of land is that the rights traditionally held by the forest communities have been progressively curtailed," and therefore, it should hardly be surprising to witness the "social unrest that has emerged in the areas affected in the form of grassroots forest protection movements which adopt tracts of forest for their preservation and regeneration" (p. 243).

The preceding arguments and examples have been raised to demonstrate the active, premeditated, and nonaccidental nature of the subversion of Adivasi human and legal rights around forest and land related issues and the related implications for exercising development on their own terms. Meanwhile, the state continues to ratify international conventions and serve up constitutional guarantees as part of a hegemonic exercise to secure state control to address the dominant interests of a global and national corporate-consumer elite. By the same token, however, as Pimple and Sethi (2005) have noted and as implied by desperate antidemocratic moves by the state such as the proposed NGO Management and Control Bill to stifle what the state of Orissa sees as anti-industry activism, there has been an increase in the response to such controls and intrusions as domination breeds its own resistance. The following section considers a potential role for popular adult education in appropriating human rights rhetoric for the purposes of repoliticizing of rights in the interests of antihegemonic Adivasi movements/struggles and counterhegemonic coalitions with other movements with intersecting agendas for social change.

APPROPRIATING HUMAN RIGHTS RHETORIC FOR COUNTER AND ANTIHEGEMONIC STRUGGLES: POPULAR PRAXIS AND THE REPOLITICIZATION OF HUMAN RIGHTS AT THE MARGINS

Contemporary neoliberal development by the Indian state under the tutelage of the international financial institutions and the interests of national/global capital has led to various types of resistances, including Adivasi movements that appear to take exception to the dominant insensitivity to cultural specificity and regional and local diversity. Speaking in relation to several similar forms of resistance internationally, Thomas (Evans, 1998, p. 178) notes that a potential common thread "running through the various examples of resistance is the rejection of neoliberal universalism, including ideas of economics, politics and *human rights* that support existing processes of hegemony or dominance." While an individualistic, ahistorical, and decontextualized version of human rights is susceptible to hegemonic manipulations and to a depoliticization of struggle around structured marginalization of social groups such as the Adivasis, alternatively, a collective, historically and sociopolitically grounded approach to human rights repoliticizes struggles and provides counter/anti-hegemonic potential. Popular praxis can be used to appropriate human rights rhetoric for collective struggles and the process of defining and securing rights can be productive in undermining prevailing hegemonic constructions in relation to Adivasis. When the state abdicates its responsibility to the people as a "regulator of social relations" that intervenes "for the development of social solidarity" (Freire, 2004, p. 25) and instead heralds a "democracy that deepens inequalities" and adopts the agency of a "liberal state that maximizes the freedom of the strong to accumulate capital even if that means poverty, at times total destitution, for the majority" (p. 24), then popular education must encourage a "political-pedagogical doing" that is "inseparable from the pedagogical political" which is "political action that involves the organization of groups and the popular classes in order to intervene in the reinventing of society" (Freire, 2004, p. 18).

Popular praxis, based on the seminal contributions of Paulo Freire and Antonio Gramsci, recognizes that adult education is political in terms of its ability to challenge oppressive social relations and hence the importance of a popular praxis that relates education to social action, research, mobilization, and organization for social change (Mayo, 1999). Indigenous scholars and educators in Northern contexts (Grande, 2004; Smith, 1999; Stewart, 2005) articulate several propositions that are instructive in relation to popular engagements with Adivasi movement activism in India. Smith (1999) emphasizes the significance of developing a local critical theory, informed by an indigenous spiritual-political project. Grande (2004) suggests that indigenous movements should engage in a coalition politics with modern progressives with agents that recognize and legitimate indigenous political aspirations and self-determination. And Stewart-Harawira (2005) reminds popular educators to ground political projects in indigenous onto-epistemmic traditions while utilizing the work of Foucault to allude to what some social movement scholars refer to as an "antihegemonic" stance where movements might seek to subvert hegemonic discourses and regimes that sustain subordination (antihegemony) but do not necessarily subscribe to (or perhaps have no modernist interest in?) the counterhegemonic project to replace the existing hegemony with a new hegemony, nor might there be a "striving for liberation" (Carroll, 1997, p. 32) from a capitalist hegemony in a Freirian-modernist sense.

Based on our experience as a small voluntary development organization (NGO), comprising outsiders and partners in Adivasi projects for social

change in South Orissa, a popular education process for Adivasi antihegemonic activism and coalitional engagements with counterhegemonic movements to repoliticize and appropriate human rights in the service of these
movements suggests to us a circumscribed "bridge-learning role" for popular
educator-outsiders pertaining to the development of a coalition politics.
First, popular educators can seek to bridge and articulate Adivasi antihegemonic concerns in relation to colonial, capitalist, and socialist subversions
to prospective counterhegemonic coalitions, in order to legitimize Adivasi
concerns around autonomy and their human rights as self-determining
agents of their own social development process. Second, in relation to
addressing the Adivasi movement, they need to articulate the political and
analytical potential of the modernist counterhegemonic project and its
potential significance for advancing both the Adivasi project and life
chances for similarly marginalized populations. In addressing this bridge-
learning role, popular educators can work with Adivasi movements to
appropriate human rights for anti and counterhegemonic ends. The following examples briefly illustrate some of these possibilities by referring to the
Orissa context.

Bridging the Adivasi Movement
to Counterhegemonic Coalitions

Adivasi movements in Orissa have for numerous reasons, some of which are
considered here, been reluctant to engage in counterhegemonic coalitions
that might assist with the process of mounting effective challenges to hegemonic manipulations of human rights commitments. Popular educators need
to recognize the grounds for this justifiable reluctance and work with the
movement to build a realistic trust around the prospects for coalitional antihegemonic opportunities. Based on the experiences in Orissa, it appears that
leftist party and nonparty groups, for instance, fail to recognize the spiritual
basis for Adivasi struggles and, in many cases, share a similar modernist disdain for their "backward ways." This has predictably distanced Adivasis from
these agents and the Left formations have lost a crucial ally in the peasant-
working class struggle in the state, as Adivasis constitute close to one-quarter
of the state population.

In order to address this development, popular educators that this author
is familiar with in the Kondh Adivasi region decided to start the coalition-
building process at the people-to-people level as opposed to trying to engage
Left-elitist party leadership elements. For example, over a period of time they
bridged the concerns of working-class unions of coolies (loaders/manual
laborers) with Adivasi struggles, as those who work as coolies often belong to
the Dalit (scheduled caste/"untouchable caste" groups) communities, many
of whom have historic cultural and economic ties with Adivasis in the

region. From small joint leadership gatherings to larger people's gatherings, such engagements facilitated the development of ties of trust and commitment that relied on the historic and cultural-economic relationship between the communities. This engagement between the Adivasi movement organization and the Dalit coolies' union eventually created a bottom-up pressure on the Left-party political leadership to which the latter provided pivotal electoral support in the region. Adivasi leaders and popular educators then found an ally in the leadership of the coolie's union and together these agents helped secure the acceptance of the party-Left leadership in relation to Adivasi participation and movement aspirations. The subsequent role for popular educators and the Adivasi movement leadership then became one of educating and ensuring that the coalition agenda continued to recognize Adivasi rights as self-determined peoples.

This position was cemented further by popular educators and the bridging role that they played in bringing together the Adivasi movement and the recent Dalit coolie's union with neighboring peasant and land-based communities and their struggles, such as the Save Chilika Movement (Andolan) of the coastal fisher folk in South Orissa, many of whom belong to Orissa's sixty-two different Adivasi groups. By organizing information exchanges, socially and spiritually significant and leadership gatherings, which have included discussions on the place of rights-based avenues for addressing Adivasi and Dalit concerns, popular educators have helped to cement lasting coalitions. These coalitions have taken on state-corporate interests and succeeded in subverting subversion as human rights and constitutional guarantees have been reappropriated on several occasions on behalf of popular struggles. For example, the Save Chilika Movement opposing the establishment of corporate aquaculture and shrimp farming operations (a US$1 billion business in India) on twenty thousand hectares of Orissa's 480km coastline despite Chilika's status as an internationally recognized wetland coastline, relied on such coalitions to secure a legal victory over one of India's biggest industrial houses. The courts, including a subsequent Supreme Court decision, prohibited shrimp culture in Chilika lake and enforced provisions under the coastal regulation zone.

When windows of opportunity arise as they do during elections, counter and antihegemonic movement interests tend to become more porous on some fronts and coalitional politics looks more viable than at other times. Popular educators need to seize these moments and engage this process in the interests of an Adivasi politics, while simultaneously contributing toward a Left counterhegemonic politics in the process. Such regionally based coalitions have succeeded in electing sympathetic parliamentary representatives who in turn have moved to help communities enhance their access to and control over land and forests as per the existing human rights and legal regimes referred to in this chapter.

Bridging Counterhegemonic Movement
Potential to Adivasi Movements

As mentioned, Adivasi movements are often reluctant to engage in counter-hegemonic political coalitions for reasons that often have to do with the failure of other movement groups to appreciate their way of life and their aspirations for political autonomy and self-determination. Ironically, such movements are often not premised on the idea of seceding from the Indian nation-state, as it does not seem plausible to break away from an entity that you did not consider yourself to be a part of in the first instance. Community constructions of nationhood, citizenship, and global citizenship are tenuous at best as Adivasi cosmic and historical attachments supercede such modernist ties. The challenge for popular educators in relation to recognition for Adivasi political aspirations is to make the case to Adivasis to consider the worth of a counterhegemonic coalitional politics to secure their vision as a society. Such opportunities often present themselves in state responses to Adivasi shows of assertion, which either: (1) expose internal weaknesses in the movement; (2) confirm the significance of Adivasi-coalition joint action; or (3) inadvertently point out new movement directions that often suggest the need for greater engagement with counterhegemonic coalitions. Popular educators can utilize state-corporate responses to movement assertions as bridge-learning moments to make the case for coalition politics to the Adivasi movement community, using these as occasions to reinterpret human rights guarantees from a populist standpoint while exposing hegemonic conceptions and applications of the same (Kapoor, 2004). Human rights discourse provides a discursive space in these instances, which has the potential to reunite these groups and simultaneously push the counter and antihegemonic struggle forward through such populist readings of rights.

A common state-corporate response is through new legislation, after court verdicts have required the state-corporate nexus to respect constitutional and legal provisions designed to protect the rights and livelihood of peasants, workers, Dalits, and Adivasis. As mentioned, the Samatha judgment referred to in this chapter has encouraged industry to pressure the state to revisit the fifth and sixth Schedules of the Constitution in a bid to undermine the successful use of these provisions by Adivasis in the state of Andhra Pradesh. Similarly, in relation to the Chilika Lake judgment, in 1997 industry lobbied the state to push through an Act of Parliament to nullify the court's decision and pass an Aquaculture Authority Bill that would make aquaculture permissible within the Coastal Regulation Zone. The PSSP struggle against the Bauxite mining proposition and similar struggles in the state of Orissa have led to the introduction of an "NGO Management and Control Bill," which aims to "blacklist" social action NGOs that are engaged in what the government views as "anti-industry lobbying" because of their relationship with movement organizations. Each of these propositions provides popular educators with tangible fodder for Adivasi movement learning pertaining to hegemonic interpretation and applications of human rights and legal frameworks and the continued significance of a counterhegemonic political activism, as Adivasi movements alone will find it increasingly difficult to roll back such developments.

CONCLUDING REFLECTIONS: CULTURE AND HUMAN RIGHTS AVENUES FOR POPULAR EDUCATION AND SOCIAL CHANGE IN ADIVASI CONTEXTS

This chapter has sought to demonstrate how hegemonic interpretations and the associated patterns of contradictory applications of national and international human rights provisions have undermined Adivasi life projects in India and Orissa. Similarly, an argument has been made that human rights discourse, in its provisions and their legal applications, can also provide avenues for a counter and antihegemonic Adivasi politics provided popular adult educator-outsiders play a bridging role to secure such possibilities. In conclusion, however, some pertinent cultural signifiers bear repeating if popular adult educators are to play a sensible and feasible role in what is often a contradictory location of insider-outsider in Adivasi struggles. First, popular educators will need to recognize the limits of a rights-based politics in its current form, given that this manifestation has predominantly germinated from a Euro-American cultural soil and is subject to material interpretations and applications that are largely policed by these nations and reproduced by the leadership of Southern countries. Galtung (1998, p. 220) makes a case in point when he notes that "the dialectic between I-cultures and we-cultures is an indelible part of the human condition," and the larger struggle toward the possibility of a "globalized human rights" and "global citizenship" (pp. 216–217) rests upon the possibility of securing "cultural equality *in* human rights" (p. 219; my emphasis), a struggle that needs to be waged by relatively disempowered "norm-objects" such as Adivasi social groups, who are objectified by a rights discourse largely controlled by "norm-senders" (e.g., UN agents) and "norm-receivers" (e.g., states, NGOs, and TNCs) (pp. 216–217).

Secondly, while popular educators pay heed to this struggle around the construction of global rights and citizenship discourse and facilitate counter and antihegemonic coalitions in local contexts, they also need to be able to recognize Adivasi cultural conceptions of the nature, purpose, and means of struggle and cannot afford to blindly ascribe to a radical political modernist zeal that disregards the Adivasi culture of protest and resistance. As Stan McKay (1992, p. 30) eloquently states in relation to the Lubicon Nation struggle in Alberta, an utterance that could just as easily have been made by an Adivasi, "The vision that moves us in the struggle toward aboriginal sovereignty is integral to our spirituality. The elders speak to us of our need for balance between the physical and spiritual aspects of our being. They would caution our political leaders not to become so caught up in the struggle for power that they compromise the spiritual heritage that shaped our being."

REFERENCES

Asian Centre for Human Rights. (2005). *Promising picture or broken future?*

Commentary and recommendations on the Draft National Policy on Tribals of the Government of India. Retrieved, September 22, 2005, from www.achrweb.org.

Blaser, M., Feit, H., & McRae, G. (Eds.). (2004). *In the way of development: Indigenous peoples, life projects, and globalization*. London: Zed.

Caroll, W. (Ed.).(1997). *Organizing dissent: Contemporary social movements in theory and practice*. Toronto: Garamond.

Evans, T. (1998). Introduction: Power, hegemony, and the universalization of human rights. In T. Evans (Ed.), *Human rights fifty years on: A reappraisal*. Manchester: Manchester University Press.

Fernandes,W., & Paranjpe (Eds.). (1997). *Rehabilitation policy and law in India: A right to livelihood*. New Delhi: Indian Social Institute.

Freire, P. (2004). *Pedagogy of indignation*. Boulder, CO: Paradigm Publishers.

Galtung, J. (1998). The third world and human rights in the post-1989 world order. In T. Evans (Ed.), *Human rights fifty years on: A reappraisal*. Manchester: Manchester University Press.

Gramsci, A. (1971). *Selections from prison notebooks*. Q. Hoare and G. Howell (Eds. & Trans.). London: Lawrence & Wishart.

Grande, S. (2004). *Red pedagogy: Native American social and political thought*. Lanham, MD: Rowman & Littlefield.

Hannum, H. (2003). Indigenous rights. In G. Lyons & J. Mayall (Eds.), *International human rights in the 21st century: Protecting the rights of groups*. Lanham, MD: Rowman & Littlefield.

Kapoor, D. (2004). Popular education and social movements in India: State responses to constructive resistance for social justice. *Convergence, 37(2)*, 55–64.

Mayo, P. (1999). *Gramsci, Freire, and adult education*. London: Zed.

MacKay, S. (1992). Calling creation into our family. In D. Engelstad & J. Bird (Eds.), *Nation to nation: Aboriginal sovereignty and the future of Canada*. Toronto: Anansi Press.

Pimple, M., & Sethi, M. (2005). Occupation of land in India: Experiences and challenges. In S. Moyo & P. Yeras (Eds.), *Reclaiming land: The resurgence of rural movements in Africa, Asia, and Latin America*. London: Zed.

Ray, R., & Katzenstein, M. (Eds.). (2005). *Social movements in India: Poverty, power, and politics*. Lanham, MD: Rowman & Littlefield.

Smith, L. (1999). *Decolonizing methodologies: Research and indigenous peoples*. London: Zed.

Stewart-Harawira, M. (2005). *The new imperial order: Indigenous responses to globalization*. London: Zed.

Shah, G. (2004). *Social movements in India: A review of the literature*. New Delhi: Sage.

South Asia Action Network. (2005). Introduction to the Kashipur struggle. www.saanet.org/kashipur/intro.htm, retrieved April 11, 2005.

Stammers, N. (1995). A critique of social approaches to human rights. *Human rights quarterly, 17(3)*, 488–508.

TEN

Human Rights Education and Contemporary Child Slavery

Creating Child-Friendly Villages When States, Communities, and Families Fail to Protect

Lynette Shultz

All liberating practice—which values the exercise of will, of decision, of resistance, of choice, the role of emotions, of feelings, of desires, of limits, the importance of historic awareness, of an ethical human presence in the world, and the understanding of history as possibility and never as determination—is substantively hopeful and, for this very reason, produces hope.
—Paulo Freire, *Pedagogy of Indignation*

INTRODUCTION

IT HAS BEEN ESTABLISHED in international law that all citizens have the right to protection from violence, exploitation, and abuse. This protection is from abuse from state as well as private actors. In the case of contemporary child slavery, it is clear that states, local communities and families have failed in their duty to protect children. This chapter examines the current increases in child slavery, the context in which this abuse happens, and presents an alternative human rights–based education project that seeks to disrupt the local and global system that surrounds the abuse of children as slaves. The child friendly village program succeeds in making the invisible visible and as a project of child protection, provides a model where, rather than *covering* children with protection, the child and his or her rights are *uncovered* to provide protection.

CONTEMPORARY CHILD SLAVERY:
A FAILURE TO PROTECT

Slavery is the total control of one person by another for the purpose of economic exploitation (Bales, 1999). This understanding has been at the core of policy and intervention since the 1800s. Slavery is not a new phenomenon, but in its contemporary form it has taken on several characteristics that place it at the intersection of forces of economic globalization and local exclusionary practices. Contemporary slavery can be understood as a global problem with local patterns based on particular social and cultural exclusions and reinforced by variances in access to political power.

Contemporary slavery is increasing in all parts of the world although exact figures are very difficult to determine because of its underground nature. Early work by Kevin Bales and nongovernmental organizations (NGOs) such as Anti-Slavery International presented important information about slavery in its contemporary form and included an estimate that at least twenty-seven million people were held as slaves (Bales, 1999, 2000). This work described a new trend in which enslaved people were "disposable" because of an abundant supply, a cheap price, a strong network supporting the practice, and lack of enforcement of existing laws (Bales, 1999, p. 118).Other research supports these findings and while the numbers in each report vary, the message is clear: slavery continues to increase at a rate that is unprecedented. In my research with grassroots community organizations working with children who have been rescued from slavery, I found a common response to the current research was that the numbers of children trafficked and enslaved are probably significantly, if not grossly, underreported in these documents. The United Nations Department of Economic and Social Affairs (UN DESA) estimates "each year 700,000 people are trafficked for the purpose of sexual exploitation and forced labour" (2002, p.1) and the United States State Department (U.S. Department of Labor, 2004) estimates between eight hundred and nine hundred thousand people are trafficked across borders each year. They also estimate forty-five to fifty thousand women and children are trafficked into the United States annually (Ibid). UNICEF (2003) produced a report based on extensive field research and estimated that 1.2 million children are trafficked each year, although this number was reported as three million in 2004 at the "Making Rights Work" conference held in Montreal, Canada, where it was also reported that trafficking in children generates profits of about $10 billion per year worldwide (Joyal, Noel, & Feliciati, 2005). Sen and Nair (2004) state, "The trade is secretive, the women [and children] are silenced, the traffickers are dangerous and not many agencies are counting" (p. 21). The International Labour Organization (ILO) (2002) estimates that 186 million children work in the worst forms of child labor, which according to the working definition, is considered slavery. The majority of these children are under the age of fifteen years (ILO, 2002). The U.S. Department of Labor (2004) provide evidence that child trafficking is for the purposes of prostitution, domestic servitude, agricultural work, mining, manufacturing, and organized begging. Bales, Fletcher, and Stover (2004) released a report that indicates there have been reported cases of slavery in ninety U.S. cities in the past five years. They also conclude that slavery is "prevalent in 5 sectors of the US economy: sex service (46%), domestic services (27%), agriculture (10%), sweatshop/factory (5%), and restaurant & hotel work (4%)" (p. 5). Their research also concludes that "forced labour persists in these sectors because of low wages, lack of regulation and monitoring of working conditions, and a high demand for cheap labour" (p. 1). Sen and Nair (2004) conclude that prevention is the key to eliminating slavery because the sale of humans is so lucrative that intervention is difficult. Community-based prevention is key because the village or local community is the starting point for trafficking and slavery. In prevention, it is essential to remove the key vulnerability factors: discrimination, poverty, and illiteracy (Sen & Nair, 2004). In addition, a shift regarding children's rights is necessary; as de Boer-Buquicchio suggests, "Children are not mini human beings with mini rights. As long as adults continue to regard children as mini human beings, violence against them will persist" (in Joyal, Noel, & Feliciati, 2005, p. 54).

The commodification of children must also be linked to wider economic policies that reflect the neoliberal ideology driving economic globalization. As countries became more closely tied to the globalized economic system through World Bank and International Monetary Fund programs in the latter part of the last century, these nations' economies and entire public sectors were restructured in alignment with the neoliberal ideology of the international financial institutions. The results of these trends have been, among other things, the collapse of many small, local enterprises that sustained individuals, families, and small communities. With the increasing global liberalism in economic systems, labor standards have been consistently diminished and local community infrastructure has been weakened, resulting in a decrease in democratic input and citizenship spaces as support for the entrepreneurial individual trumps social development or social action. It is at this point that the vast increase in slavery is located. "Slavery emerges when economic vulnerability combines with high population growth and a lack of regulation or control over the use of violence" (Bales, 2000, p. 9). Local communities, with economic livelihoods devastated by global neoliberal economic policy and with public sector policy and programming minimized,

also according to neoliberal structural adjustment programs, have few material or social resources with which to respond to the new global economic reality into which they are thrust. Slavetraders and slaveholders, functioning
within this free market system, find easy access to marginalized people, lax
regulations, and few enforcement agents.

Despite organizations such as the ILO having identified the persistent
and growing problem of child slavery, it is increasing with little progress on
prevention or intervention. Joyal,Noel, and Feliciati (2005) speak directly to
the problem:

> Children victims of trafficking play music and beg in our squares, offer sex-
> ual services in our avenues and train station, clean our restaurants and col-
> lect vegetables in our fields. They are everywhere but seem to be invisible
> to our eyes, our hearts, and our policies. (p. 52)

The state, local communities, and families have failed to protect these
children who become engaged in a system that often includes trafficking,
extreme violence, and coercion. This failure is in part caused by the general
reality that children's issues tend to be ignored, tied to women's issues, or
downplayed through a logic of patrimony. Denial of the existence of child
slavery is a key finding in research and Sen and Nair (2004) describe "a conspiracy of silence by all concerned, which does not exclude family, community, religious institutions, and political parties, and, at times, even CBOs
[community based organizations] and NGOs [nongovernmental organiza-
tions]" (p. 380). In recent interviews with staff of NGOs working with children, a tension of how even to speak about these children was evident:

> No we don't use the term slavery. Because we understand that term comes
> with a historical, political context and a historical time period. . . . In our
> experience, we say children who are enslaved do exist. That's just how we
> put it, children who are enslaved do exist. But we do not use the term *slav-
> ery*. (Interview, 2005)

> We do not use the term *slavery*. We are a leading child rights organization
> and therefore we are sensitive to the terms used about children, for children,
> or in the words of children. So used in the context of labor, we talk about
> the worst forms of child labor; in the context of child soldiers, we still put
> in the form of worst form of child labor. In the sex trade, we talk about chil-
> dren who are exploited, because all children are exploited; there are really
> no worst forms of child labor, in the sex trade all forms are unacceptable. In
> the context of child trafficking, we talk about, we call them, children who
> have been trafficked. (Interview, 2005)

> Of course it's slavery—in its worst forms. There is no doubt that these chil-
> dren were slaves. However, slavery is a very political term. Because slavery

is banned, no one wants to call it slavery. The government can't say, "We have slavery" to the rest of the world. So we don't use it and you shouldn't either. (Interview, 2005)

When the people and organizations, at national, local, and family levels, that are set up to protect children are silent, if not complicit, it makes clear the need to intervene in alternative ways including working to empower children themselves. This requires a shift in how we frame children's rights and their ability to claim these rights.

In most places, children occupy a position of both diluted rights and limited citizenship. As highlighted by Brysk (2005), there is a tension between the social logics of children as property or projections of their parents or sociocultural communities and the logics of the human rights of children as a universal principle affirming both human dignity and equality. The patrimonial view of children holds that "children [are] the bearers of a group identity for the family, ethnic, or nation, which trumps their rights or needs as individuals" (Brysk, 2005, p. 34). Understandings of children as commodities or property of their parents exist within most societies and in a vast majority of family relationships, and this position poses few problems as families negotiate ways to protect and socialize children; however, it is also this understanding of children in relation to others that operates most often when children are sold or contracted into slavery. This patrimonial invisibility serves to create both the vulnerability and the space for exploitation. "Although coercion and family failure may sometimes be factors, it is important to recognize that in most cases trafficking is deliberately promoted by children's families, from some combination of ignorance, desperation, exploitation, or even custom" (Brysk, 2005, p. 42). Coupled with the global trafficking networks and a global silence on labor exploitation, there is little fear of reprisal for those who enslave and little hope of intervention for those enslaved. Particularly problematic is the destruction of agency that the experience of slavery imposes.

FRAMING CHILDREN'S RESPONSES IN A HUMAN RIGHTS AND GLOBAL CITIZENSHIP APPROACH

Given the vast numbers of children involved and the fact that the problem of child slavery exists in most countries and reflects age, gender, class, ethnicity, and caste discriminations, it is necessary to look for alternative ways to frame children's positions within family and the wider community. Can a child rights approach mediate this contested space?

The movement of human rights from a distant legal process to the center of community interactions has taken place over the last fifty or sixty years

and can be understood as a generational process of human rights development and application (see Evans, this volume). Jochnick (1999) highlights
the important shift that human rights have presented:

> States are either bound by those norms that achieve the distinction of cus-
> tomary law or those that they explicitly consent to through treaties. How-
> ever, human rights law has in large measure defied these narrow categories
> by suggesting an additional foundation: human dignity. (pp. 59–60)

Human dignity is not a new concept, nor a Western concept, and can be
found in religious and cultural texts from all places and times. Human dignity
as a foundation of social actions and interactions makes claims on all actors
regardless of custom or consent. When human rights–based work is framed as
efforts to universalize respect for human dignity, it provides an alternative way
to link local, national, and global efforts but also takes human rights into areas
formerly involving only state actors. Jochnik (1999) suggests that moving
human rights beyond the state-centric paradigm serves two purposes. First, "It
challenges the reigning neo-liberal extremism that infects much of the public
discourse about development and poverty, providing a rhetoric and vision to
suggest that entrenched poverty is neither inevitable nor acceptable" (p. 57).
In the case of child slavery, the attitude that *there is no alternative* permeates the
thinking and policy approaches in communities and states around the world. If
the strong local and global networks that perpetuate child slavery are to be
interrupted, the whole approach to exploitive child labor must be reframed. A
human rights frame based on the universalistic concept of human dignity can
provide the avenue for social change based on a vision of justice based on
human dignity (Stammers, 1999). Second, those actors that function outside
state mechanisms, such as transnational corporations, international financial
institutions, or warlords, can be held accountable within the human rights
regime. Human rights provides a means for human dignity to trump customary
practice that is significant in the context of child slavery, which owes much of
its existence to customary practice revealed as action, inaction, or silence.

Within a local context, a human rights approach provides access to those
rights and privileges we come to understand as citizenship through the transformation of individual and social agency of marginalized individuals and
groups. As Sen (1999, 2005) suggests, agency is key to development and is
both an individual ability to project oneself into the social world and a social
commitment toward individuals. Agency includes voice (deliberative
agency); ability to question (critical agency); and the ability to act (constructive agency). Because power is embedded in everyday social relations,
shifting power extends these relationships. A human rights frame provides a
tool to make this shift inclusive of those who are marginalized and excluded
from the social, political, and economic rewards of participating in society.
Human rights, then, becomes a means to extend individual and social agency.

What might this look like in practice? One example of using a human rights approach to prevent child slavery is being carried out by one branch of an Indian coalition, the South Asian Coalition on Child Servitude (SACCS).

THE BAL MITRA GRAM PROGRAM

> The emancipation of children who have been abused in exploitive work lies in changing the mindset, behaviour, and priorities of the village community.
>
> —Bal Mitra Gram, Policy Statement

The South Asian Coalition on Child Servitude (SACCS) aims to create a child friendly, child slave free, society through education, rehabilitation, and Bal Mitra Gram (Child Friend Village) programs. The Bal Mitra Gram (BMG) concept was adopted in 2000 as part of a way to make villages and wards in India child labor free. The particular villages chosen as sites for the program have current conditions that make exploitive child labor and child slavery particularly prevalent. These conditions include a history of child slavery, economic vulnerability, as well as social and cultural conditions that create a particularly vulnerable group of marginalized people who suffer discrimination. This discrimination is usually based on caste, religion, class, and gender. The process of becoming "child friendly" has four phases.

Elimination and withdrawal of child labor from the village. During this stage, community members, including children, are engaged in a social mapping project that helps to identify who the children are in the village and where they are. As this participatory mapping process proceeds, very important discussions take place regarding child labor, children's human rights and the right to education, and issues of equity, discrimination, and justice. The program leaders take an activists position and begin to bring more and more people "to the table" including those who have traditionally been marginalized by caste, class, gender, age, or ability. These inclusive discussions lead to defining what the particular village would look like if it were "child friendly." To assist in this process a human rights framework is introduced and becomes helpful as a tool and a language with which to identify and discuss local issues. The community identifies which children are "missing" due to being taken for exploitive labor through kidnapping, sale, or parental permission, and alternatives to child labor are developed. This leads to the second phase, "enrollment of all children in school."

Enrollment of all children in school. In relation to non-poor children, the benefits of schooling are seldom debated. Most middle and upper-class children everywhere in the world experience expectations that they will become educated, and there is corresponding pressure on school systems to provide quality education to these children. However, for poor children, there continues to be a question of whether education is a secondary concern after finding employment. In the BMG project, there is no distinction between the right to education for rich or poor, and the benefits of education are promoted to all parents and community members. The second stage of BMG involves working with the formal school sector and nonformal education providers in new ways. Inclusive community meetings, facilitated initially by BMG leaders, become places where deliberation and dialogue take place. It is clear that these are new processes and many school staff members discuss how they had never before been invited to community meetings. The BMG process engages children, teachers, and community members in discussions about the quality and organization of the school program. Often the local school had not taken advantage of current government schemes initiated to improve the quality of education programming. Through community discussions, information regarding government schemes and community expectations was aired openly. Previously, educators often felt no responsibility for children who were not attending and most felt that this was a parental responsibility. However, because the BMG process engages the wider community in supporting children's participation in school, the pressure to send children to school starts to come from many places including neighbors, the school, other children, and other local community members. Often this pressure is the first that some parents have felt to send their children to school rather than to work.

> I didn't know. Now I understand that MY children can also go to school.
> (Informal conversation with parent in BMG village, 2004)

When I spoke with community members about their community after participating in BMG they felt very strongly that they needed to promote their community as one where all children attend school. As a result, they would challenge children out of school or parents who were not sending their children. This new norm of inclusivity that created a shared responsibility for education was evident through the BMG communities I visited. Community schemes were established to help extremely poor families to recover the money that children would have been earning had they been working, often only two or three rupees per day. Accessing government funds for free school midday meals also helped, as the money children would have earned often was just enough to pay for their food. For those children vulnerable to being sent into slavery, their families no longer needed to worry about the cost of education and the cost of the main meal of the day, and so one of the "push factors" for selling children was eliminated.

As the BMG became more established, the community involvement resulted in other educational initiatives such as working with the schools to provide locally created materials in the village language, support for vocational education based on the local economic context, and training in environmental education initiatives.

Establishment of the Bal Panchayat (Children's Assembly). This part of the program is founded on a belief that right from childhood, children are capable of making decisions and taking leadership in the issues that affect them. Through the Children's Assembly, children learn the processes of democratic decision making, citizenship engagement, and social action. All children in the community are involved and there is particular pressure from children for village-wide attendance, including those traditionally marginalized (at least in the adult world) by caste, class, religion, or gender. The children become engaged in the real issues of their community and are trained in group processes that reflect democratic and human rights, and in engaged citizenship activities such as lobbying, public speaking, and making group decisions. These activities begin around the issues of abusive child labor and are initiated by BMG leaders, but quickly, as the children learn how to have a voice, the children themselves begin to take the lead in addressing the many issues of their communities. The BMG leaders continue to assist the children in accessing the information they need, such as current government policy, and the children soon learn valuable research skills. While the issues are often related to school experiences, in several villages that I visited the Children's Assembly was responsible for getting good water, improved toilets, and safe places to play for the school and village children. In one case, the Children's Assembly was responsible for holding head teachers accountable for money collected for school fees when these were to have been eliminated. In one school, the children's parliament challenged the school head who had taken the school TV and VCR to his home rather than deliver it to the school. The students don't stop at the school, but continue to bring forward issues from the community. The following are some of the questions raised at Children Assembly meetings:

> Why is there no bridge across the river for children to cross safely to get to school? Why is there no boundary around the electrical generator near the playground? Why are the children of this family not in school? Why do these children not have enough food? (Interviews and field notes, 2005)

Children are very involved in initiatives to end child labor and to improve the quality of education, and have the opportunity to engage with children from other villages and at a national level. The ability and resourcefulness of children in examining these issues becomes a precedent for engagement in other issues in the community.

Bal Panchayat becomes part of the formal governance structure of the community. During the final stage of becoming "child friendly," the children's assembly becomes a formal part of the governance structure of the community. The goal is to have the Bal Panchayat members as regular and full participants in local meetings and to have their ideas taken seriously. There is also an annual meeting of members of BMG children's assemblies and the Indian national parliament. At this meeting, children are able to present their concerns to the prime minister and MPs and to engage in dialogue and debate about important issues. The participation of the children brings the framework and the language of human rights into the governance of the village affairs. In BMG villages, it is quite reasonable to hear issues being discussed using human rights language to frame and claim participation, access and distribution.

> Due to discrimination, extreme poverty, inappropriate development schemes, children are not provided the necessary skills and knowledge they need for community life. Until and unless a child is politically, socially and economically secure in his/her environment, talking of child protection is meaningless, and for that reason these issues need to be collectively addressed and made into a mass movement amongst the local people. (Community organizer, 2004)

The child friendly village program transforms many established ideas and practices within village life and seeks to position children as citizens with full rights. Children are engaged very actively and authentically in understanding and acting on their social, moral, political, and economic context. They learn in a very participatory way, about the context, their position within it, and how change happens. As a human rights–based initiative, process matters; it is not just about creating laws, or enforcement, but how the process of inclusive dialogue and participation based on a universal understanding of human dignity, takes place. Children are generally excluded from participating in the social and political working of communities in any real way, so the BMG model provides an example of a very different role for children.

In addition, the BMG program breaks the silence on child slavery in what can be understood as the enactment of deliberative agency.

> [T]he biggest obstacle is the culture of silence. . . . Because children will say that very, very strongly. People know things are going on but for some strange reason they tend not to pay attention to it and the reasons for that are multiple. I was involved in research on child sex tourism and people kept quiet. (Interview, 2005)

Through the participation in the stages of becoming "child friendly" it becomes acceptable for children, parents, and community members to speak about the impact of exploitive labor on their children, families, and community. The culture of silence around slavery plays a part in perpetuating this practice. Parents, many already marginalized by poverty and discrimination, feel they have no place and no voice to complain. Many are embarrassed by their situation and feel hopeless in making any change. Schools tend to add to the problem of silence despite the mandate for universal education, making reentry back into the school system more difficult for children who have missed school due to exploitive work. Shields (2004) describes the pathology of silence in relation to school communities. Educators' "pathologization of [the lived experience of students] is covert and silent, engendering in students and their families feelings that, somehow they and their lived experiences are abnormal and unacceptable within the school community" (p. 112). By beginning the BMG process around the issue of exploitive child labor and openly presenting child labor as an unacceptable practice the issue is opened not only for discussion but for action.

> The panchayat and the people have been given the collective right to make schemes for economic development and social justice. This law gives the villagers an opportunity to make their village child labor free. BMG support groups also lay stress on the formulation of schemes at the grass roots level by the villagers. Recognition of child laborers as well as on their rehabilitation is given special emphasis. As a result of such initiatives there has been an increase in the involvement of various sections of the villagers in the formulation of various useful schemes. (Interview, 2005)

Another area of transformation is the active participation of children, which results in bringing children into the center of the policy process. This shift in both normative and cognitive structures challenges norms of child participation and constructive agency. Children very ably engaged in the governance of their communities. Their input helps to clearly identify issues and strengths of the local system and provides pressure to make the education program of good quality and locally relevant. This presents new ideas about trusteeship of education. Very often this role has been played by adults within the community, but the BMG model indicates that children also have the capacity to be effectively involved in monitoring and guiding community education programs. A radical position for children in education!

The BMG program provides an example of how children are capable of being subjects of their lives, a key premise of the Convention on the Rights of the Child. The program allows a strong link to be made between personal/individual and social action. Political and social literacy are key aspects of the process, and children are able to understand and participate in both political and social aspects of community life. The children's identities as engaged citizens are reinforced through participation and through the process of recognition by the wider community.

In addition, the protective capacity of schools becomes a community asset during the BMG process. When school-community relationships are weak, schools can become places of both real and perceived exclusion. Forging strong relationships between formal educators and community members requires challenging established patterns of relations and engaging in new ways of decision making and problem solving.

CONCLUSIONS

If child slavery is to be disrupted, it is clear that significant changes in how children are positioned within their communities must take place. Addressing child protection is most effective when it is based on children's rights within the wider context of human rights and the experience of the local community. The BMG program provides a model of transformational human rights education that changes not only the relationship between children vulnerable to being exploited through child slavery but also the relationships between children and adults in general. In this way, children's agency is expanded, including deliberative agency, the children's ability to exercise their voice, their critical agency or ability to raise critical questions about the issues that affect them, and their constructive agency, the ability to take action. The program uses a human rights framework to engage children, families, and the wider community in working to eliminate child labor and exploitive work from the community. Children are actively involved in the democratic process in authentic ways. Established norms of participation are shifted as children become community animators and leaders in the social and political life of the community. This process becomes part of the education system as children grapple with the right to education for all children and make their demands clearly to the relevant adults. There are few other models of children playing a strong trustee role in protecting and enhancing local education. The strengthening of children and of the community as a whole enables them to change both thinking and practices that exploit children. In child friendly villages, children experience the protection and security of a school and community that places them actively at its center. . . . Indeed a transformation!

REFERENCES

Bales, K. (1999). *Disposable people: New slavery in the global economy*. Berkeley/London: University of California Press.

Bales, K. (2000). Slavery in the age of globalization. *Journal of International Affairs*, 53(2), 461–484.

Bales, K., Fletcher, L., & Stover, E. (2004). *Hidden slaves: Forced labor in the US*. Report for Free the Slaves, Washington, DC, & Human Rights Center, University of California, Berkeley, CA.

Brysk, A. (2005). *Human rights and private wrongs: Constructing global civil society*. New York: Routledge.

Cowen, M., & Shenton, R. (1996). *Doctrines of development*. London: Routledge.

Freire, P. (2004). *Pedagogy of indignation*. London/Boulder, CO: Paradigm Publishers.

International Labor Organization (ILO) (2002). *A future without child labour*. Geneva: ILO Office.

Jochnick, C. (1999). Confronting the impunity of non-state actors: New fields for the promotion of human rights. *Human Rights Quarterly, 21(1)*, 56–79.

Joyal, R., Noel, J., & Feliciati, C. (Eds.). (2005). *Making children's rights work: National and international perspectives*. Final report of the conference held in Montreal on November 18–20, 2004.

Sen, A. (2005). *The argumentative Indian*. New York: Farrar, Straus & Giroux.

Sen, A. (1999). *Development as freedom*. New York: Anchor Books.

Sen, S., & Nair, P. M. (2004). *A report on trafficking in women and children in India, 2002–2003*. New Delhi: Institute of Social Sciences, National Human Rights Commission, UNIFEM.

Shields, C. (2004). Dialogic leadership for social justice: Overcoming pathologies of silence. *Educational Administration Quarterly, 40(1)*, 109–132.

Stammers, N. (1999). Social movements and the social construction of human rights. *Human Rights Quarterly, 21(4)*, 980–1008.

UN DESA (United National Division for the Advancement of Women, Department of Economic & Social Affairs). (2002). *The UN response to trafficking in women and girls*. New York: United Nations.

UNICEF. (2003). *Trafficking in human beings, especially women and children, in Africa*. Florence: Unicef Innocenti Research Centre.

U.S. Department of Labor. (2004). *The U.S. Department of Labor's 2003 findings on the worst forms of child labor*. Washington, DC: U.S. Department of Labor, Bureau of International Labor Affairs.

ELEVEN

Toward Minority Group Rights and Inclusive Citizenship for Immigrants

The Role of a Voluntary Organization in Vancouver, Canada

Shibao Guo

INTRODUCTION

COMMUNITY-INITIATED voluntary associations play a valuable role in immigrant societies, such as multicultural Canada. They are, however, not always seen as benign, self-motivated, or altruistic institutions. Where immigrants are all too frequently viewed as a drain on societal resources, ethnic organizations are also viewed as threatening national unity, diluting Canadian identity, and promoting ghettoization and separatism. Other critics raise specific questions about it, such as whether the state should use taxpayers' money to fund these organizations. Still others argue that all Canadians should be treated equally, and that allocating special resources to support such organizations would undermine Canadian democratic principles and erode norms and practices of democratic citizenship.

This chapter explores, in detail, the way in which one ethnic organization in Vancouver, called SUCCESS—United Chinese Community Enrichment Services Society—was founded in 1973 for exactly the opposite reasons. The failure of the government and mainstream organizations to provide accessible social services for Chinese immigrants led to its initiation. The chapter investigates the role of SUCCESS in building a support and citizenship community for Chinese immigrants in Vancouver. It examines the founding, historical development, and social contributions of SUCCESS.

This chapter falls into six parts. The first examines the theoretical framework, followed by a review of the historical, social, and political context in which SUCCESS emerged. The third focuses on the research design. The fourth analyzes the historical development of the organization and the provision of programs and services. The fifth reports the major changes in the organization, and finally the social contributions of SUCCESS.

THEORETICAL FRAMEWORK

The Citizenship Debate

The success of contemporary Western societies such as Canada can be partially attributed to adherence to liberal democratic principles, including fairness, justice, and the protection of individual rights and freedoms. However, Canada is becoming an increasingly ethno-culturally diverse society. The 2001 Census of Canada (Statistics Canada, 2003) reveals that as of May 15, 2001, 18.4 percent of Canada's total population were born outside the country, and that 13.4 percent identified themselves as visible minorities. People come to Canada from different social, economic, and cultural backgrounds. In the process of adapting to the new society, they have heterogeneous needs and encounter many barriers. We usually find ourselves in a debate over whether liberal democracy can accommodate such needs, the role ethnic organizations should play in the settlement and adaptation of immigrants, and the relationship between minority group rights and democratic citizenship. At the center of this debate lies the concept of citizenship, particularly in relation to immigrants' membership in the national community.

Two schools of thought are usually represented in this debate: traditional liberalism and cultural pluralism. Traditional liberals (Bissoondath, 1994; Gwyn, 1995; Rawls, 1971) advocate a culturally neutral state, where citizens deal fairly with each other and the state deals equally with all, regardless of how we conceive our ends. They believe in universal rights and citizenship, and maintain that the promotion of minority group rights restricts individual rights and freedoms and erodes the norms and practices of responsible citizenship. Rawls's (1971) "justice as fairness" is a good example of this argument. He places the protection of individual rights, along with nondiscrimination provisions, before collective goals. Traditional liberals also oppose multicultural policies. In his critique of multiculturalism, Bissoondath (1994) argues that maintenance of ethnic heritage and identity is injurious to national allegiance and unity. He rejects using taxpayers' money to fund ethnic organizations. Bissoondath (1994) also points out that, instead of promoting integration, ethnic organizations dilute Canadian identity and encourage ethnic

"ghettoization." When translating liberal universalism into practice, traditional liberals tend to adopt a difference-blind approach in addressing immigrants' needs and barriers, maintaining that people are essentially the same,
and therefore, require similar modes of service and intervention. According to
Bissoondath, Canada should not aim at preserving differences but at "blending them into a new vision of Canadianness, pursing a Canada where inherent differences and inherent similarities meld easily" (p. 224).

The liberal perspective has been criticized as "unrealistic," "unacceptably 'thin,'" and "unfair" (Bloemraad, 2000). Bloemraad maintains that
thought experiments concerning an "original position" are unrealistic
because such a position never existed; furthermore, they ignore the critical
point that no one is born an atomized, rational actor. She continues to argue
that, because it fails to recognize that being part of a community is a primordial good, the liberal conception of citizenship is unacceptably thin. A
person's ethnic and cultural heritage must be recognized as part of the individual so as to encourage participation by all (Walzer, 1982). Bloemraad also
criticizes the liberal ideal of universal citizenship as unfair. According to
Tamir (1995) and Young (1995), governments cannot be culturally neutral.
The notion of a neutral state embodies a dangerous and oppressive illusion.
Strict adherence to the principle of equal treatment merely sustains the status of privileged groups and perpetuates oppression and inequality (Young,
1995). Taylor (1993, 1994a, 1994b) also adds his criticism of liberal neutrality. He fears that liberal neutralism prevents citizens from pursuing certain legitimate collective goals through their political institutions. He maintains that a single-principle neutral liberalism cannot suffice, and that it has
to allow space for other goods. He notes further that the reality of plural
societies may require us to modify neutral liberalism. As an alternative,
Young (1995) and Taylor (1994) propose "differentiated citizenship" and
"deep diversity" respectively to acknowledge and accept plural ways of
belonging. The multiple conceptions of citizenship act as a means to guarantee group rights and group representation.

Minority Group Rights

According to Kymlicka and Norman (2000), minority groups can be divided
into four categories: (1) national minorities; (2) immigrant minorities; (3)
religious groups; and (4) *sui generis* groups. These groups have different histories, needs, aspirations, and identities, and face different kinds of challenges.
For example, Canada's national minorities (i.e., Aboriginal peoples and
French Canadians) are different from immigrants (Kymlicka, 1995, 1998).
The former are seeking various forms of self-government and demanding special recognition to maintain their status as culturally distinct and self-gov-
erning societies within Canada, whereas immigrants wish to integrate into

mainstream society. Although immigrants want to modify the institutions and laws of mainstream society to make them more accommodating of cultural differences, their goals differ from those of national minorities. In Canada, ironically, one of the major mechanisms for accommodating cultural differences is "the protection of civil and political rights of individuals" (Kymlicka, 1995, p. 26) that are highly suspicious of collective goals, which are insufficient to meet the needs of ethnic groups. These common rights need to be supplemented by specific "group rights" that recognize and accommodate particular ethno-cultural practices and identities.

The rights of ethno-cultural minorities, or minority rights in short, can be defined as "a wide range of public policies, legal rights, and constitutional provisions sought by ethnic groups for the accommodation of their cultural differences" (Kymlicka & Norman, 2000, p. 2). The heterogeneous nature of ethnocultural groups determines that there are three categories of group-specific rights: self-government, polyethnic, and special representation rights (Kymlicka, 1995, 1998). Levy (1997), on the other hand, regards Kymlicka's classification of group rights as too broad. He classifies minority group rights into eight categories: exemptions, assistance, self-government, external rules, internal rules, recognition/enforcement, representation, and symbolic claims. In this context, assistance rights are more relevant to this research. According to him, "Assistance rights are claims for help in overcoming obstacles to engaging in common practices" (p. 29). Two common clusters of assistance rights are discussed here: language rights, and subsidies to a variety of cultural and linguistic institutions and associations.

Because of language difficulties, speakers of the minority language may not be able to interact with the state or receive state protection and benefits. They may be prevented from voting, using the courts and the schools, or having access to the bureaucracy. Accordingly, they need special provisions to overcome this obstacle, but special provisions are costly. Supporters of assistance rights argue that the costs are less important than the injustice that takes place because of speakers of the minority language being denied access to the activities and services to which they are entitled. Another group of assistance rights is subsidies to a variety of cultural and linguistic institutions and associations. These could be direct subsidies or special tax credits as contributions to such associations. These special state measures are designed to help cultural groups preserve their cultural integrity and heritage to the same degree as the majority culture.

Minority rights are beyond the common provisions of civil and political rights of individual citizenship in a liberal democratic society. Proponents of minority rights (Kymlicka & Norman, 2000; Tamir, 1995; Taylor, 1994; Young, 1995) typically see group rights as supplementing individual rights. They argue that the promotion of group rights can actually enhance citizenship. They point out that minority groups seek these rights to allow them to do things or get access to services that members of the majority culture already enjoy. They seek special provision because of culturally specific disadvantages or because the desired common activity is out of the reach of members of nondominant groups. Minority rights are needed to prevent the ongoing stigmatization of ethno-cultural minorities, to encourage alienated groups to come to identify with the larger society, and to become full members of the community. They show that refusal to grant recognition and autonomy to such minority groups is likely to provoke even more resentment and hostility, alienating them further from their identity as citizens of the larger state. Kymlicka and Norman (2000) also emphasize that the relationship between the minority group rights and democratic citizenship is more complicated than it appears, that it requires actual empirical investigation in specific contexts, and that no conclusion should be drawn a priori.

HISTORICAL, SOCIAL, AND POLITICAL CONTEXT

The Chinese immigrant group is one of the oldest in Canada, and its history is probably the most unsettling (Li, 1998). The first group of Chinese arrived in Victoria on June 28, 1858, from California in search of gold and new development opportunities. Originally, they came predominantly from the southern Chinese coastal provinces of Guangdong (or Kuangtung) and Fujian (or Fukien). Most of them were single men with rural origins. As the gold fields petered out, the Chinese found employment as domestic servants, coal miners, and seasonal workers in the salmon canning industry (Tan & Roy, 1985). Chinese workers were used extensively during the construction of the Canadian Pacific Railway (CPR).

The proliferation of the Chinese on the West Coast was perceived as a threat to the mission of the government to build a white *British* Columbia. The Chinese signified an ancient and medieval baggage of distinctions between "West" and "East," civilized and barbarian, master and slave, Christian and heathen, white and nonwhite (Anderson, 1995). With the completion of the CPR, the Chinese were no longer welcome. In 1885, the government of Canada imposed a $50 head tax on all incoming Chinese, increased to $100 in 1900, and to $500 in 1903. When it was found that it was not effective enough to keep the Chinese out of Canada, the federal government passed a restrictive Chinese Immigration Act in 1923, which virtually prohibited all Chinese immigration into Canada until its repeal in 1947. Besides the head tax and the 1923 Chinese Immigration Act, the Chinese also faced other kinds of discrimination. Since they were not allowed to vote, they were prohibited from entering certain professions such as law, medicine, or accounting. Further, they were denied the opportunity to acquire Crown land (Tan & Roy, 1985).

The founding and historical development of SUCCESS mirrored, and was influenced by, the national immigration policy. From Confederation to the 1960s, the selection of immigrants was based on racial background, with the British and Western Europeans being the most "desirable" citizens, the Asians the "unassimilable" and, therefore, "undesirable." After World War II, the Canadian immigration policy continued to be "highly restrictive" (Knowles, 1997) despite external and internal pressures for an open-door policy.

In the mid-1960s, Canada was experiencing "the greatest postwar boom" (Whitaker, 1991, p.18). Skilled labor was required to help Canada build its expansionary economy, but Europe as the traditional source of immigrants was not able to meet the needs of Canada because of the economic recovery there. Thus, the Canadian government turned its recruitment efforts to the traditionally restricted areas—Asia. In 1967 a "point system" was introduced by the Liberal government, which based the selection of immigrants on their "education, skills and resources" rather than their racial and religious backgrounds (Ibid., p.19). According to Whitaker, this new system represented "an historic watershed," and "it did establish at the level of formal principle that Canadian immigration policy is 'colour blind'" (Ibid., p.19). However, the new selection method was criticized for being "in favour of some racial groups and against others" (Mattas, 1996, p.100). Whitaker (1991), however, believes that the new system might have stacked the deck against poor immigrants from third world countries.

Whitaker pointed out further that the "point system" was successful in reversing the pattern of immigration to Canada away from Europe toward Asian and other third world countries. By the mid-1970s there were more immigrants arriving from the third world than from the developed world, the largest number coming from Asia, followed by the Caribbean, Latin America, and Africa (Ibid., p.19). Among the Asian group, many were from Hong Kong.

To understand the founding of SUCCESS, besides understanding the historical, social, and political context in the receiving country, it is also important to review the context from which the immigrants came. According to Wong (1992), there have been three major waves of emigration from Hong Kong since the end of World War II. The first occurred between 1958 and 1961 owing to dramatic changes in Hong Kong's agriculture. The second wave was triggered by a political crisis, the 1967 riot. It was a spillover of the Cultural Revolution (1966–1976) in China. It began with a demonstration led by local communists, but ended with violence and terrorism. Threatened by bombs and political instability, thousands left Hong Kong for popular destinations, in particular the United States and Canada. Many of them were members of the Hong Kong elite.

The third wave of emigration described by Wong began in the 1980s. According to the 1984 Sino-British Agreement on the future of Hong Kong, the colony would become a special administrative region under the rule of

China. Many of the residents who were worried about their future began to leave Hong Kong. Among them, a large number found homes in Canada. Wong described this latest group of emigrants as "predominantly 'yuppies'— young, educated, middle class professionals" (Wong, 1992, p. 4).

RESEARCH DESIGN

The central guiding question for this research was: How did a community-initiated voluntary organization such as SUCCESS respond to the changing needs of an ethnic community in a multicultural society? Two major qualitative research methods were used to conduct this study: document analysis and personal interviewing. The selection of research methods derived from the nature of this research as an interpretive study and its attempts to understand people's lived experience with the organization. The document analysis included SUCCESS annual reports, newsletters, the minutes of its annual general meetings, important speeches, and program brochures. Twenty interviews were conducted with the executive, board members, and program directors. Time and space did not permit interviews with clientele, so their views of this organization are not represented here. In addition to the two major methods, site visiting and participant observation as a volunteer were used as complementary methods to help me contextualize what was read and heard about the organization. Multiple data sources and methods indicated that this study adopted a triangulation approach which ensured the credibility of the research. For the analysis of the research, a four-stage process was developed: (1) identifying main points, (2) searching for salient themes and recurring patterns, (3) grouping common themes and patterns into related categories, and (4) comparing all major categories with reference to the major theories in the field to form new perspectives. The four-stage process assured that there was frequent interplay between the data and theory.

HISTORICAL DEVELOPMENT

Among the Chinese immigrants who arrived in the 1960s, many did not speak good English. In particular, among the group who came under the family reunion category, many arrived in Vancouver with little or no English at all. Owing to their language difficulties and cultural barriers, many had problems accessing mainstream social service agencies for assistance. In 1973, SUCCESS was founded out of this context in response to the failure of government agencies and mainstream organizations to provide accessible social services for newly arrived Chinese immigrants from Hong Kong.

To facilitate an understanding of the historical development of SUCCESS between 1973 and 1998, its twenty-five-year history has been divided into three stages. This division was made on the basis of a general review of the history of SUCCESS, its programs and services, and its organizational development. Stage One, from 1973 to 1979, is the founding and establishing stage. Stage Two, from 1979 to 1989, is the developing and maturing stage. Stage Three, from 1989 to 1998, deals with its expansion and transformation.

During Stage One, following its establishment, the society successfully sponsored its first project, the Chinese Connection Project. SUCCESS provided direct and referral services to meet the needs of individual immigrants. Meanwhile, they worked with mainstream organizations to help them provide better services to non-English-speaking Chinese clients. In addition, SUCCESS also participated in advocacy activities, such as forming a special task force to pursue discussions on the publication of the Green Paper, which contained proposed new immigration policies in the Citizenship Act. Volunteer development also began during this stage. Voluntarism, mutual help, and self-help were manifested through sponsoring refugees from Vietnam in collaboration with other Chinese ethnic organizations. All their programs and services were very popular.

Despite high popularity of the society, SUCCESS encountered financial difficulty when the Chinese Connection Project came to an end in 1977. However, the society did not disappoint its clients and decided to continue with its services. Board members, staff, and volunteers all worked together to overcome the difficulties and rebuild the society. The rebuilding process ended by winning recognition from mainstream organizations in joining the United Way. This also marked the end of the founding and establishing stage and the beginning of the developing and maturing stage.

Demographic changes among Chinese immigrants in Vancouver in the 1980s contributed to the extension of SUCCESS programs and services to Vancouver South and Richmond during Stage Two. The big increase of Chinese immigrants from Hong Kong was reflected both in the volume of its services and budget.

Significant developments during this stage include: (1 the first Walk With the Dragon Walkathon event in 1985, (2) joining the United Way of Lower Mainland in the same year, (3) approval in principle of the proposal to build a permanent SUCCESS Social Services Complex and Extended Care Facility for seniors, (4) advocating for social justice and participating in the debate over W5 Campus Give Away and the Dim Sum Diary incidents, and (5) strengthening its public relations, fundraising, membership, and volunteer development. As a result of its dedicated hard work and compassion, it won a number of awards and recognition from the Chinese community and community at large. Although its influence on mainstream society was not obvious at this time, it had become a well-established organization by the end of Stage Two.

Stage Three was characterized by expansion and transformation. During this stage, there was an increasing number of immigrants from Hong Kong,

Taiwan, and Mainland China. Among the most recent group, many were business and independent immigrants. Their needs for services were different from their early counterparts. To respond to the new demographic changes, SUCCESS expanded its programs and services to business and employment training, as well as set up special centers to accommodate the needs of Mandarin-speaking immigrants. Furthermore, the society extended its program and services to other ethnic groups.

Following the opening of its first two branch offices, Fraser and Richmond Offices, during Stage Two, SUCCESS set up another six branch offices in Stage Three in order to meet the changing needs. The completion of the New Social Service Centre, home to its head office, was interpreted by many as a sign of permanence and stability, a symbol of pride and a sense of belonging. By the end of Stage Three, SUCCESS had developed into a holistic, multiservice agency providing a comprehensive array of programs and services based on community needs.

PROGRAMS AND SERVICES

By the time it celebrated its twenty-fifth anniversary, SUCCESS's programs and services had expanded into six areas: Community Airport Newcomers Network (CANN), Language Training and Settlement Services, Family and Youth Counselling, Small Business Development and Training, Employment Training and Services, and Group and Community Services.

The Community Airport Newcomers Network (CANN) was established in 1992 to help newly arrived immigrants and refugees with their presettlement and integration through the provision of welcome reception, resource orientation, and referral services. It was fully funded by Citizenship and Immigration Canada. Many immigrants who received their services found that it was useful to have people who spoke their own languages greet them and help them with the landing procedures and obtain necessary settlement information upon arrival.

Language Training and Settlement Services have always been the core of SUCCESS programs and services. The division provided direct information and referral services, workshops, new immigrant orientation, language training, citizenship classes, and Mandarin services. It also organized special support groups to help recent independent immigrants. These programs and services aim to bridge the gap between immigrants and mainstream society, help new immigrants overcome language and cultural barriers, and facilitate adjustment and integration.

Family and Youth Counselling was founded in the early 1980s as a family program and later expanded to include counselling services. Beginning in the 1990s, SUCCESS began to offer these services in its branch offices. Family counselling was the core program of this division. In the last few years,

SUCCESS organized workshops on emotional intelligence (EQ), a forum on child issues, and thirteen-episode TV programs on family life education. Its programs and services served two major purposes: help immigrants with family and relational issues, and advocate on immigrant family services. All of its staff members in the program were bilingual in English and Cantonese or Mandarin Chinese because of the significance of providing counseling in the clients' native languages.

Small Business Development and Training was formally launched in 1995 in response to the needs of proliferating business immigrants. Their programs included the Youth Entrepreneurial Development Program, business information and referral services, and business ventures with corporations. The objective of these programs was to help participants become self-sufficient through setting up their own businesses during the training. The long-term benefits of these programs were to help immigrants with their economic integration. Expanding its programs and services to small business training was regarded as an extension of SUCCESS's original mandate, not a contradiction. This division basically served three different groups of clients: ordinary citizens from the local community, employment insurance recipients, and newly arrived immigrants.

SUCCESS Employment Training and Services was originally set up to assist immigrants to find jobs and settle in Canada, including helping immigrants upgrade their English, learn job searching skills, and prepare for resumes and job interviews. In more recent years, Employment Training Programs have shifted, becoming open to everyone without targeting any particular ethnic group. From its past experience, SUCCESS Employment Training and Services has developed its own approach. The holistic approach was a collaborative endeavor with other sections of SUCCESS services, such as language training and counseling. It also involved people from outside SUCCESS, such as business partners and government agencies. This approach gained recognition across Canada by people in the field.

The Division of Group and Community Services looked after a wide range of programs, including seniors' programs, women's programs, civic education, and community development. This division also liaised with the media and Chinese community organizations, and promoted volunteer and membership programs. Over the past years, SUCCESS has built partnerships with 150 mainstream organizations, such as community centers, hospitals, health boards, police, school boards, and the media. Group and Community Services has made its contribution in the areas of advocacy and public education.

MAJOR CHANGES IN SUCCESS

SUCCESS experienced great changes between 1973 and 1998. These changes were manifested in the growth of the organization, the expansion of programs and services, and changes in its mandate. First, the fiscal growth of SUCCESS during its first twenty-five years was most evident. When it was founded in 1973, the organization employed only four full-time professional social workers. By 1998, it had a professional team exceeding two hundred. At its initial stage, it was funded with less than one hundred thousand dollars a year; when it celebrated its twenty-fifth anniversary, its annual budget had reached eight million dollars. The number of clients receiving its programs and services skyrocketed from its initial two thousand client contacts a year to more than two hundred thousand by 1998. Physically, the organization has grown from the very beginning in a three hundred square foot office in Chinatown to an organization with multiple satellite offices in the Greater Vancouver area, with headquarters in a 26,000 square foot Social Service Building of its own.

Other important changes were seen in its programs and services. In the 1970s, its lack of resources limited it to providing basic settlement services such as language interpretation and information services. By the 1990s, it was providing a whole range of programs, including airport reception, settlement services, language training, counseling services, small business development and training, employment training and services, and group and community services. It was no longer just a single-focus organization providing only settlement services; it had become a well-established multiservice community organization. Some of these programs have remained constant throughout its twenty-five years of existence because needs have remained more or less unchanged. For example, ESL programs within the Language Training and Settlement Services area have remained important for all non-English-speaking immigrants, to help them acquire the language skills necessary for full participation in society. Programs in the Business Development and Employment Training areas are responding to increases in the number of business and professional immigrants. Its holistic approach helps immigrants become competent socially, culturally, linguistically, and economically.

Further changes which were not as noticeable were those in its mandate. SUCCESS was established in 1973 as a demonstration project, which was supposed to end in three years. Its mandate was mainly to help non-English-speaking Chinese immigrants by providing basic immigrant settlement services, with the assistance of bilingual social workers who could speak both English and Chinese. Its situation in 1998 demonstrated that SUCCESS had become a multicultural and multiethnic organization. Its clientele comprised immigrants from non-Chinese ethnic backgrounds, including those from mainstream society. To reflect the demographic changes among its clients, its professional team has also become ethno-culturally inclusive. Their programs and services were made available in many languages other than Cantonese and English.

The study has also demonstrated that the changes that took place in SUCCESS incorporated many aspects of the organization. SUCCESS has grown exponentially and become strong enough to be noticeable not just in the Chinese community but also in the mainstream society. It played multiple roles with a three-pronged focus: providing professional services and adult education programs, advocating on behalf of immigrants, and facilitating citizenship education and community development.

Likewise, the current study reveals that many social forces have contributed to the evolution of SUCCESS. First, the profile of immigrants changed owing to changes in Canadian immigration policies, such as the adoption of the "point system," the introduction of the business immigrant category, and the opening of the immigration division in the Canadian Embassy in Beijing. One consequence of the most recent policy change was the increase of professional and business immigrants, especially those from Taiwan and China. Second, the needs of newly arrived immigrants differed from their early counterparts and SUCCESS responded to meet these changing needs. Another force that influenced the changes in SUCCESS was government funding. Through funding requirements, the government encouraged SUCCESS to extend its programs and services to other ethnic communities. Other elements that contributed to the changes in SUCCESS included an internal democratic electoral system, professionalism, a politically neutral stand, and timing. Finally, and most important, SUCCESS had a dedicated team, including early founders, board members, volunteers, and staff members. It was their shared compassion, empathy, dedication, and common experience that were formative influences in propelling SUCCESS to its current stage.

The Contributions of SUCCESS

During its first twenty-five years of existence, SUCCESS has contributed tremendously to the ethnic Chinese community and Canadian society at large. Its contributions have touched both practical and theoretical fields of immigration, citizenship education, and integration. Its social impact has been extensive.

First, this study challenges the argument that minority group rights restrict individual rights and freedoms. This investigation has clearly demonstrated that minority group rights, in contrast, supplement and further enhance individual rights and freedoms. It is evident that an area that SUCCESS has had a great impact on was the Chinese community itself. Chinese immigrants benefited immensely from its programs and services. By providing culturally and linguistically appropriate services, SUCCESS has increased the access of Chinese immigrants to settlement and other social services, which they were entitled to but deprived of, owing to the failure of the state and mainstream social service agencies. SUCCESS acted as a mediator between the individual immigrants and the state. It provided a means to investigate the dynamic between individual immigrants' agency and the structural or institutional constraints they face in exercising that agency. As a transitional institution, it has helped immigrants ease the process of settlement, adaptation, and integration. To many immigrants, SUCCESS was a stepping stone for them to integrate into mainstream society. Meanwhile, it is also an important entrance for government agencies and mainstream organizations to approach a hard-to-reach ethnic community. Furthermore, it helped create a safety network, a home, and a community to which Chinese immigrants felt they belonged. The experience of SUCCESS has shown that ethno-racial organizations can be an effective alternative to mainstream organizations, because they are more closely connected with and responsive to ethnic community needs.

Second, the study challenges the view of universal citizenship. It confirms the argument that granting equal individual rights alone is not sufficient to achieve inclusive citizenship. To build a society to which all citizens feel they belong, universal citizenship has to be complemented by differential citizenship. The special programs and services that SUCCESS provided for immigrants were not unjust privileges; they were the first step in the process for immigrants to achieve fairness, justice, and equality. The whole process of the historical development of SUCCESS displayed the collective efforts of the Vancouver Chinese community in responding to unjust and unfair treatment of an ethnic group. Allocating the necessary resources and support to Chinese immigrants helped correct the disadvantages that Chinese immigrants suffered within difference-blind institutions. It also enhanced democratic and independent citizenship because failure to recognize and accommodate their special needs was more likely to alienate further the Chinese from identifying with the larger society and becoming full members of the community. Clearly, the study provides an alternative model to interpret citizenship and democracy.

Furthermore, it built a citizenship learning community. This study demonstrates that SUCCESS adopted a community-based participatory approach in promoting new citizenship learning. It built an infrastructure that incorporates activities that require engagement and collaboration among a number of stakeholders. Besides acquiring knowledge and skills, more importantly it has helped immigrants foster a sense of critical consciousness while educating them about their rights and responsibilities. In this learning community, learning is fundamentally sociocultural and sociopolitical. It involves constructing complex social relationships between the immigrant community and society at large.

In addition, the study reveals that the role of SUCCESS in citizenship education is two-sided. Through its community development events and activities, SUCCESS has contributed to sensitizing mainstream organizations about their service approaches and changing public attitudes toward immigrants. It has helped enhance mutual understanding between immigrants and mainstream society, hence shortened the social distance between the two groups. That SUCCESS has played a significant bridging role between the two communities is clearly one of its most important contributions.

REFERENCES

Anderson, K. J. (1995). *Vancouver's Chinatown: Racial discourse in Canada, 1875–1980*. Montreal: McGill-Queen's University Press.

Bissoondath, N. (1994). *Selling illusions: The cult of Multiculturalism in Canada*. Toronto: Penguin.

Gwyn, R. (1995). *Nationalism without walls: The unbearable lightness of being Canadian*. Toronto: McClelland & Stewart.

Bloemraad, I. (2000). Citizenship and immigration: A current review. *Journal of International Migration and Integration, 1(1)*, 9–37.

Knowles, V. (1997). *Strangers at our gates: Canadian immigration and immigration policy, 1540–1997*. Toronto: Dundurn Press.

Kymlicka, W. (1995). *Multicultural citizenship: A liberal theory of minority rights*. Oxford: Clarendon Press.

Kymlicka, W. (1998). *Finding our way: Rethinking ethnocultural relations in Canada*. Toronto: Oxford University Press.

Kymlicka, W., & Norman, W. (2000). *Citizenship in diverse societies*. New York: Oxford University Press.

Levy, J. T. (1997). Classifying cultural rights. In I. Shapiro & W. Kymlicka (Eds.), *Ethnicity and group rights* (pp. 22–66). New York & London: New York University Press.

Li, P. S. (1998). *The Chinese in Canada*. Don Mills: Oxford University Press.

Matas, D. (1996). Racism in Canadian immigration policy. In C. E. James (Ed.), *Perspectives on racism and the human services sector: A case for change* (pp. 93–102). Toronto: University of Toronto Press.

Rawls, J. (1971). *A theory of justice*. London: Oxford University Press.

Statistics Canada (2003). *2001 census: Analysis series*. Ottawa: Statistics Canada.

Tamir, Y. (1995). Two concepts of multiculturalism. In Y. Tamir (Ed.), *Democratic education in a multicultural state* (pp. 3–14). Oxford: Blackwell.

Tan, J., & Roy, P. E. (1985). *The Chinese in Canada*. Ottawa: Canadian Historical Association.

Taylor, C. (1993). Shared and divergent values. In G. Laforest (Ed.), *Reconciling the solitudes: Essays on Canadian federalism and nationalism* (pp. 155–186). Montreal & Kingston: McGill-Queens' University Press.

Taylor, C. (1994a). The politics of recognition. In A. Gutmann (Ed.), *Multiculturalism: Examining the politics of recognition* (pp. 25–73). Princeton: Princeton University Press.

Taylor, C. (1994b). Reply and re-articulation. In J. Tully (Ed.), *Philosophy in an age of pluralism: The philosophy of Charles Taylor in question* (pp. 213–257). Cambridge: Cambridge University Press.

Walzer, M. (1982). Pluralism in political perspective. In M. Walzer (Ed.), *The politics of ethnicity* (pp. 1–28). Cambridge: Harvard University Press.

Walzer, M. (1995). Education, democratic citizenship, and multiculturalism. In Y. Tamir (Ed.), *Democratic education in a multicultural state* (pp. 23–31). Oxford: Blackwell.

Whitaker, R. (1991). *Canadian immigration policy since confederation.* Ottawa: Canadian Historical Association.

Wong, S. L. (1992). *Emigration and stability in Hong Kong.* Hong Kong: the University of Hong Kong.

Young, I. (1995). Polity and group difference: A critique of the ideal of universal citizenship. In R. Beiner (Ed.), *Theorizing citizenship* (pp. 175–207). Albany: State University of New York Press.

TWELVE

Traditional Peoples and Citizenship in the New Imperial Order

Makere Stewart-Harawira

INTRODUCTION

MY OBJECTIVE IN THIS CHAPTER is to examine some of the political and institutional constructions of the notions of citizenship in the context of contemporary formations of imperialism, and to do so largely from an indigenous perspective. Drawing on the work of Michel Foucault, I begin the chapter with a review of historical constructions of citizenship and the category of "populations" as peoples to be governed. This is followed by a brief analysis of the historical relationship between international human rights law and citizenship as it pertains to indigenous peoples. A discussion of some key aspects of the recent shifts in the nature of the state and implications of those shifts provides the context for developing my main argument, the need for a new model of citizenship; one which is underpinned by a new political ontology for global order and in which Indigenous ontologies are critically important.

CONSTRUCTING "CITIZENSHIP"

Like most political concepts, the concept of global citizenship today is contested in terms of its ascribed meanings, importance, and usage.[1] James Tully identifies two overlapping yet distinctive meanings in the literature on global citizenship, each framed slightly differently within policy and curriculum documents. One version of citizenship, most commonly associated with constitutionalism and the rule of law, interprets citizenship in terms of opportunities associated with status and consequential rights and privileges. The other is defined in relation to democracy and is framed in terms of the right and obligation to engage in or "exercise."

Historically speaking, the notion of global citizenship, or of being a "world citizen," has perhaps much in common with the idea of the ancient Stoics, many of whom articulated a concept of world citizenship, or *cosmopolites*—citizen of the universe (Dower, 1998, p. 71). This perspective is frequently articulated by participants in global social movements such as the antiglobalization movement and ecological movements. Most commonly, however, and certainly in the legal sense, notions of citizenship are associated with the relationship between the individual and the nation-state.

Foucault's analysis of the development of governmentality provides a useful background to the trajectory of the developing relationship between the state and society and the way in which "the economy" as the essence of government became the defining feature of state-society relationships and ultimately, citizenship (Foucault, 1991, pp. 87–104). One of the distinctive features of the period of the sixteenth century was what Foucault describes as "the introduction of economy into political practice." A core feature of this "art of government" as applied to states was the establishment of forms of "surveillance and control." Foucault explained this using the analogy of the priority given by the father as the head of the household to the family economy. In the same sense, the introduction of the economy into government as applied to states, saw "the economy" become the very essence of government. Linked to this principle, he suggests, is that of "the right disposition of things."

By the eighteenth century, demographic expansion, the increasing abundance of money and the expansion of agricultural production led to the development of what was seen as the problem of populations and governance. This saw a shift in the focus of governance to the interrelationships between "population, territory and wealth," and the requirement of intervention (Ibid., p. 101). This moment, says Foucault, saw the birth of political economy. It also saw the birth of new technologies of power that relied on discursive and disciplinary strategies for their effectiveness and were indispensable in controling populations. Education and confinement were key sites for the embedding of these strategies.

In the eighteenth century, the global economy was constructed around Enlightenment notions of luxury, consumption, and commercial society (Rosow, 1994). The Scottish Enlightenment philosopher David Hume regarded the expansion of international trade for the purpose of satisfying the need for consumption as integral to the creation of civil order (Ibid.). This then legitimated the de-territorialization and re-territorialization of indigenous peoples' territories as a specific requirement of the spread of capitalism. The principle of individual ownership based on labor, which was given such impetus in Locke's *Second Treatise on Government*, provided the legitimation for the dispossession of indigenous peoples from their own territories and the allocation of citizenship rights on the basis of land ownership. During the seventeenth and eighteenth centuries, dissimilarity between indigenous and nonindigenous peoples became the dominant ideology by which moral exclusion from "the family of nations" was operationalized. As the polygeneticist ideologies of Voltaire and others gave way to doctrines of social evolutionism, the division between sedentary and hunter-gatherer peoples as the criteria for distinguishing civilized from noncivilized or savage societies became the justifying principle for imperialism and for the exclusion of particular groups from the world of nations.

This division enabled the enactment of genocidal practices upon indigenous peoples within colonial nation-states to continue without fear of punitive legal measures. It also became the legitimizing principle for statements such as that by Thomas Paine, who in 1776 said of America that "happy as she pleases she hath a blank sheet to write on" (cited in Chomsky, 1997, p. 239), and for the declaration of Australia as *terra nullius*, or unoccupied land, by the Royal Navy's First Fleet when under Captain James Cook it claimed to have acquired the continent for the British Crown by right of discovery. In this manner legal norms and discourses redefined relationships between indigenous peoples and states. In colonized territories, these norms concretized the reconstruction of indigenous peoples' status from sovereign nations to dependent populations within international law, where they were recognized at all.

SUBJUGATION THROUGH
LEGISLATION AND EDUCATION

In 1900, the Australian Constitution Act created the Commonwealth of Australia. Aboriginal peoples were deliberately excluded from that jurisdiction. In 1902, the state of Queensland forbade the entering of Aboriginal people onto the electoral rolls. Similar provisions were legislated throughout all Australian states. In 1944, Western Australia established elaborate procedures by which for Aboriginal peoples could be deemed to be no longer Aboriginal and thus to qualify as citizens. This echoed legislation passed in New Zealand in 1912 that allowed certain Maori (males), subject to certain qualifying requirements such as land ownership, to apply for citizenship and by doing thus, to no longer be deemed Maori. Aboriginal peoples throughout Australia were not granted citizenship rights until the period of 1962 to 1965.

Similar policies were enacted in North America. The 1776 Declaration of Independence saw obligations to First Nations under the Royal Proclamation of 1763 received into U.S. law (the proclamation set aside vast tracts of land in British North America which were recognized as belonging to Indian tribes and nations (Tully, Ibid.). The 1867 British North America Act, which created a confederation of colonies, gave the federal government jurisdiction over First Nations peoples and their lands. The Indian Act passed in 1976 under the Gradual Civilization Act of 1957 had as its primary objective the ultimate assimilation of First Nations peoples as wards of the state. In the fifty years between 1871 and 1921, "land surrender treaties" signed with the First Nations of Western Canada ensured the undermining of any substantive ability to be self-sufficient and ensured dependence upon the federal government. It was not until 1973 with the *Calder vs. the Attorney General of BC* decision regarding the Nisga'a Nation that any substantive recognition was given to Aboriginal title which could not be extinguished by law or by a treaty. In Aotearoa/New Zealand, violent land wars having failed to exterminate Maori or to sufficiently subdue them, assimilatory policies in which colonial education for Maori was central, continued to prevail until the mid-1980s.

Across the colonized world, colonial provision for native education was a key tool for the subjugation of traditional indigenous ways of knowing and being and for the application of new "biotechnologies" that aimed at constructing and subjugating sovereign indigenous peoples as docile populations to be governed. Through these processes, indigenous cosmologies and ways of knowing were marginalized if not eradicated, and the essential qualities and characteristics of indigenous community life such as extended family structures, shared ownership of resources and collective methods of decision making were targeted for extinction.

Church residential schools such as those provided for Native education in Canada and the denominational boarding schools for Maori in Aotearoa/New Zealand were sites within which the exercise of "technologies of power" aimed at transforming autonomous, independent indigenous communities into resources for the production of capital. The enclosing of indigenous children away from the community not only sought the production of healthy, docile, and productive populations and frequently, cheap labor. One of its main objectives was the inculcation of colonial ideologies of individualism and the subjugation of what in New Zealand was called, "the beastly communism of the pa" (a fortified Maori village).

THE COLONIZATION OF INDIGENOUS KNOWLEDGE

The extinguishing of aboriginal land rights, the denial of the validity of treaties signed between sovereign nations, the discursive construction of sovereign indigenous nations as "populations" within states constructed over indigenous peoples' traditional lands, and the disestablishment of indigenous frameworks for the study of specialist and metaphysical knowledge were accompanied by the disciplining of minds and bodies. The recruitment, training, education, and employment of indigenous peoples and minorities viewed as fundamental to achieving the goal of their construction as docile and productive providers of labor was accompanied by the targeting of the fundamental elements of indigenous cultural values and forms of knowledge as a means for dismantling indigenous political and social structures. In conjunction with legislation that outlawed indigenous traditional ceremonies and structures, education was the primary tool for the submerging of indigenous peoples' highly developed "inner" ways of knowing under a layer of colonizing ideologies (cf. Wilmer, 1983; Thiong'o, 1986).

I want to pause here to look at what is meant by "indigenous ways of knowing." To begin with, it is important to bear in mind that indigenous peoples' ontologies and cosmologies are far from being homogeneous. Nonetheless, it is possible, while avoiding the pitfalls of essentialism, to define certain key principles that are held broadly in common. For instance, Carl Urion of the Dearborn River Cree refers to traditional knowledge as "living knowledge" (Urion, 1999). Rather than being limited to a "codified canon," Urion states, traditional or indigenous knowledge is an expression of life itself, of how to live, and of the connection between all living things (Ibid). Vine Deloria Jr. (1999) of the Lakota Nation identifies indigenous conceptions of knowledge as intrinsically connected to the lives and experiences of human beings, individuals, and communities. Deloria draws a comparison between forms of Western scientific knowledge, which draws conclusions by excluding some forms of data and including others, and traditional and indigenous systems of knowledge in which all data and all experience is relevant to all things.

A fundamental commonality within all indigenous ontologies is the notion of an interrelationship between all forms of existence. This key principle of interconnectedness governs indigenous understandings of and relationships to the physical world and to the world of metaphysics. Another critical principle is the inseparable nature of the relationship between the world of matter and the world of spirit, often articulated through indigenous narratives that are frequently interpreted by the Western world as myths. This integral relationship is demonstrated in the words of Iroquois leader Oren Lyons (1984) when he declares, "The primary law of Indian government is the spiritual law. Spirituality is the highest form of politics, and our spirituality is directly involved in government."

Related to this is the understanding that every individual element of the natural world, each individual rock and stone, each individual animal and plant, every body of land and of water, has its own unique life force. This life force, which Maori refer to as *mauri*, is an essential element of all forms of wellness. There are many implications, interpretations, and meanings that connect to the concept of *mauri*. One is the concept of each living thing being guarded by its own supernatural being, explained by Maori scholar Mason Durie as an expression of the need to acknowledge and protect the life force present in all aspects of the natural world. As an expression of interrelationships, Durie (20001, p. 88) states, *mauri* or life force "spirals outwards seeking to establish communication with higher levels of organization and to find meaning by sharing a sense of common origin." This concept underpins the principle of guardianship, which defines the relationship of indigenous peoples to the natural world. Often mistaken as an articulation of ownership, this principle recognizes the obligation of indigenous peoples to utilize and care for their traditional environment in sustainable ways and that the land and waters can never be permanently owned in the Western sense.

The twin principles of balance and reciprocity connect to the interconnectedness of existence and preexistence. Balance and reciprocity are expressed in the relationship between the dimensions and layers of existence comprising being and nonbeing, in the deep recognition of the dual nature of every action, of action and counteraction, of male and female, light and dark. Like the principle of balance, reciprocity recognizes that nothing occurs without a corresponding action. Reciprocity means deeply acknowledging the gifts of the other and acting on this recognition in ways that deeply honor the other. At its deepest and most fundamental level, reciprocity requires first acknowledging and elevating the *mana*, that is, the status, the "being" of the other. To do otherwise, that is, to attempt to elevate oneself above the other, is in fact, to demean and reduce one's own *mana*, and thus oneself.

These, then, were the kinds of understandings that the education systems instigated by missionaries in the first instance, and colonial state apparatuses in the second instance, sought to eradicate, along with languages, customs, and social structures of collectivity. Importantly, indigenous peoples were far from passive victims in this process but developed multiple strategies for resistance. Somewhat ironically, schooling itself not infrequently became an important site of such resistance, as revisionist historians such as Maxine Stephenson (1993) and Judith Simon (1990) have described. In New Zealand, for instance, despite being a primary target for policies that aimed to eradicate extended family structures, schooling nonetheless became an important avenue for the strengthening and maintenance of both extended family structures and Maori language use.

Most notably, from the 1970s onward, the assertion of traditional indigenous values and pedagogies which was central to indigenous peoples' strategies of resistance became a main plank in the development of education strategies and policies by indigenous peoples for indigenous peoples. The legitimacy of indigenous ontologies and epistemologies was the foundation of demands for the recognition of indigenous peoples' rights within international law and contributed in large measure to ideological changes within international human rights law during the latter part of the twentieth century.

HUMAN RIGHTS IN INTERNATIONAL LAW

By the mid-twentieth century, the geographical landscape of the world had been changed many times and the Westphalian state was part of a new international order of sovereign states, in which international relations were mediated by the balance of power. It was in this context and against the background of two horrific world wars that the United Nations and the human rights framework were born. In any discussion of universal human rights and the enshrining of human rights within international law, there are some critical points that should be kept in mind if we are to understand these events in proper perspective. One of these is the history of the development of these twin covenants. The second point is that human rights include cultural rights and that these rights are embedded in both covenants.

In the years following World War II, the United Nations Universal Declaration of Human Rights together with its twin covenants became broadly regarded in the Western world as the foundation stone of liberal democracy. Yet the elaboration of the UN Declaration of Human Rights, a nonenforceable document, within documents that are legally enforceable in international law was hotly contested by states throughout the twenty years of its development. In fact the inclusion of human rights in the Charter of the United Nations was due only to "the effort of a few deeply committed delegates and the representatives of some 42 private organizations" (Roberts & Kingsbury, 1993).

The trajectory of the development of these human rights instruments was fraught with contestation over tensions between the principle of state sovereignty and the notion of individual and collective human rights. There was a span of twenty years between the original drafting by the UN's Economic and Social Council (ECOSOC) of an International Bill of Rights and the 1966 voting in the UN General Assembly on the twin human rights covenants, the principles of which were originally formulated within the Declaration of Human Rights in 1948. It was a further ten years before the required thirty-five votes were received for these covenants to become international law. These tensions over the original drafting of the United Nations Declaration of Human Rights led to some of its principles being removed to create what were to become twin human rights covenants, the International Covenant on Economic, Social and Cultural Rights (ICESCR) and the International Covenant on Civil and Political Rights (ICCPR) and its Optional Protocol.

The legally binding obligations on signatory states that are contained in the covenants include certain minimum provisions for all "peoples." The first of these rights is that of self-determination by which peoples may "freely determine their own political status and freely pursue their economic, social and cultural development and destiny." This includes the right of peoples to dispose of their own natural resources and wealth, and not to be deprived of their means of existence. The covenants also share a prohibition against discrimination on the grounds of race, color, sex, language, religion, political or other opinion, national or social origin, property, birth or other status. One of the significant aspects of this is that these are rights that accrue to all peoples (emphasis mine). The other significant aspect is that who counts as "peoples" to whom these and other rights accrue, is one of the most hotly contested debates within international law, particularly between indigenous and tribal peoples and states. All people, as far as state-centric international law is concerned, are not "peoples" with the international human rights that such a designation entails. Indigenous peoples, tribal peoples, are not, we are told, peoples, in the international law sense of the world, but populations. And populations, like territories, are objects of governance.

Since their entry into force in 1976, the covenants have provided indigenous peoples with a forum for the pursuit of justice within the international arena. To date, these pursuits have been largely unsuccessful. Indigenous peoples across the globe define their rights in terms of fundamental collective rights, yet there is no provision in the covenants for the acknowledgment and protection of collective rights within international law. Further, there is considerable resistance to the notion that collective rights should be provided for in international law. Kymlicka (1989) points out that some measures that define the special status of indigenous peoples, such as in Canada, do not involve collectively exercised rights but in fact modify or differentially distribute individual rights. He notes that there seems to be enormous difficulty in accommodating the idea of collective rights within the moral ontology of liberalism (Ibid., p. 139). The difficulty for indigenous peoples is that the human rights covenants and their protocols are one of the only possible avenues within the United Nations system available to indigenous peoples as a means of seeking redress, yet they function in ways that mitigate against the fundamental collective rights of indigenous peoples. The two key reasons for this are, firstly, the contested nature of state sovereignty and its interpretation within international law and secondly, the relatively recent shift from collective rights to the recognition of individual rights, a shift that has in the main occurred only since World War II.

Roberts and Kingsbury (op. cit.) point out in their historical analysis of the development of the United Nations Declaration on Human Rights and its covenants that the construction of indigenous peoples as "minorities" or "populations" within sovereign states enables injustices perpetuated upon indigenous peoples in colonized territories to be invisibilized within a general human rights discourse and functions to mask many of the injustices perpetuated on groups and individuals. The Vienna Declaration issued from the 1993 UN Conference on Human Rights and signed by 171 countries reemphasized the notion of human rights as a universal concept. Nevertheless, ideological power relations continue to dominate the way in which tensions between the notions of state sovereignty and human rights are played out.

In this respect, Yongjin Zhang's (1997) discussion of human rights in the post–Cold War period highlights the increasing prominence accorded to human rights in the context of world peace and international security. Military interventions authorized by the United Nations such as in the cases of Somalia (1991, 1992), Iraq (consistently since 1998), and Kosovo, are legitimated on the basis of their importance in preventing human rights abuses and disruption of the international order. Zhang points out that the challenges to state sovereignty represented by such interventions demonstrate the increasingly strategic role of human rights in international relations and a widening international consensus concerning the need for protection of and respect for human rights. Nevertheless, he notes, although the entrenchment of human rights within international law has to a limited extent compromised state sovereignty, it has not yet resulted in human rights being accorded a higher priority than the assertion of state sovereignty.

The ongoing problematic between human rights, state sovereignty, and international law was highlighted in the Australian government's refusal, in 1999, to allow a UN Human Rights Commission investigation onto Australian soil to investigate its inhumane treatment of Aboriginal peoples including its policy of mandatory imprisonment for petty crimes, for reasons of "foreign policy and democracy" (Brace, 2000). The disjuncture between human rights rhetoric and practice by states was again underscored in respect of Australia's leadership in the human rights interventions in East Timor, interventions that were initiated in response to enormous public pressure.

The political economy underpinning protestations of state sovereignty and complicity in human rights abuses was highlighted in the contradiction between this well-publicized intervention and twenty-five years of silent complicity in human rights abuses in East Timor, regarding which Australia's contractual arrangements with Indonesia and Canada to exploit what was believed to be a large reservoir of oil in the Timor Gap resulted in a lengthy twenty-five-year period of social amnesia. In this light, evidence released that Australia was fully informed by Indonesia three days before the attack on the Timorese town in Bilbo in October 1975 in which five Australian journalists were killed (Hopkins, 2000) problematizes the integrity of states' foreign policy and the political economy underpinning compliance with international human rights norms by industrialized nation states. The geopolitical rationale was provided by the then U.S. Ambassador to Indonesia when he stated that American support of Indonesia's invasion of East Timor, an act that resulted in the deaths of more than two hundred thousand indigenous Timorese people, was viewed as essential in order to ensure that "this vast stretch of territory representing Indonesia not fall into anti-American hands" (Milibank, 2000, 2002; also Robie, 1989; Chomsky, 1999, 2000). U.S. President Gerald

Ford and U.S. Secretary of State Henry Kissinger's tacit consent to the 1975 invasion of East Timor by Indonesia,[2] demonstrates the prioritizing of political expediency over human rights including citizenship rights.

INDIGENOUS PEOPLES AS
CITIZENS OF THE NEOLIBERAL STATE

In addition to seeking the renewal and revitalization of their languages, cultures, and identities, indigenous peoples had been actively engaged in seeking acknowledgment of some form of the same right to self-determination that, according to the Declaration of Human Rights and its covenants, is granted to all peoples everywhere. These activities and strategies of indigenous peoples have had a marked impact globally and locally. Locally, the biggest impact has been in states' relationships with indigenous peoples and in the reconfiguring of indigenous self-determination within an economic paradigm.

By the end of 1989 the bipolarism of the cold war had ended and the neoliberal state had emerged, having been birthed firstly in Aotearoa/New Zealand under the influence of neoliberal policies initiated by the then minister of finance Roger Kerr. The reconfiguring of the state under the influence of neoliberal economics and the rule of the market saw significant changes in the way states conducted their affairs. In Aotearoa/New Zealand, state initiatives to reincorporate Maori into what was rapidly becoming a neoliberal state was driven by the state's recognition that without the development of new and different relationships with Maori, investment confidence would be undermined. Familiar colonial tactics of divide and rule under the guise of treaty settlements saw smaller tribes disenfranchised as larger tribes headed by state-appointed elites negotiated away their traditional lands, resources, and customary rights in a process that commodified genealogies as well as natural resources. In some cases, traditional lands and sacred places became the commodities of corporatized tribal bodies.

As James Tully has outlined, the treaty negotiated between representatives of the *Nisga'a* Nation of Northern British Columbia and the Supreme Court of Canada arose from the assertion during the 1970s of the right of the *Nisga'a* Nation to collectively use and occupy their traditional lands. Because this treaty case provided for the people of the *Nisga'a* Nation full incorporation of the *Nisga'a* people into Canadian society, that is to say, full citizenship status including the right to vote and the right to pay taxes, it is worthwhile briefly examining its outcome here.

The treaty between the *Nisga'a* Nation and the federal government of British Columbia was concluded in 1998 after twenty years of official negotiations and more than one hundred years of struggle for recognition and redress by the *Nisga'a* Nation, the resultant treaty provided for the full incorporation of the *Nisga'a* people into Canadian society. That is, full citizenship rights. Tully (2000) notes that this was the time in the history of North America in which an indigenous people (as represented by 61 percent of the eligible voters) voluntarily relinquished their rights and status as indigenous peoples.

In addition to surrendering more than 90 percent of their territory, the people of the *Nisga'a* Nation agreed to the transformation of their status to one of "a distinctive minority with group rights within Canada" (Ibid., p. 50). In return for a voluntary relinquishment of 93 percent of their traditional territories and the right not to pay taxes, and for a compensatory settlement sum which equated to roughly eleven dollars per person, the *Nisga'a* Nation were granted Aboriginal title in the form of an estate in fee simple with certain proprietary rights over the remaining 7 percent, some rights with respect to trap lines, wildlife, and migratory birds outside this area, and the right to pay taxes and receive citizenship entitlements to training. This saw the complete extinction of Aboriginal title over 28,751 square kilometres of *Nisga'a* traditional territories. Through this process, the federal government of British Columbia were able to accrue more than $1 billion of foreign investment that had been waiting in the wings (see also Stewart-Harawira, op. cit., pp. 196–198).

I turn now to look at some issues involving what some have termed the new global empire.

CITIZENSHIP AND THE POSTMODERN STATE—
OR THE NEW LIBERAL IMPERIALIST ORDER

One of the characteristics of Empire, Hardt and Negri suggest, is that it resides within a context—in this case, a world context—that "continually calls it into being" (2000, p. 181). In their words, the Gulf war provided the conditions in which U.S. initiative saw hegemony reorganized in preparation for a new imperial project of network power (Ibid. pp. 179–180). In the words of Secretary of Defense Rumsfield, the Gulf war provided a great strategic opportunity, "the kind of opportunity that World War Two offered—to refashion the world" (cited in Bacevich, 2002, p. 227).

Richard Cooper, previously Tony Blair's senior foreign policy advisor and now Director-General of External and Politico-Military Affairs for the Council of the European Union, also advocates the notion of empire as the solution to the crisis of the global order (Cooper, 2002; 2003). Cooper draws a parallel between empire in the ancient world and that of the new. In the ancient world, he declares, the condition of empire was "order, culture and civilization" whereas outside the empire, all was "barbarians, chaos and disorder." Similarly, he argues, the security and order of the postmodern world—he defines the EU as the best example of a postmodern state and, interestingly,

Canada also comes into this category—is threatened by what he terms the "modern" and "pre-modern" zones (2003, pp. 16–54). The threat of the modern zone which comprises the classical state lies in the disintegration of the balance of power and the supremacy of nationalism. The risk constituted by the premodern world of chaos and instability is that having lost the monopoly or legitimacy of the use of force, the premodern state provides a base for non-state actors involved in illegitimate activities.

Under these conditions, Cooper insists, the rebirth of empire is essential to the maintenance of global order and the defense of the postmodern state. Hence, he advances the notion of a "double standard" as necessary and legitimate in the defense of the new, voluntary, postmodern imperialism. Inside empire, the conditions of interdependence and openness are safeguarded by mutual surveillance and mutual interference. In the case of the "more old-fashioned kinds of states," the behavior of earlier imperial forces is appropriate. Deception and the preemptive attack are legitimate and necessary behaviors for the maintenance and defense of empire. The "Just War" is a legitimate use of force upon those who remain outside the walls.

New forms of surveillance have become one of the central critical issues in the contemporary forms of imperialism that have emerged over the last two decades. One of the embedded contradictions of globalization that has accompanied the privatization of goods and services and the liberalization of trade is that between the discourse of freedom and the tightening of individual liberties. In regard to this, Deleuze's concept of societies of control encapsulates the multilayered technologies of control that have accompanied the transformation of the Keynesian Fordist state to a transmission belt for global capital. It thus provides a useful framework within which to examine the shift in the extension of power over individuals and populations through multilayered networks of electronic technologies, legislation, and discursive shifts in the concept of democracy. According to Deleuze, the shift from "disciplinary societies" in which confinement was the main technology toward "control societies that . . . no longer operate by confining people but through continuous control and instant communication" (Deleuze, 1995, cited in Peters, 2001) is reflected in a shift in technologies of control.

SOCIETIES OF CONTROL:
SURVEILLANCE AND CITIZENSHIP

The September 2001 attack on the World Trade Center opened the door to a significant removal of civil rights including privacy rights, intellectual freedom, and citizenship rights in many countries across the globe. Officially entitled "Uniting and Strengthening America by Providing Appropriate Tools Required to Intercept and Obstruct Terrorism (USA PATRIOT ACT) Act of 2001," the U.S. Patriot Act is far-reaching in its impact. Ostensibly designed "[t]o deter and punish terrorist acts in the United States and around the world, to enhance law enforcement investigatory tools, and for other purposes," the act removed wide-ranging freedoms previously protected under the U.S. Constitution.

The unconstitutional nature of the Patriot Act is evidenced in the finding by a U.S. federal judge that parts of the act are in violation of the First and Fifth Amendments to the U.S. Constitution. In a ruling handed down in January 2004, U.S. District Judge Audrey Collins said the ban on providing "expert advice or assistance" is impermissibly vague, in violation of the First and Fifth Amendments. As written, the ruling stated, the law does not differentiate between impermissible advice on violence and encouraging the use of peaceful, nonviolent means to achieve goals. By thus placing no limitation on the type of expert advice and assistance that is prohibited and banning the provision of all expert advice and assistance regardless of its nature, the judge declared, that section of the U.S. Patriot Act is unconstitutional.[3] Nonetheless, the U.S. Patriot Act has had global reverberations.

The globalization of new forms of terrorism has seen the normalization of escalating levels of monitoring and control. In the United States this includes extending the use of "pen-registers that record numbers dialled, and trap-and-trace devices such as email" (Hitz & Weiss, 2004, p. 17) for the use of which warrants are not required because they are "not considered searches under the Fourth Amendment." Biometric technologies for the recording of fingerprint and iris patterns for border controls have become an acceptable level of monitoring not only in the United States, but also in countries such as Canada and New Zealand.[4] In the United States, the sweeping reforms in response to the terrorist attack on the World Trade Center in September 2001 prompted past inspector general of the CIA Brian J. Weiss to comment:

> The challenges ahead to civil liberties are significant. New technologies for data search and pattern recognition, combined with greater investigative freedom, have enormous potential for abuse. Even if used within the law, the capability of the government to search and correlate large amounts of data on its citizens . . . frightens most Americans (Hitz & Weiss, 2004, ibid.).

What then of human rights? In the context of these new forms of imperialism that are endeavoring to shape the world for the foreseeable future, how can we develop educational systems and processes that address these issues of human rights?

EDUCATION FOR HUMAN RIGHTS:
A NEW ONTOLOGY OF GLOBAL CITIZENSHIP

Of the multiple discourses of globalization that proliferated during the last three decades of the twentieth century, the most pervasive is the neoliberal notion of inevitability or "there is no alternative," generally interpreted as no alternative to the redrawing of the global political landscape, to the hollowing-out of the nation state and to the establishment of a neoliberalist, market-based global economy and political order. Yet there are indeed alternatives.

As Nigel Dower pointed out (See chapter 4 this volume), the transformation of the global political and economic framework has been accompanied by the emergence of an increasingly broad social movement of resistance that is global in membership and in impact. This new global movement represents a critical opportunity for intervention. The second world superpower, Hardt and Negri's joyous multitude, "a global biopolitical subject of absolute democracy" has unlimited power for bringing about change and may yet, by its refusal to countenance the horrors of an unjust unilateralism, be the downfall of globalized domination. Hardt and Negris's model of cooperation is based on the hybridity and flexibility of a multitude joined together in a joyous movement of constituent power that Passavant and Dean refer to as "self-organized democracy" (Passavant, 2004, p. 11). However, this model falls short of articulating a deep understanding of interconnectedness, such as that which lies at the heart of indigenous ontologies. Traditional indigenous ontological principles provide an ontological framework for world order that is grounded in a new eco-humanism, at the root of which is understanding of the deep interconnectedness of existence and of our shared spiritual reality.

To secure human rights for all requires an urgent re-visioning of the way in which we understand the past, present, and future, of the way in which we view relationships, and, in particular, of the form and shape of global order. It involves matching the outward exploration of existence with an inward exploration of the meaning of being, of the nature of being human and of the purpose of existence. It involves a new vision of our collective purpose on the earth. Falk (2002) applies the nomenclature "citizen pilgrims" to those engaged in this kind of endeavor. It is this very endeavor, I believe, that sits at the heart of transformative education, of education for global human rights. It is an education of hope, an education indeed of the possible.

NOTES

Some of this material originally appeared in Makere Stewart-Harawira, *The New Imperial Order. Indigenous Responses to Globalization* (London: Zed Books; Australia and New Zealand: Huia Books, 2005). I am grateful to Zed Books in London, England, and Huia Books in Wellington, New Zealand, for permission to reuse some material.

1. James Tully, Two Meanings of Global Citizenship: Modern and Diverse. Presented at The Meanings of Global Citizenship Conference, Liu Centre and Trudeau Foundation, UBC, September 2005.

2. Evidenced in recently declassified documents of the U.S. State Department posted on the Web site of the National Security Archive at George Washington University.

3. CNN Law Centre, at http://www.cnn.com/2004/LAW/01/26/patriot.act.ap/.

4. NZ Customs Service, Contraband. *New Zealand Customs Service Magazine*, September 2003, pp. 8–12.

REFERENCES

Bacevich, A. J. (2002) *American empire. The realities and consequences of U.S. diplomacy.* Cambridge & London: Harvard University Press.

Brace, B. (2000). *The Guardian,* 31 July 2000; see also UN Human Rights Committee Press Release HR/CT580, 21 July 2000, regarding the Report of the Human Rights Committee re mandatory sentencing of Aboriginals in Australia.

Chomsky, N. (2000). *Rogue states. The rule of force in world affairs* (pp. 51–61). Cambridge, MA: South End Press.

Chomsky, N. (1999). *The umbrella of US power. The universal declaration of human rights and the contradictions of US policy* (pp. 39–40). New York: Seven Stories Press.

Chomsky, N. (1997). *Perspectives on power. Reflections on human nature and the social order.* Montreal, New York, London: Black Rose Books.

Cooper, R. (2003). *The breaking of nations. Order and chaos in the twenty-first century.* New York: Atlantic Books.

Cooper, R. (2002). The new liberal imperialism. http://www.observer.co.uk/Print/0,3858,4388912,00.html, accessed 3/10/02.

Deloria, V. Jr. (1999). *Spirit and reason. The Vine Deloria reader.* Colorado: Fulcrum Publishing.

Dower, N. (1998). *World ethics. The new agenda.* Edinburgh: Edinburgh University Press.

Durie, M. (2001). *Mauri Ora. The dynamics of Maori health.* Auckland, NZ: Oxford University Press.

Falk, R. (2002). An emergent matrix of citizenship: Complex, fluid, and uneven. In N. Dower & J. Williams (Eds.), *Global citizenship. A critical introduction* (pp. 15–30). New York: Routledge.

Foucault, M. (1991). Governmentality. In G. Burchell, C. Gordon, & P. Miller (Eds.), *The Foucault effect. Studies in governmentality* (pp. 87–104). Chicago: The University of Chicago Press.

Hardt, M., & Negri, A. (2000). *Empire.* Cambridge: Harvard University Press.

Hitz, F. P., & Weiss, B. J. (2004, Spring). Helping the CIS and the FBI connect the dots in the war against terror. *International Journal of Intelligence and Counter-Intelligence, 17(1),* 17.

Hopkins, A. (2000). Special report: Australia and East Timor. *The Guardian,* September 13, 2000, online at http://www.guardianunlimited.co.uk/Print/0,3858,4062928, 00.html, accessed 14/09/00.

Kymlicka, W. (1989). *Liberalism, community, and culture*. Oxford: Oxford University Press.

Lyons, O. (1984). Spirituality, equality, and natural law. In L. Little Bear, M. Boldt, & J. A. Long, (Eds.), *Pathways to self-determination. Canadian Indians and the Canadian state*. Toronto: University of Toronto Press.

Milbank, D. (2001). East Timor invasion got US go-ahead. *Washington Post*, 7 December, online at http://www.globalpolicy.org/security/issues/etimor/2001/1206kissinger.htm, accessed January 2002.

Paine, T. [1776], cited Chomsky, N. (1997). *Perspectives on power. Reflections on human nature and the social order* (p. 239). Montreal, New York, London: Black Rose Books.

Passavant, P. A. (2004). Introduction: Postmodern republicanism. In P. Passavant & J. Dean (Eds.), *Empire's new clothes. Reading Hardt and Negri*. New York & London: Routledge.

Peters, M. (2001). *Poststructuralism, Marxism, and neoliberalism. Between theory and politics* (p. 98). Oxford: Rowan & Littlefield.

Phillips, L. *A new journey: The Nisga'a treaty*. Video Documentary, Lanyon Phillips BBDO, British Columbia.

Robie, D. (1989). *Blood on their banner. Nationalist struggles in the South Pacific*. Leichardt, NSW: Pluto Press.

Roberts, A., & Kingsbury, B. (Eds.). (1993). *United Nations, divided world: The UN's roles in international relations*. Oxford: Clarendon Press; New York: Oxford University Press.

Rosow, S. J. (1994). Nature, need, and the human world: "Commercial society" and the construction of the world economy. In S. J. Rosow, N. Inayatullah, & M. Rupert (Eds.), *The global economy as political space* (pp. 17–36). Boulder, London: Lynne Rienner.

Shirres, M. P (1997). *Te Tangata. The human person*. Auckland: Accent Publishers.

Simon, J. (1990). *The place of schooling in Maori-Pakeha relations*. IRI PhD Thesis Series Number 1. International Research Institute for Maori and Indigenous Education, University of Auckland, New Zealand.

Stephenson, M. (1993). Karakariki School: A revisionist history. Unpublished MA thesis, School of Education, University of Auckland.

Stewart-Harawira, M. (2005). *The new imperial order. Indigenous responses to globalization*. London: Zed Books; Australia & New Zealand: Huia Books.

Thiong'o, N. (1993). Decolonising the mind: The politics of language in African literature [London: James Currey, 1986]. Reprinted in L. Chrisman & P. Williams (Eds.), *Colonial discourse and post-colonial theory* (pp. 435–455). London and New York: Harvester Wheatsheaf.

Tully, J. (2000). The struggles of indigenous peoples for and of freedom. In D. Ivison, P. Patton, & W. Sanders (Eds.), *Political theory and the rights of indigenous peoples*. Cambridge: Cambridge University Press.

Urion, C. (1999). Recording first nations traditional knowledge. Unpublished paper, U'mista Cultural Society.

Wilmer, F. (1993). *The indigenous voice in world politics. Since time immemorial.* Newbury Park, London, New Delhi: Sage.

Zhang, Y. (1997). Human rights and the post-cold war international society. In R. Wilkinson (Ed.), *Culture, ethnicity, and human rights* (pp. 39–54). Auckland, NZ: NZ Institute of International Affairs.

THIRTEEN

Human Rights Imperialism

Third Way Education as the
New Cultural Imperialism

Jerrold L. Kachur

INTRODUCTION

WESTERN POWERS INTERVENED militarily in Yugoslavia (1999), Afghanistan (2001), and Iraq (2003) using "human rights" as a justification for transgressing the sovereign borders of three nation-states. These three recent imperialist assertions of power mark the rise of new international norms in considering interstate relations and the legitimate use of military force. With the end of the cold war, the emergence of the United States as the sole superpower, and the American focus on the War on Terror following 9/11, a more nuanced understanding of the positive and negative relationships among imperialism, education, and human rights is necessary for imagining and implementing progressive education policies and practices.

Many eyes are turned on George W. Bush's administration with its enunciation of The Bush Doctrine, a defiant superpower nationalism justifying the hegemon's right to unilateral preemptive self-defense. The official document is called *The National Security Strategy of the United States of America* (NSS 2000). The doctrine immediately caused alarm at home and abroad because it dismissed deference to international law and cooperation. These "gunboat" imperialists use human rights talk to mask raw political economic interests when other justifications fail. However, this chapter looks at "human rights imperialism" as "humanitarian interventionism" in the Third Way thinking of center-left liberals who take human rights talk seriously yet find themselves constantly compromised (e.g., UK prime minister Tony Blair and U.S. president Bill Clinton). Third Way thinking is problematic. It dangerously reduces public politics to personal morality. Following the work of Callinicos (2001, 2003), Chandler (2002), Teeple (2005), and Mandel (2004), I take a critical realist humanist stance and argue that while human rights discourse may provide an important normative resource, the problem with "humanitarian interventionism" is not because human rights have not been fully applied or that the Great Powers manipulate or co-opt international agencies to do their bidding but because human rights discourse tends to undermine public politics, mistrust non-Western peoples' capacity for self-governance, and breed cynicism among the Westerners about their democratically elected governments and international institutions.

HUMANITARIAN INTERVENTIONISM: A LESSER OF TWO EVILS?

By 2004 the American electorate provided public support for George W. Bush's militarily occupation of Iraq without the consent of the United Nations Security Council. In this new era, "real American freedom" means fighting terrorism and making money at the same time but without the support of the UN. An intuitive response to Bush II and the new mandarins of American power is an unreflexive defense of international law and cooperation to resist this kind of hardcore approach to American imperialism. This approach wishes for a return to the Nixon-to-Clinton years and diplomacy based on weak multilateralism and a new emphasis on humanitarian interventionism. However, social regulation via human rights shifts power from political participation to outside administrators as the basis for state legitimacy and economic development—in other words, adherents facilitate technocratic politics but present themselves as democratic. This "new humanitarianism," as a new ethics, promotes an elite theory that denies people dignity and respect by presuming that they are inherently evil and require moral regulation from above. As politics, it degrades democracy because it compensates for the decline of mass politics and a shrinking public sphere by denying the autonomous capacity of people for rational decision making. It deinstitutionalizes the capacity of human beings to collectively solve the problems that confront them in their everyday lives.

Canadian liberalism is consistent with the center-left thinking of Tony Blair and Bill Clinton. In September 2005 Canada proudly persuaded the UN member nations to enshrine a new policy called "responsibility to protect" (or "R2P") that partially establishes the conditions for UN (or international organizations) interventions when states are unwilling to protect their own people from mortal threat (Ibbitson, 2005, p. A4). India, China, Russia,

African governments, and other South countries provided the most resis-tance and treated the initiative as a self-righteous Western justification for neocolonialism. More significantly, they saw it as marking the UN's shift away from defending the equal and sovereign rights of every member state, regardless of size. However, Western powers, foreign policy analysts, and human rights NGOs identified that the protection of a government's sover-eign rights could mean sacrificing the human rights of the ruled to their own oppressive rulers. Humanitarian interventionism meant caring for the people affected by the atrocities in the post–Cold War period: East Timor, Somalia, Bosnia, Herzegovina, Kosovo, Chechnya, Rwanda, Liberia, and Darfur.

The new policy was passed when Canada, with the moral support of Rwanda, agreed to specify that outside collective force could be used to pro-tect a threatened population only in cases of "genocide, war crimes, ethnic cleansing and crimes against humanity" and if the UN worked with "the rel-evant regional organizations," such as the African Union.

While R2P might not pass the Security Council deliberations, Ibbitson (2005, p. A4) captures the sentiment of many proponents of humanitarian interventionism on the Left and Right:

> [I]f there is ever to be collective peace for all the peoples of the world in this century, then countries that have the power to protect must eventually agree collectively on their responsibility to protect. Sovereignty must give way to human rights; the hypocritical excuse that mass slaughter is "an internal matter" should become a call to arms.

Simply stated, where governments cannot be trusted not to engage in geno-cide, war, ethnic cleansing, and crimes against humanity, bring in outside administrators to implement "human rights" legislation and back it up with the necessary military force and UN sanction.

Most certainly, genocide and ethnic cleansing are horrific acts of brutal violence and humans must act to end or at least reduce their occurrence. However, even if the violence has captured Western attention, it is unusual to make such a significant reversal in international law to facilitate "human-itarian intervention." Why all the attention and this particular remedy for violence around the world?

According to the 2005 Human Security Report (HSR 2005) almost all forms of political violence are down since 1992. Battle deaths from civil and external wars since the end of the Korean War show a clear but uneven decline from a high in of seven hundred thousand in 1950 to a low of one hun-dred thousand in 1992 and twenty thousand in 2002. Furthermore, in spite of massacres in Rwanda and Bosnia, acts of genocide dropped by 80 percent between 1988 and 2001. Human rights abuses have fallen in five of six regions in the developing world since the mid-1990s and the number of coups have declined about 60 percent since 1963. However, while the total terrorist attacks per year had a clear uneven downward trend from a high of about 650 in the mid-1980s to about two hundred in 2003, internationally significant terrorist attacks have been on the rise, from a low of about twenty in 1982 to a high of about 180 in 2003. Yet terrorist casualties are a minimal fraction of the death toll from war. While people might believe that violence has increased, it hasn't. It has been on a continuous decline in the world.

However, if humanitarian intervention addresses a nonexistent problem, why is a reversal in the foundation of international law necessary to justify military action? Fen Hampson et al. (2005, p. A21) proposes that the "use of force and coercive diplomacy" may be needed to bring the remaining intractable forces (e.g., in Congo, Kashmir, Palestine, etc.) to their senses or else they will remain a breeding ground for terrorism, regional instability, and potential nuclear conflict. He suggests that the only other option for these "hardened cases" is "laissez-faire." Furthermore, in anticipation of the release of the UN's annual Arab Human Development Report, Elie Nasrallah (2005, p. A19) suggests more specifically that despotism and the use of state security apparatuses has left Arab societies "in the dark ages as far as modernity and democratization are concerned." And, "the Arab world today needs a road map for salvation, emancipation, reform, peaceful change, modernity, democratization, empowerment, and above all a working formula to separate state and religion." He adds, one of the key results on inaction is schools that stifle children: "imprisons the mind, destroys the spirit and cripples potential" (Ibid.).

The nature of despotic regimes and the consequences for such kinds of schooling may well be true; however, this kind of approach juxtaposes doing nothing with "coercive diplomacy" or military interventionism without acknowledging other options for liberation and who is "emancipating" whom or attributing any Western responsibility for the dire state of affairs in the region.

Who is the object of invention? Michael Mandel (2005, p. A15) points out that the greatest innovation in human rights was the basic legal document for the trial of the major Nazi war criminals. The London Charter of the International Military Tribunal defined "Crimes Against Peace," as "the planning, preparation, initiation or waging of war of aggression, or a war in violation of international treaties, agreements or assurances" (Ibid.). The crime of aggression is not in modern international criminal codes and the lead country in keeping it out has been the United States. The reason, Mandel says, is straightforward if one takes the 2003 Iraq war as an example, because it exemplifies the quintessential war of aggression: it falls short of any justification in self-defense or authorization by the Security Council of the United Nations. Aside from the insistence of the U.S. government that this is a "humanitarian intervention," itself rather dubious legal grounds for war, under international law sixty years ago, the United States would be guilty of "crimes against the peace" and charged with thousands of murders (Mandel, 2004, 2005).

Maybe there is an American alternative to the Bush Doctrine? To focus on only George W. Bush or to treat the Republican Party as the War Party does identify specific individuals and organizations as representatives of their countries. However, as Mandel (2004) identifies, in the specific cases where the United States has been the aggressor in crimes against peace since World War II, both Republican and Democratic administrations have been involved. A closer look at the Yugoslav war (1999) under the presidency of center-left Bill Clinton shows that in this war or "policing action," the UN sanctioned "transgression of state sovereignty" against non-Western peoples and justified US/NATO actions with reference to "humanitarian interven- tion." The roles and justifications between West and non-West were reversed when compared to the 1991 Gulf war. But Yugoslavia could not get redress as Kuwait expected and received (Chandleer, 2002; Cockburn & St. Clair, 2004; Teeple, 2005). Nevertheless, to focus only on internal U.S. politics or the United States as a "rogue nation" or how military acts are justified misses broader systemic structures that inform actions and consequences: the nature of global capitalism and Great Power conflict and the function of interna- tional agreements that legitimate or delegitimate wars and "policing" that nation-states undertake.

According to David Chandler (2002),

> "[I]nternational justice" and the human rights–based approach are a reflec- tion of the dismissal of sovereign political equality. The inequalities of international law are increasingly institutionalizing international political inequality. . . . [T]he idea that non-Western peoples and states cannot be trusted at the most basic level of the administration of law and government is increasingly articulated by Western policy-makers and NGOs. . . . The problem that the advocates of "international justice" have to grapple with is that without sovereign equality there can be no international law. The position at the moment seems to be that the United States government believes that the US military should not be limited by its NATO allies and that NATO should not be constrained by the views of non-NATO states, but this position has not been forwarded as part of any new system of inter- national regulation. . . . It seems [then] that the only principle of the new post-UN order is that intervention may be used to coercively enforce "international justice" if the United States thinks that this would be a good idea. (pp. 151–153)

To reiterate: The Bush Doctrine of "pre-emptive unilateral action," the Nixon-Clinton soft multilateralism of "collective defense against sovereign aggression," and the emerging "humanitarian responsibility to protect" share a common imperialist logic while allowing a divergence of opinions, strate- gies, and tactics underpinned not by authentic international consensus but by "The Washington Consensus"—American hegemony and trilateral imperial power. Underpinning this hegemony and power is a common sensibility: a reduction of sovereign power of peoples and and a turn to individualistic human rights to regulate human behavior. As the basis for state legitimacy and economic development, this approach shifts power from public partici-pation in politics to outside administrators.

THE NEW CULTURAL IMPERIALISM

A critical realist approach to imperialism includes Marxian, poststructuralist, and critical theory insights into global power (Achcar, 2002; Callinicos, 2001, 2003; Cockburn & St. Clair, 2004; Cox, 1996, 2003; Held & Koenig-Archibugi, 2004; Held, 2004; Hardt & Negri, 2000; Negri, 2002; Harvey, 2003; Magdoff, 2003). The new imperialism assumes changed economic cir-cumstance as a result of global corporations. "The extraction of surplus, the race for control of raw materials and resources, the creation of economic dependencies in the global periphery and the unending contest among rival powers, [now] manifest themselves in new and transformed ways" (Magdoff, 2003, p. 14). One change is the new political economy of knowledge pro-duction, raising fundamental issues that go beyond traditional education debates. New conflicts are played out in the marketing of services, the pro-tection of intellectual property rights, and raises questions about who will benefit from the investment returns in education. I argue that Third Way education is the most advanced form of cultural imperialism because it accounts for profiting from cultural commodification.

Three key questions informed this exploration of humanitarian inter-ventionism, education, Third Way ideology, and global security liberalism: (1) Why did Blair, a right-of-center social democrat, join Bush II, a religious neoconservative to fight the Iraq war (2003)? (2) What might this tell us about the nature and functioning of human rights discourse and humanitar-ian intervention in facilitating rather than challenging American imperial-ism? And (3) how might this alert us to some central problems in the use and abuse of a human rights agenda for the world and education in a post-9/11 world? In the prescient *Education as Cultural Imperialism*, Martin Carnoy (1974) answers a question: "Education for development or domination?" He suggests:

> In the non-industrialized economy, the school is an institution that not only keeps the individual from self-definition, but keeps the entire society from defining itself. The schools are an extension of the metropole structure, just as are the economy, polity, and social structure. . . . (p. 72)

He concludes once this system of "equal opportunity" has been implemented, the social structure *among* nations will also be maintained with developed country-promoted efficiency reforms, that is using, scientific management to match work equally with schooling measured in number of students, years of schooling, and job placement. "As an important side-effect, the multinational corporations and other foreign investors use foreign, vocationally trained labor to compete with US workers. . . . [M]anagers are imported from the United States or Europe, so local workers never learn the necessary skills to run the firms by themselves. This industrial division of labor . . . is part of their ideological thrust into the Third World" (p. 334).

The development of American power and political strategies as a global hegemon, before and after the end of the cold war, has been well documented (Cox, 1996, 2002; Gowan, 1999; Teeple, 1995). With the national bourgeoisie of the third world now integrated into global circuits of power, with Western-educated managers from North and South now directing the industrial processes, and with Southern elites no longer trustworthy to deliver social control over a burgeoning urban working class and mobile and volatile underclass, the national security liberalism of the 1970s is morphing into global security liberalism for the twenty-first century.

Global security liberalism enhances American influence in the world. At its core, security is connected to the development of American interests in global capitalism and support for human rights and democratic governments abroad. In this sense a commitment to liberalized, deregulated, and privatized markets in goods, services, labor, and ideas (i.e., neoliberal economic globalization) also includes a commitment to an integrated international order based on the principles of democratic capitalism backed up by the military force of the United States as guarantor of order and enforcer of law. True belief in the "religion" of global security liberalism, like most religions, is not one of choice but habituated disposition and ritualized action, consistent with the cultural milieu one is socialized into as a child. It is also why it is difficult for Westerners to imagine a world without global security liberalism any more than it was possible for the Spanish and Portuguese to imagine a sixteenth-century civilization without Counter-Reformation Catholicism.

THE POVERTY OF "THIRD WAY" THINKING

In analyzing human rights imperialism, it seems rather straightforward to understand the neoconservative commitment to human rights as a hollow and cynical cover for American world domination or a return to Gunboat Diplomacy in opening doors for capitalist markets. That is, in the neoconservative case it was not really about human rights but rather about what Noam Chomsky (1987) calls a proxy for defending the American "fifth freedom" as the "national interest": the unrestrained right of U.S. corporations to make money whenever or wherever they so desire and with a defense of "democracy" as free market and free trade capitalism. However, New Labourite Blair's commitment to the rights of the "international community" to "humanitarian intervention" is more intriguing. As a center-left politician he is like the more open-minded Jesuit missionaries who had a concern for New World natives as "humans" so as to justify their potential for conversion to The Cross.

I raise the religious allusion because the history of human rights is closely tied to faith-based movements or politically influential leaders who took their religious faith seriously (Lauren, 1998; Mead, 2000, 2004). Paul Lauren (1998, pp. 4, 5) even introduces the first chapter of his expansive history of human rights with a quotation from *Genesis* 4:9: "Am I my brother's keeper?" and grounds the movement in the world's great "religious visions: brothers, sisters and duties beyond borders." However, when I talk about a religious discourse, I don't necessarily mean it draws on religious content even if it does that, too. But I suggest that religious thinking is a way of thinking, a logic of thought, and that any discourse can function *religiously*—and this is the way I want to talk about the center-Left's Third Way thinking about human rights, both its content and function.

Humanitarian interventionism has a religious calling with deep roots in the American colonial missionary movement in the nineteenth century and the Wilsonian politics of ethnonational self-determination during the break-up of empires in the aftermath of World War I. It also informs the consolidation of comparative and international studies in American universities and the consequent cold war discourse around the "liberal security state" that now emerges as the ideology of empire: "humanitarian interventionism" and the global security state (Callinicos, 2001, 2003; Mead, 2000, 2004; Said, 1978).

Third Way thinking is the marker for a cluster of liberal, liberal democrat, social democratic, and multiculturalist positions (Hombach, 2000). These "center-Left" intellectuals are against the New Right of Reagan and Thatcher and any marriage of neoliberal economics to social conservatism. They are also against the Old Left promotion of economic statism: either Soviet-style state socialism or Roosevelt's New Deal welfare state socialism. Or better, these new "competitive progressives" promote the notion that they are not against but *beyond* the Old Left-Right paradigm. If social democracy is a halfway house between communism and neoliberalism, Third Way thinking is a halfway house between social democracy and neoliberalism. Political exemplars of the center-left politicians are, in the UK, Tony Blair's New Labour; in Germany, Gerhard Schröder's New Center; and in the United States, Bill Clinton's New Democrats. Intellectual defenses are wide-ranging in defending a kind of neopragmatism or neoprogressivism, some liberal, some social democratic, many who believe global capitalism can be humanized, and some who are quite explicit in their defense of human rights imperialism (Callicinos, 2001). Variation of this theme would include left-wing social democrats such as Jürgen Habermas (1996) and David Held (2004)— who are probably too discomforting for the Blairites and Clintonians. Closer to center-left thinking are intellectuals such as Anthony Giddens (1998, 2000, 2003) and liberals like Andrea Dworkin (2000), Michael Ignatieff (2000, 2003, 2004), and Amartya Sen (2003). Unlike traditional socialists or the left social democrats, the center-left thinkers and the Third Way leaders such as Blair and Clinton no longer assume that global capitalism can be transcended through social reform or revolution. As much as they are for peace and against violence, they believe that global capitalism can be contained, constrained, and harnessed for economic development and social justice. The more conservative Third Wayers believe "left" liberalism or ethical socialism should be used to humanize capitalism. If anything remains of socialism it is not as either an economic system or even a political system. Third Wayers reduce the political to the moral; political change is about social values. They are strangely silent about transforming economic or political power. This ethical socialism or left liberalism commits itself primarily to "community" and to a particular definition of community as an ethical commitment to the market. Secondarily, Third Wayers value liberty and equality though these are reduced to "economic opportunity" and "individual responsibility" respectively. Thus, in Blair's (2000) antistatist and antieconomic ethical socialism his key concern is the affirmation of community values. Blair spoke to the Global Ethics Foundation on June 30, 2000:

> [We advance] the belief in the equal worth of all . . . and in our mutual responsibility in creating a society that advances such equal worth. Note: it is equal worth, not equality of income or outcome; or simply, equality of opportunity. Rather it affirms our equal right to dignity, liberty, freedom from discrimination as well as economic opportunity. The idea of community resolves the paradox of the modern world: it acknowledges our independence; it acknowledges our interdependence; it recognizes our individual worth.

Concomitantly, economic opportunity is provided by efficiently functioning markets. According to Callinicos (2001) and Chandler (2002), center-left Third Wayers believe that neoliberal globalization is here to stay and they are committed to the productivity of innovations in information technologies and "knowledge capitalism." Consistent is a commitment to "endowment egalitarianism" where the state acts to equalize "the background distribution of productive endowments so that the market interactions lead to a greater initial equality of income, lessening the need for subsequent redistribution" (White, 1997, cited in Callinicos 2001, p. 48), but access to only one productive endowment is to be equalized: skills through improved education and training. In addition, paid employment is seen as the route to opportunity (e.g., this approach defines Blair's and Clinton's approach in promoting welfare-to-work programs for the long-term unemployed; see, e.g., O'Connor, 2001).

So "knowledge economy" competitiveness depends on the skills of the workplace and success or failure in the economy depends on access to knowledge and new information technologies more than to economic capital. Individual liberation arises from the enhancement of the value of labor rather than the abolition of private capital. The virtuous reward of economic effort means that social justice and economic efficiency are not in conflict: justice and enterprise live together. Read most contemporary documents on education and knowledge distributed by the OECD or World Bank or even the UN and you will find a hotbed of Third Way thinking about social justice. The marriage of neoliberal economics harnessed to the social development model is the Third Way definition of "social justice."

Callinicos (1991) summarizes how this development model has failed: (1) paid employment is not the key to reducing inequality because most disadvantaged groups (e.g., disabled, elderly) cannot work, most marginalized cultural minorities are ascribed to certain work, and income depends not on the skill requirements but on the nature and remuneration of the job, and (2) educational disparities reflect and reproduce wider economic inequalities and these have to be tackled at the source (e.g., maldistribution of household wealth), and (3) so under the Third Way model socioeconomic inequalities of income and increased poverty have been greatly exacerbated (not eliminated or even moderated) and tend to mirror the worst disparities produced under the capitalist watch of the New Right in the North and military regimes in the South. With the traditional social democratic strategy of reducing poverty through the provision of universal benefits or humanitarian aid financed by a progressive taxation ruled out, governments are left with regressive strategies of indirect taxation and privatization of social services to local communities and families. It is doubtful whether the Third Way's egalitarian aspirations can be grafted to neoliberal economics or that enterprise and justice can be harmonized or that this neo-modernization project will in fact deliver the goods to non-Western peoples. In regard to individual responsibility, the notion of a socially just community takes on a form of moral authoritarianism. Here rights and duties are emphasized, with concept of duty given priority over rights. Here "respect for others" and "responsibility to them" is treated as a prerequisite for a strong and active community where discussion of socioeconomic inequality and redistribution remains a taboo topic (or reduced to "culturalized" concept, e.g., culture of poverty), almost completely displaced by the politics of identity and cultural recognition. Thus, "free economy, strong state" are tied together. Neoliberal economics is the working assumption of Third Way approaches to human capital, and most approaches to cultural capital, and identity. There is disdain for political economic analysis.

For Third Wayers, unemployment is (in these virtuous neoliberal circumstances) a consequence of the dysfunctional behavior of individuals who refuse to work, and this behavior must in turn be caused either by their individual moral faults or by a more pervasive "culture of poverty." Thus, if cultural capital is a precondition for the development of human capital and market payoff, school failure and economic marginalization are treated as a sign of cultural weakness or the consequence of cultural disrespect or discrimination and not the product of the way global political economic capitalism functions.

For Third Wayers, the state's role becomes the authoritarian enforcement of dutiful relations for community integration where cultural respect for "difference" becomes synonymous with inclusion in various sets of market relationships. Inclusion, here, means the right to the job or credential markets (not to eat or experience a meaningful education or job). This narrow but dynamic idea of "postmodern" communities treats stable communities as enemies of innovation, talent, creativity, diversity, and experimentation. A nostalgic sense of strong communities is the enemy of knowledge creation and blocks the source of economic growth. Community is reduced to "social capital" and a marketable commodity. They also forget that it takes more than a local community to raise a child. The 2004 *United Nations Development Report, subtitled Cultural Liberty in Today's Diverse World,* oozes Third Way thinking. The report takes a "humanitarian" approach to balance cultural identities, rights, and commodities within a human rights perspective. But its commitment to private property rights and global free trade thus strengthens the commodification of "culture" as the new hot property without negatively assessing the consequent cultural disintegration.

Third Way thinkers have a self-image of a global society where identity, commodities, and rights adhere to each other and where harmony reigns at the center. In advanced capitalist countries the agonies of the twentieth century have been eclipsed because enterprise and justice are reconciled with a common disdain for the "moral deficit" of the poor at home and abroad. Global citizenship is construed with market participation and discourse shifts to overcoming "marginalization" through "inclusion" in the market and normalization of an entrepreneurial character rather than ending economic exploitation or political oppression. Public political problems are reduced to personal moral problems. This is Western *humanitarian* neoliberalism gone global.

However, it is imperative that when there is evil, tyranny, and violence in the periphery, it is necessary for these liberal capitalist societies to awaken from their self-satisfied complacency to mount police actions to contain the disorder. What marks the 1999 Balkan war between US/NATO and Yugoslavia is that it was justified as an act of humanitarian warmaking and was unlike the Gulf war in 1991when the transgression of territorial sovereignty of Kuwait was the primary justification. According to Blair (1999), the Yugoslav war was a just war, based not on any territorial ambitions but on *values.* It was not just about the plight of victims and functioning of globalization. It was about politics and security. He stated in a speech to the Economic Club of Chicago in April 1999:

> We are witnessing the beginnings of a new doctrine of "international community." By this I mean the explicit recognition that today more than ever before, we are mutually dependent, that national interest is to a significant extent governed by international collaboration and that we need a clear and coherent debate as to the direction that his doctrine takes us in each field of international endeavor. Just as within domestic politics, the notion of community—the belief that partnership and co-operation are essential to advance self-interest—is coming into its own; so it needs to find its international echo.

In the abstract, who would disagree? However "the international community" and "global security state" take a particular form today: underpinned not by authentic international consensus but by American hegemony and trilateral imperial power. The moral superiority of justice made for non-Westerners is self-evident in Third Way thinking. It should be remind Westerners that Christian soldiers can sing more than one tune. And this cause is worth fighting for.

LIBERALISM: A FIGHTING CREED

History will judge whether Bush's logic is just an accident of history, the idiosyncratic response of a particular administration to international law and global governance, or, rather, a prescient moment of historical transparency, one that reveals the deeper logic of a global hegemon that is discovering that it has won the wars of imperial succession against Britain, Germany, and the USSR and it can now do whatever it wants, in any way it wants, whatever the rule of international law (Mead, 2004). Or can it?

If this dynamic is more about the functioning of a global hegemon than George W. Bush and his neoconservative compatriots out of control, then promoters of human rights might have to think again about their strategies for taming the tiger or any other newly emerging tiger—such as China—or a coalition of tigers. Faith placed in a Democratic hopeful might also be misplaced given that the Nixon-to-Clinton soft-multilateralism coincided with military interventions, both legal and illegal in terms of international law around the world. And it might be good to recall the many imperialist adventures and occupations in Indian Country, Latin America, the Philippines, and around the world—justified with the humanitarian side of Manifest Destiny (Mead, 2000, 2004; Scowen, 2003).

So let us return to the question: Why would Blair, the Third Wayer, believer in human rights, and ethical socialism sign on with Bush, the neoconservative "warmonger"? To do good deeds: make money and foster humanitarian care. But why might this "caring" intervention fail? Most likely for much the same reason that Bob Woodward (1994) reveals describing when the well-intentioned Bill Clinton was unable to push through his modest domestic reforms when his economists told him in his first year that he had to cut the federal budget by $140 billion to persuade nervous bond markets and the Federal Reserve Board to let interest rates fall. In his words, with anger and disbelief, he responded: "You mean to tell me that the success of the program and my re-election hinges on the Federal Reserve and a bunch of fucking bond dealers" (Woodward, 1994, p. 84). This is the tale of well-intentioned liberal reformers, their humanitarianism defeated by capitalist economic constraints. In this case, imposed notably through the flight of capital on the financial markets. The fight for social democracy will have to have higher standards than this limited idea of "social reform" whose downside is a best-case version of humanitarian governance imposed at the global level but always compromised by the financiers and bondholders and other kinds of co-commitments entailed in neoliberal capitalism.

For Third Wayers, humanitarian interventionism or human rights imperialism is not a screen for some baser instinct that suddenly drives their alliance with neoconservative militarism but rather the way they define their own virtuousness in articulating a theory of global capitalism and social justice when considering their notion of social justice as congruent with neoliberal economic development and an ethics of community valuation. For Hardt and Negri (2000, 2002) "multilateral humanist intervention" is *Empire*. It is "global security liberalism" in its multiplicity of political forms of capitalist globalization; it is a policy option for enlightened capitalists. But is this distinction between enlightened and unenlightened capitalists accurate? I think not. Whether they can even take up the enlightened route without recourse to violence is another matter—and a crucial point for some of the more explicit and realistic center-left humanitarians such as Harvard scholar Michael Ignatieff (2003) who calls for a softer and kinder imperialism— *Empire Lite*—and points out that liberal North Americans must not shrink from the use of violence and force. It can be necessary for its survival but it must be measured, not as a program of torture and revenge. Here we see liberalism as a fighting creed and not the sanitized version taught to us in grammar school where only bad guys are aggressively violent. He asks a question, in *The Lesser Evil*, that all Third Wayers and others should ask themselves: "What lesser evils may a society commit when it believes it faces the greater evil of its own destruction? This is one of the oldest questions in politics and one of the hardest to answer" (2004, p. 1).

CONCLUSION

The political fallout of the end of the cold war was not the end of serious interstate conflict. Nor was it simply the transcendence of national governments with more countries drawn into multilateral processes of "global governance" between equals. And the peace dividend that materialized was not translated into poverty reduction, health and education services, and housing and infrastructure. Violence is down but the costs of fighting terror are up. Rather, the end of the cold war marked the consolidation of global capitalism and the exceptional predominance of American military power. Any analysis of human rights and education that does not account for the dynamics of global capitalism and Great Power conflict may find its promotion of the human rights discourse used as a proxy for unilateral and preemptive imperialism of the old form or else implicated in the defense of the international community and the construction of human rights imperialism in the new form, the global security state.

Is "imperialism" good or bad? I have left this question unanswered in order to assess the legitimacy of "humanitarian interventionism" as a progressive ideology that has historically denied its aggressive nature, forewarning the difficulties it might unleash if human rights are tied too closely to it. Following Callinicos (2003), I emphasize that human rights activists will fail if they identify the enemy as merely globalization and not global capitalism; if they fail to analyze the core institutions of global capitalism such as the multinational corporations, the leading capitalist states, and the international institutions that refract their interests; if they fail to see how the requirements of capitalist reproduction set the limits to its regulation and reform of nation-states and global governance; if they fail to identify the primary axes of capital and labor over secondary but necessary axes of cultural identity; if they fail to look for and participate in anticapitalist movements (based on a coalition of organized labor, other social movements, and a defense of the environment) where alternative models of society will emerge; and if they fail to comprehend that transcending capitalism requires a revolution of global social relations.

Furthermore, even if necessary, it is insufficient to transform schooling as the means to achieve revolutionary goals; and it is most likely impossible to escape human rights imperialism when educational reform follows Third Way thinking. What is missed in this blending of enterprise and justice, democracy and human rights, is that these activities are quite different, often based on competing theoretical and moral foundations. Furthermore, within the existing framework of international law and political decision making, the real dynamics and fundamental distinctions between personal morality and political agency are not critically considered. In addition, human rights discourse increasingly replaces needs-based aid with rights-based intervention, and rights-based discourse is increasingly informed by religious thinking, where the mysteries of revelation give access to the self-evident power of human rights to transform the world and theoretical and philosophical justifications for human rights claims are treated as disruptive and unhelpful to the cause.

Third Way thinking is a powerful new form of cultural imperialism even if it promotes ethical communities, economic opportunities, and self-sufficiency through society and schooling. I have pointed out another way, the politics of critical realist humanism, emphasizing public participation and collective self-organization to solve the global problems that cause the unnecessary suffering of humans in their daily lives.

REFERENCES

Achcar, G. (2002). *The clash of barbarisms*. New York: Monthly Review Press.

Axworthy, L. (2004). Let's head off Armageddon in the Artic. *Globe and Mail*, 9 November, p. A17.

Blair, T. (1999). Doctrine of the international community. Speech to the Economic Club of Chicago, 22 April 1999. Online: www.fco.gov.uk, pp. 2, 3, 4, 9.

Blair, T. (2000). Values and the power of community. Speech to the Global Ethics Foundation, Tubingen University, 30 June 2000. Online: www.number-10.gov.uk, p. 4.

Callinicos, A. (2001). *Against the Third Way*. Cambridge: Polity.

Callinicos, A. (2003). *The new mandarins of American power*. Cambridge: Polity.

Carnoy, M. (1974). *Education as cultural imperialism*. New York: Longman.

Chandler, D. (2002). *From Kosovo to Kabul*. London: Pluto.

Chomsky, N. (1987). *Turning the tide* (2nd ed.). Montreal: Black Rose.

Cockburn, A., & St. Clair, J. (2004). *Imperial crusades*. London: Verso.

Cox, R., with Schechter, M. (2002). *The political economy of a plural world*. New York: Routledge.

Cox, R., with Schechter, M. (1996). *Approaches to world order*. Cambridge: Cambridge University Press.

Dworkin, R. (2000). *Sovereign virtue: The theory and practice of equality*. Cambridge: Harvard University Press.

Giddens, A. (1998). *The third way*. Cambridge: Polity.

Giddens, A. (2000). *The third way and its critics*. Cambridge: Polity.

Giddens, A. (2003). *The progressive manifesto*. Cambridge: Polity.

Gowan, P. (1999). *The global gamble*. London: Verso.

Habermas, J. (1996). *Between facts and norms*. Cambridge: MIT Press.

Hampson, F. O., Crocker, C. A., & Aall, P. (2005). If the world's getting more peaceful, why are we still in danger. *Globe and Mail*, 20 October, p. A21.

Hardt, M., & Negri, A. (2000). *Empire*. Cambridge: Harvard University Press.

Hardt, M., & Negri, A. (2004). *Multitude*. New York: Penguin.

Harvey, D. (2004). *The new imperialism*. Oxford: Oxford University Press.

Held, D. (2004). *Global covenant*. Cambridge: Polity.

Held, D., & Koenig-Archibugi, M. (Eds.). (2004). *American power in the 21st century*. Malden, MA: Polity.

Hombach, B. (2000). *The politics of the new centre*. Cambridge: Polity.

HSR (2005) 2005 Human Security Report. Oxford: Oxford University Press. Available Online: http://www.humansecurityreport.info/.

Ibbitson, J. (2005). Kudos to Canada for 'major breakthrough' at UN. *Globe and Mail*, 15 September, p. A4.

Ignatieff, M. (2000). *Virtual war: Kosovo and beyond*. Toronto: Penguin.

Ignatieff, M. (2003). *Empire lite*. Toronto: Penguin.

Ignatieff, M. (2004). *The lesser evil*. Toronto: Penguin.

Lauren, P. G. (1998). *The evolution of international human rights*. Philadelphia: University of Pennsylvania Press.

Magdoff, H. (2003). *Imperialism without colonies*. New York: Monthly Review Press.

Mandel, M. (2004). *How America gets away with murder*. London: Pluto Press.

Mandel, M. (2005). Making war illegal. *Ottawa Citizen*, 26 August, p. A15.

Mead, W. R. (2004). *Power, terror, peace, and war*. New York: Alfred A. Knopf.

Mead, W. R. (2000). *Special providence*. New York: Routledge.

Nasrallah, E. M. (2005). Hope for a new Arab world. *Ottawa Citizen*, 20 October, p. A19.

NSS (2002)) *National Security Strategy of the United States of America*, September 2002. www.whitehouse.gov, pp. 17–18.

Negri, A. (2002). Folly of our masters of the universe." *Guardian*, 18 December. Cited from A. Callinicos (2003). *The new mandarins of American power* (p. 101). Cambridge: Polity.

O'Connor, A. O. (2001). *Poverty knowledge*. Princeton: Princeton University Press.

Said, E. (1978). *Orientalism*. New York: Vintage.

Scowen, P. (2003). *Rogue nation: The America the rest of the world knows*. Toronto: M & S.

Sen, A. K. (2003). *Development as freedom*. Paris: O, Jacob.

Teeple, G. (1995). *Globalization and the decline of social reform*. Toronto: Garamond.

Teeple, G. (2005). *The riddle of human rights*. Amherst, NY: Humanity Books.

Woodward, B. (1994). *The agenda*. New York: Simon and Schuster.

FOURTEEN

Citizenship and its Exclusions

The Impact of Legal Definitions
on Metis People(s) of Canada

Cora Weber-Pillwax

INTRODUCTION

IN THIS CHAPTER I will speak to some experiences that are shared by many Metis people across Canada. However, I will contextualize this discussion through a story describing the experiences of a family living on a Metis Settlement in Alberta. The use of pseudonyms and the creation of a composite narrative based on a number of actual incidents and situations will protect the identities of real persons and real groups and communities. While they are not necessarily representative of Metis life in general, these experiences do display certain characteristics that are common and recognizable to other Metis people, no matter where they live within the geographical boundaries of Canada. Members of this particular family have been denied the rights to citizenship, as this concept is commonly understood. Since citizenship as a theoretical area is not my field of academic focus, I will frame this discussion around the basic description of the four components of citizenship as outlined by Darren J. O'Byrne in *The Dimensions of Global Citizenship: Political Identity Beyond the Nation-state* (2003).

In sharing the story of the Lajimodiere family as the foundation of my discussion, I am relying heavily on shared personal stories (Clarisse and Jeremy Lajimodiere and their mother, Dorothy Lajimodiere), some basic theory from O'Byrne, my own knowledge of the legal and social histories of

Metis people in Alberta and, probably most importantly, my own common sense in synthesizing these sources of information in what I hope is a respectful manner.

DEFINITIONS OF CITIZENSHIP

Citizenship is a word that is popularly used. Its meanings, however, apply not only in political contexts but in everyday experiences. This likely explains why most people will confidently use the term with a very personal and individual definition or understanding of that term and its application. According to O'Byrne, the discourse of citizenship has a long history, going back to the Greek philosophers who saw it as "the active realization of the ideal community" (p. 3). In a general sense, most people would agree with O'Bryne that "[c]itizenship is generally understood as a form of belonging: but a specific form of belonging, reliant upon certain rights and duties which betray its contractarian assumptions" (p. 2). Another element present in Canadian versions of "citizenship" is an implied direct relationship between the individual and the state, a relationship that implies particularly the political involvement that is seen as central to citizenship. The four components of citizenship, then, that are perceived as essential to O'Byrne are: membership, rights, duties, and participation.

Membership becomes the driving question, as citizenship is understood to imply citizenship *of* some entity, usually some bounded territory or nation-state. Significant questions related to membership are: "Who determines membership?" and, "How is such membership described, denied, or terminated?" O'Byrne cites Hall and Held (1989) in stating that "the politics of citizenship emerge essentially over inclusion and exclusion." Inclusion and exclusion factors have been the primary concern of indigenous social and political notions of citizenship for hundreds of years. In the early years of indigenous peoples' subjugation under Europe-as-colonizer and then under the new Dominion of Canada, citizenship was not extended to any peoples except Europeans and their recognized descendants. The politics of identity and identification emerged more forcefully, demanding formal political and social address, with increasing numbers of offspring from the marriages/unions of European men and First Nations women. These marriages were so common and widespread that by the 1700s, the descendants were numerous enough that they were choosing to intermarry amongst their own and a new and distinct people were being born.

This chapter will focus on the contemporary lives of individuals who self-identify as members of the Metis people of Canada, the people identified by anthropologists such as Jennifer Brown as the "new" people of the 1700s. Membership within the group known as *Metis* has been a highly contested area in the last decade. The reasons for this are complex, tied to historical state actions as well as social events enacted by the Metis themselves.

Within O'Byrne, rights are described as the three types cited by Marshall (1950):

- Civil rights that are necessary for individual freedom/liberty—of person, of speech, thought, and faith, to justice provided by the legal system
- Political rights that support the right to participate in election of a governing body, allowed for by the democratic system
- Social rights that include the rights to welfare, education, health, security, and well-being as a member of a civil state

Generally, however, the rights of citizenship have been seen as arbitrary and fluid, leading to ongoing debate as to how these are to be defined and/or determined. Agreement has rested on the state-assigned nature of civil liberties, and this characteristic is seen clearly in the Canadian Charter of Rights and Freedoms (1982), where Section 1 addresses the "reasonable limits" on citizens' individual rights and freedoms.

The rights and freedoms of Aboriginal peoples of Canada are recognized in both Sections 25 and 35 of the Constitution Act, 1982. Section 25 of the Constitution Act says that the guarantee shall not be construed to abrogate or derogate from any Aboriginal, treaty, or other rights or freedoms, whether these derive from the Proclamation of October 7, 1763, or through land claims agreements or treaties. Section 1 exceptions to this rule do not apply to Aboriginal rights as these may be defined pursuant to Section 35 of the Canadian Constitution. These sections (25 and 35 of the constitution) are in place as a direct outcome of signed treaties/agreements where Aboriginal peoples gave up their lands to the state in exchange for certain types of protections and services, such as protection and maintenance of languages and cultures, education, and health services.

Duties of citizenship can be a fairly large and unresolved issue in indigenous communities. Personal dialogue and discussions with Aboriginal community members over many years have shown that many people do not feel any sense of duty to the state at all. There is almost invariably, however, a sense of duty, including loyalty and commitment, to the community or the people of which the one is a member. What I have observed in many years of educational involvement with northern Aboriginal communities is that most of the people do not have any sense of citizenship as it is commonly stressed in relation to the state. On the First Nation reserves, as late as 1982/83, many people had never had occasion to consider meaningful participation in an election system in their communities. The opportunity for "Indian" participation in election of school board trustees was new to the people, for example, and they did not trust that this opportunity would not negatively impact their treaty rights. Considering that the treaties had been federally administered since the 1800s and that education had been seen as a federal responsibility tied to the treaties, Aboriginal community apprehensions about the long-term outcomes and impacts of newly introduced election processes were reasonable.

The significance of democratic election processes as elements of citizenship remains largely outside the experiences of many First Nations persons, excepting in the instance of election of a chief and council where these processes often do not reflect notions of citizenship and democracy as Canadian society describes these. These election processes themselves are not always perceived as citizens' participation for purposes of forming representative government. They are more often perceived as opportunities for individuals to get together in support of a family member in the acquisition of power and status. In my observations and experience, most Metis and First Nations persons will not openly discuss their personal views of democracy and citizenship as these relate to the forms of "approved" and "legislated" self-government that guides the development in their own communities. The reason for this, I suggest, is that these concepts or notions of "democracy" and "citizenship" are so far removed from the lived reality of Aboriginal existence that they are, in truth, only abstract notions, having little or nothing to do with daily experiences and Aboriginal lives.

It is of note that many First Nations people have made public statements and take strong political positions that they are not citizens of Canada, but only of their own respective nations. This position is not often verbalized or opened for discussion.

LEGAL IDENTITIES OF METIS PEOPLE(S)

Until the Supreme Court ruling in *Powley* (2004), there was no mention of Metis as peoples in any context; the term *Metis* was understood to refer to a people, and Metis were seen as one nation, or one people. In *Powley*, the Court ruled that Metis individual hunting rights are connected to and must be tied to a traditional Metis community. This meant that thereafter, the identification of Metis as peoples rather than as one people might become another factor underlying the identity and membership issues that surround the determination of Metis citizenship in Canada.

With some exceptions, most Metis hold the view that they are citizens of Canada. To many Metis, Louis Riel continues to be honored as the most loyal of citizens to his country, Canada. With his leadership as a model, these people feel a strong commitment to the well-being of this country and these lands. This perspective is consistent with another common claim that Metis are the original citizens of Canada and in fact are the only indigenous peoples who have sprung from this land and belong to no other land.

Having made these perhaps contentious statements, I will move now into a story that exemplifies how legal definitions of identity and citizenship have plagued Metis lives for centuries. The foregoing commentary about First

Nations peoples or "Indians" has been necessary in order to contextualize the experiences of the Lajimodiere family, the subjects of this story. As is true for all Metis, our lives are not separate from the lives of our First Nations relatives. Within these blood connections lie the shared suffering and the shared respect for different interpretations of similar experiences. The political maneuvering of the state in its nation-building agenda has not robbed the Metis of their claim to citizenship as they choose to define it, nor has it in any way dissuaded them from continuing to assert their own identities and ways of relating to one another and to others.

BACKGROUND

Metis elders will talk about the human need for a sense of "belonging." From the stories about their experiences in the political struggles of the Metis people in northern Alberta and especially of those people on the Metis Settlements, I have always understood this sense of belonging as that force that underlays or motivates the struggle for land and self-determination by all Aboriginal peoples, and, particularly in this case, by the Metis.

I was born and raised a "halfbreed" and much later realized that the other identifying label that could be applied to my family and me was "Metis." We were, after all, descendants of the Michif of the Northwestern Territories and of the "halfbreeds" who had to choose to identify as White or Indian in the eastern United States. All of this genealogical information was gathered long after I was an adult and I am still finding information that helps me to understand how my people were scattered across the continent and made homeless because their notions and practices of citizenship were not in line with those of the state. The Michif, like their cousins the Cree, believed that the land would provide for all of their needs if it was respected. The people lived in ways that respected the land and the animals that were taken off the land for sustenance of their families and communities. When the European settlers came and wanted the lands where they had always lived, the Michif fought for their rights and freedoms as good citizens of their own homeland. Their story forms a familiar part of the history of western Canada, but it is rarely told from the perspective of the Metis citizenry of the day. The story has not changed much.

There are eight Metis Settlements in Northern Alberta. These were lands set aside for Metis people in the early 1930s through the Metis Betterment Act, pursuant to the report of the MacEwan Commission on the welfare of the halfbreed population. Following the establishment of the Metis colonies, as they were called then, Metis lives were controlled in the same manner as those of the Indians who lived on reserves. Where the Indian agent controlled almost every aspect of Indian life on reserve lands, the colony supervisor controlled the lives of the Metis on the colony lands. An individual did not come and go off the land (or out of the community) without a written pass approved by the supervisor. This system of social control was in place until the mid-1970s.

In the mid-1980s, the provincial government moved to negotiate an out-of-court settlement on a lawsuit initiated by the Federation of Metis Settlements re: Metis ownership of natural resources on Settlement lands. After a long struggle during which Settlements memberships were split for and against the proposed accord, the people voted through referendum in 1989 to accept a form of self-government that offered a modified form of municipal powers and gave up all claims to the natural resources that represented the only certain economic base for the future of themselves and their communities. Membership ambiguities that existed before the accord led to uncertainty with respect to the "citizenship" right of Settlement members to vote in the referendum. The problem of membership ambiguities persists and becomes evident in issues related to the civil, political, and social rights of citizenship on Metis Settlements, notwithstanding that recent changes to the legislation delegate authority to Settlement Councils to grant membership not only to Metis, but also to Inuit and Indian persons as well. This membership by implication includes the citizenship right to vote in the election of a governing body, the civil rights to freedom of speech, thought, and justice, and the social rights that encompass or address the members' security and well-being.

Metis opposition to the accord in the late 1980s was based primarily on the struggle to ensure the right of the people to know and understand what they were being asked to vote upon. The demand was that the negotiation process be guided by the principle and practice of informed consent. Many of the Metis could not read and/or could not understand the legal and formal language that was used in the documents being circulated. Where lay versions of the documents had been written, these were generally inaccurate and not representative of the full content and implications of the originals. The community meetings were dominated by lawyers and government consultants who relied on prepared responses that maintained oppositions within the Metis citizenry, the intended beneficiaries, collectively, of the proposed accord. Information and accessibility to information would likely have led to open dialogue, direct explanations, and responsive clarifications, all of which would have eliminated many of the subsequent issues that continue to tear apart the Metis Settlement communities. To an insider involved in the situation, it was obvious that direct and open dialogue or explanations could not be provided because if the people had understood fully or even minimally the significant aspects of the proposed agreement, the accord would never have been supported to the extent that it was. While facing threats of various types, as well as being uninformed and misinformed, the people voted.

Two years later, a majority of the Settlement members voted against the Charlottetown Accord, which would have entrenched that same provincial legislation, the Alberta-Metis Settlements Accord, into the Constitution of Canada. Did the provincial government notice that the same people who voted in favor of the Accord now voted against its entrenchment in the Constitution of Canada? Did the government understand that statement? Because the Charlottetown Accord failed, the province has not fulfilled its promise that the provincial accord legislation would be entrenched in the Constitution of Canada and thereby guarantee ownership of the land to the General Council on behalf of all Metis in Alberta. The significance of this point lies in the fact that this promise of protection of the land through entrenchment in the Constitution of Canada was the most compelling argument used to "sell" the accord to the Settlement people. This argument was convincing in that the Metis people on the settlement lands had in their history watched helplessly as four of the twelve original colonies had been taken away from them by the "stroke of a pen"—a provincial minister's pen. The "stroke of a pen" expression was used on multiple occasions as a threat to the people, suggesting that if they did not support the accord, they stood in danger of losing the remaining settlement lands through the subsequent wielding of that dreadful pen.

So how has the history of this period of conflict in Metis life in Alberta been recorded? The book that was contracted as a record of the process was written by a lawyer who had worked for the government law firm involved directly in the negotiation of the accord. The actions of the provincial government and the federal government throughout this whole process were consistent with that of a conquering nation but not consistent with a country that claims to hold to the principles of a Charter of Rights and Freedoms for its citizenry.

The description of this negotiation process for Settlement Metis self-government shows clearly that the people's notion of citizenship as socially constructed was not considered in the state operationalization of its own definition of citizenship as a part of a nation-building agenda. For the Metis in this situation, the concept of self-determination as a right of citizenship—Aboriginal citizenship—has been over the past decade reframed or translated into the language and policies of Aboriginal "self-government" as described by the state. The adoption of such terminology to describe the accord outcomes has serious legal implications for Metis claims to Aboriginal rights and entitlements in the future, yet these are not being discussed with the people who are and will be most directly affected.

THE STORY

I have heard "Metis" referred to as "bois brule." This refers to the growth that comes after a fire has gone through an area of land. The elder used the word *scourge*, saying that after the scourge had destroyed everything, the new growth came. "These," he said, "were the Metis as described by the Cree people." He also said that the Metis were or embodied the first treaty, signed by their DNA. This was a powerful description of people who have often been described in words such as "halfbreed" or "quarterbreed," like cattle or livestock. Another fairly derogatory translation of the Cree term for Metis—*Apihtogosan*—is "half-a-person." An elder explained to me that, in fact, the term *Apihto-ni-go-sisan* means "half my son/daughter," referring to the name used by the old people when they talked about the Metis sons and daughters that were born to them. How beautiful that explanation would have been in the past to a young person who was being ridiculed and called "mongrel" because his/her bloodline was being called into question by European notions of blood "purity." How beautiful it is today to us when our children continue to be called "mongrels" and our young married women "country wives." The shame is often misdirected, it is true, from those who perform actions of shame toward those who are the victims of those shameful acts.

The grandfather of the Lajimodiere family was born in Lac la Biche, one of the main centers of Metis settlement in the late 1700s and early 1800s. He traveled and settled in the area of St. Albert where Lajimodiere, father of Clarisse and Jeremy, was born. Joseph eventually married Dorothy Jacobs, an Indian woman of a small reserve in northern Alberta. When Dorothy married Joseph, a Metis man, she lost her rights of treaty and her status as an Indian. She was forced to leave her home community, and was no longer recognized as a member of the community where she had grown up. The family established residence as close to the reserve boundaries as possible so as to maintain continued access and connections with immediate and extended family living on the reserve. At that time, "outsiders'" access to the reserve was obtained primarily through permission of the Indian agent. Dorothy eventually moved with her husband and family to one of the large lakeside Metis communities in Alberta.

In the early 1950s, again the family moved. This time they moved to one of the Metis Settlements, planning to settle down and build a life of self-sufficiency and independence on the land. The father had been recruited, because of the low membership on the land and the supervisor's threat to the people that they stood very close to losing their rights to the Settlement lands. The family's arrival into the community assisted in the preservation of Metis interests in the lands of the colony/Settlement and prevented the dissolution and loss of the land through provincial government actions, actions that had already happened to four other Metis colonies/Settlements.

In the mid-seventies, the Settlement was again threatened with closure or dissolution. Jeremy Lajimodiere went to the provincial government and petitioned on the basis that the membership count was low for the Metis Settlement because the women had not been counted. Jeremy took in the new counts that included the women of the community. Prior to this, the practice of registering women as members and property holders had been actively discouraged and even disallowed by the Settlement supervisor. The formal registration of the women meant that their rights as citizens of the colony and their inclusion in Settlement affairs could now be openly recognized. This action on behalf of Metis women supported the collective interests of the Settlement, yet neither the significance of such action for the advancement of Metis women nor for the betterment of the Settlements has been recorded in the histories of the Settlements. They are carried in the oral histories of the people and their significance generally remains uninterpreted.

In the late 1900s, as part of the executive of the Federation of Metis Settlements, Jeremy Lajimodiere had been elected to protect the interests of the eight Settlements. The federation established one voice to negotiate with the government and industry for the benefit of the Metis people on every Settlement. The people had realized that they were being played off against one another in the development and implementation of government policies and practices. They saw that they needed to sit together as one organized body in order to be strong and to be heard and heeded in action. It was from this federated body that a lawsuit was initiated against the provincial government when the Settlements discovered that resource funds had not been going into their Settlements account as had been directed by the Metis Betterment Act. The lawsuit was initiated to bring back to the Settlements those funds that had accrued from the harvesting and development of natural resources on Settlement lands. The complexities of this litigation have been discussed in depth by legal scholars and are certainly beyond the scope of this chapter. It is mentioned here only to contextualize and describe the type of relationships that Jeremy Lajimodiere has maintained historically with the Settlement and governance structures of his community.

In 1985, the Federal government enacted Bill C-31. Through this amendment (Bill C-31), Canada's Indian Act was brought into accord with the provisions of the Canadian Charter of Rights and Freedoms (1982), assuring equal treatment to men and women. The effects of C-31 are at present the subject of several inquiries, examining the problems created on Indian reserves because of the increase in population as Bill C-31 Indians returned or attempted to return to "their" home reserves, the threat C-31 membership poses to band sovereignty, and the limitations of funds, land, housing, and other resources to support "new" memberships on the reserves.

The amendment brought about by Bill C-31 permitted the reinstatment of women and children as Indian band members if they had lost status because of sexual discrimination. Dorothy Jacobs, the mother of Clarisse and Jeremy Lajimodiere, had married Joseph Lajimodiere, a non-Indian person, and had thus lost her status as an Indian band member. Under Bill C-31, Dorothy and several of her children did seek reinstatement as status "Indians" under the Indian Act. In the case of Jeremy Lajimodiere, he made application to be registered as an Indian under the Indian Act just prior to the final reading of the Alberta-Metis Settlements Accord legislation and his application was dealt with after the accord legislation was passed as Alberta legislation in 1990.

This legislation granted authority to each of the eight Settlement Councils to recommend removal of membership from any Metis Settlement member whom they believed to be registered under the Indian Act. A list of names of the Lajimodiere family, including Dorothy, Jeremy, and Clarisse, was submitted by the Settlement Council to the provincial minister responsible for the Settlements with a recommendation for removal of membership. When the minister did not act on the recommendation, the case was taken to trial and several members of the family had their memberships removed by order of the provincial courts.

Jeremy Lajimodiere was one of the brothers who had his membership removed through the actions of the Settlement Council. Following that decision of the courts and follow-up actions by the Settlement Council, water services were cut off to his house and he could no longer access community supports and services that were normally available to other community members. Basic services were not denied to Dorothy Lajimodiere nor to any one of Jeremy's siblings despite their own losses of membership. Why was Jeremy singled out for this type of alienating treatment?

A matriarch of her community and her extended family, Dorothy Lajimodiere suffered social stigma and alienation from community members with whom she had formed and maintained relationships over decades. She also lived through extreme psychological distress caused by rejection from Settlement Council supporters. She continues to live in the community despite ongoing tensions caused by the definitions and labels associated with citizenship and membership dictates of the state.

Clarisse Lajimodiere talked about her own problems with self-identification as a Metis. She cannot identify any longer as a Metis. There has been too much pain and suffering caused by the actions of the Metis Settlements General Council and the Minister of Aboriginal Affairs. She has watched her family being destroyed by the provincial legislation and by the Settlement Council, which has acted with discrimination against her family. She noted that other persons who are registered as "Indians" continue to reside on Metis Settlement lands with full membership, and rights of such membership being granted by the Settlement Council, the same council that had recommended removal of membership and rights from several of her own family.

Clarisse described injustice in her family's situation. She shared how two brothers registered as "Indians" under Bill C-31—one because he could not afford his medications for diabetes and another who was being sued and threatened with jail because he could not pay his Alberta Health Care premiums. Her view was clear that basic human needs should not be used to constitute reasons for using legal and political authority to remove all rights to citizenship, community membership, and personal identity. Today, in the Lajimodiere community, there are several brothers and sisters who live on the Settlement where they have lived all or most of their lives. However, these siblings no longer have the rights of citizenship to participate in decision making that affects and impacts on their lives. They do not have the right to vote for their choice of a representative in any form of local government. Although they are Indians by virtue of their formal and legal connections through treaty with the Wabasca Lake Cree First Nation, they have not applied to vote at the First Nations reserve because that is not their social community. In at least one respect, they have no citizenship status anywhere.

Clarisse has seen the pain of her mother as she was rejected and put out of her home community twice in her one lifetime. When Dorothy was a young woman and married outside the "Indian" membership of Sucker Creek, she was ordered off her own home territory. Now she is in her nineties, and after living in her Metis community for more than fifty years, she is again facing the threat of being legally ordered off her home property where she and her husband raised their family and from the community where her husband and other family members are now buried. Clarisse has watched and shared the pain of her family. She knows that she cannot identify herself as she has known herself to be for all of her life.

Her assessment is simple: government legislation has split families through legal identification mechanisms and this has resulted in intense suffering as well as ongoing undermining of basic Metis family structures and personal and familial well-being. Jeremy's personal views were and are somewhat different from those of Clarisse. He also very clearly expressed that he has been Metis all of his life and he remains Metis. No legislation will change that. Further, he described himself with clarity as a Metis and member of the Settlement based on the fact that he and his family saved the community from dissolution twice in his lifetime. He stated that he would fight for his right to be who he is, despite the legislation that has tried through legal means to rob him of his identity. In the meantime, he lives with the reality that his membership and some elements of his identity have been legally removed by the Settlement Council with the result that he cannot attend political meetings and express his opinions or participate in decision making that affects his life and the life of his family.

CONCLUSION

Acknowledgments have to be extended to the persons who shared these significant aspects of their lives. The case raises some serious questions about citizenship in Alberta and Canada, especially in relation to Metis people on Settlements. The relevant legislation with respect to Metis Settlements in

Alberta is constructed in such a manner that Settlement member opposition to local political positions and/or councils can lead to open and direct retaliation and severe personal injustice and property loss, with no accessible and financially feasible recourse to the courts or the provincial minister for assistance or resolution.

I believe that it is the design of the legislation that permits the minister to ignore situations where provincially delegated authority contributes significantly to the denial of basic rights of citizenship at the local levels of governance. Under present legislation, Settlement Councils have the delegated authority to either enforce and support or undermine and destroy the concepts associated with citizenship rights. Of most serious consequence is that the legislation directly and indirectly impacts upon and contributes to the destruction of Metis individuals, families, and communities. At the same time, critical scrutiny and analysis of the legislation reveals that its design benefits the provincial and federal governments in their control and unchallenged claims to natural resources on Metis Settlement lands. The intricate web of legislation, both provincial and federal, has initiated in many ways and continues to maintain in the Metis communities insidious paralysis and genocidal processes that advantage the state in its consistent refusal to acknowledge the outstanding rights and entitlements of Metis as Aboriginal peoples. This state positioning almost guarantees that the civil, political, and social rights of citizenship for Metis people will likely remain at the level of rhetoric and discussion on state planning agendas.

As long as Metis people must struggle for survival as individuals and families with distinct identities and ways of being, we cannot engage in the struggles that are necessary for political justice and the establishment of our rights of citizenship even in our own communities. We can only hold the ideals in our hearts and look in shame at the beauty of our country, Canada.

REFERENCES

O'Byrne, D. J. (2003). *The dimensions of global citizenship: Political identity beyond the nation-state*. London & Portland, OR: Frank Gass.

R. v. Powley [2003] 2 S.C.R. 207 (S.C.C.).

Charter of Rights and Freedoms, Part I of the *Constitution Act, 1982*, Schedule B to the *Canada Act, 1982* (U.K.) 1982, c.11.

Constitution Act of Canada 1982, Schedule B to the *Canada Act 1982* (U.K.) 1982, c. 11.

FIFTEEN

An Introduction to Librarianship
for Human Rights

Toni Samek

Even in Canada, a free country by world standards, books and
magazines are banned at the border. Books are removed from the
shelves in Canadian libraries, schools, and bookstores everyday.
Free speech on the Internet is under attack.
—Book and Periodical Council, 2004

—Where they have burned books, they will end in burning
human beings.
—Heinrich Heine

THE MAIN INTENTION of this chapter is for students, educators, administrators, policymakers, and stakeholders in education to consider reconceptu-
alizing their understanding of librarians in schools and in society. Library and
information studies communities can also benefit, for example, by being open
to such topics as inquiry-based learning, democratic education, curriculum
reform, the politics of the textbook, and human rights education. The message is simple: the partnership of educators and librarians is a fundamental
step in the path toward the development of education for human rights and
global citizenship.

Alberta Learning is currently promoting inquiry-based learning, "a
process where students are involved in their learning, formulate questions,
investigate widely and then build new understandings, meanings and knowledge. That knowledge is new to the students and may be used to answer a

question, to develop a solution or to support a position or point of view. The knowledge is usually presented to others and may result in some sort of action" (Branch & Oberg, 2004, p. 1). The benefits to students, community, and society are numerous, including: treatment of authentic (real-life) problems within the context of the curriculum and/or community; promotion of student curiosity; active use and interpretation of data and information; teacher-students/teacher-librarian collaboration; connection of community and society with learning; and student ownership of learning (Branch & Oberg, 2004, p. 4). Furthermore, these benefits support UNESCO's Human Rights Education Program (1945–), which identifies the following conditions (UNESCO, 2004): teacher-student society connections; advocacy; meaningful authentic learning experiences; engagement of students in knowledge construction; instructional accommodations to social transformations; access to education; quality education that addresses cultural diversity, multilingualism, intercultural understanding and exchange; curriculum reform; democratic school management; and community involvement.

However, as is the case with human rights, inquiry-based learning is difficult to achieve for a variety of reasons. For example, it requires: articulated administrative vision; commitment despite competing pressures; champions; resources and space; teacher collaboration (teacher-librarian cooperation); teacher (librarian), student, parent trust; small interdisciplinary teams; and intrinsic value for problem solving throughout the school/school system. In other words, "success with inquiry-based learning often requires a change in school culture [and the role of the library therein]" (Branch & Oberg, 2004, p. 2). Furthermore, it is difficult to imagine how teachers can effectively build a culture of inquiry without embracing some of the basic tenets promoted by the library community, such as access to information and intellectual freedom. Vice versa, the efforts of teacher librarians and school library media specialists (and ultimately librarians in general) are at risk of being stymied within school culture, without broad teacher support for critical inquiry–based learning.

Christine Hopkins (2005) refers to this two-way street as "mutual political advocacy." In an e-mail posting to a progressive librarians listserv under the subject line "Librarians & Teachers?" Hopkins wrote: "Teachers' unions, we all know, are extraordinarily powerful organizations with real political clout. Isn't there some way librarians can get more connected with teachers' unions and educate teachers to refer students to libraries and librarians and come out to support library bonds and staffing, etc. Couldn't there be some kind of quid pro quo of mutual political advocacy?" The answer is yes!

The theory and practice of intellectual freedom are essential underpinnings of critical inquiry and informed citizenship, both important goals of our education system. However, our teachers are hard-hit by related sensitive social issues, such as book challenges, Internet access and child protection, principles of intellectual freedom in the aftermath of terrorist attacks, the impact of cutting teacher-librarians, and working with community leaders to deal with concerns about school resources. English language arts teachers are the hardest-hit of our educators for a number of reasons: (1) the resources and curriculum they use are challenged regularly, (2) the intellectual works they choose are subject to broad interpretation, (3) the students they teach represent every level and age group, and (4) they are rapidly losing their best professional consultants on intellectual freedom issues—teacher-librarians. (Alberta currently employs only about seventy professional teacher-librarians, down from approximately five hundred.)

In a nation where such cuts to our school systems have reached the point of national crisis, there exists a very real threat to intellectual freedom and cultural democracy. For this reason alone, teachers and librarians need to support one another all the more. Teachers need the library community's help with school policy, curriculum, resources, community relations, and media response in the context of sensitive community climates. And for the kids who will grow up (we hope) to vote and participate in civic engagement, teachers and librarians need to come together to ask such questions as: What happens to intellectual freedom in an era of intense privatization and heightened legalistic atmospheres? What happens to the public's "right to know" in the context of society's competing political, economic, and ideological agendas? What happens to the notion of informed citizenry when informed consent is dubious? These questions are not indicative of safe professional ground for any of us. Within librarianship, for example, 2004/2005 Canadian Library Association (CLA) President Stephen Abram (2004) recently described information professionals as "subversives" (p. 173).

This activist interpretation of the librarian in society is rooted in what preeminent American library activist E. J. Josey calls *positive aggression*. So while librarianship is often stereotyped as a quiet feminized profession, it is, in essence, an outspoken vehicle for principled engagement—and at times, positive troublemaking. In this view, librarians self-identify as activists, freedom fighters, agents of democracy, watchdogs of government, providers of space and place for the public sphere, promoters of authentic opinion and the right to know, educators for literacy (in all its forms), advocates of cultural democracy, facilitators of active transparency (information meeting you fully at the time of need), preservers of cultural and civic identities, providers of access from all points of view, and, at the core, supporters of human rights including the rights of the child and the girl-child. For example:

> Libraries have emerged in different forms over the course of human history, yet their significance has never been more strongly felt than in the last twenty years with the increased central role of information technology and the explosive growth of the Internet. As a result, many individuals feel lost and misguided among what seems to be a ceaseless flow of

information, resulting in a social demand for librarians and information professionals. These professionals service the public by demonstrating the proper usages for information technology, providing order to the array of informational media, and accepting the responsibility of cultural preservation that the library traditionally maintains. By fulfilling these duties, librarians and information professionals become "cultural warriors" capable of defending the professional integrity of the industry amid profiteers of information technology, while simultaneously creating cooperative efforts between the technological productions of technologists and the public service unique to librarianship. (Save Library and Information Studies, 2005)

Librarianship is a profession that, at its core, works in the "production, collection, interpretation, organization, preservation, storage, retrieval, dissemination, transformation and use of information," cultural records, recorded knowledge, and ideas (Capurro & Birger, 2003, p. 389). Intercultural information ethics prompts library workers to be mindful of unfettered cultural records for all peoples, ethical and related issues, and implications for social change and the development of human rights. It considers social and political development, cultural development, and economic development. In each aspect, there is contestation and threats to social justice, especially in the contexts of pluralism, heightened legalistic atmospheres, and competing political, economic, and ideological agendas. The Internet, for example, has great potential for resistance, counterdominance, and empowerment, but also serves as a powerful conveyor and perpetuator of flat culture, standardization, homogenization, consumption, colonialism, toxic trade, and perhaps most importantly deafening silence.

The international intercultural ethics community is largely committed to an optimistic vision for an Internet culture that is grounded in public sphere, authentic opinion, community, human welfare, and ultimately human development at the local level. It embraces intercultural information ethics as a tool for bringing to light value choices in the power struggle over human need versus profit. It views cultural distinctiveness as a priceless foundation for a so-called knowledge society.

The direct implication for teachers (and librarians) is to be extra mindful, in general, of the contexts (e.g., historical, epistemological, political, social, ideological, legal, economic) of information and resources used both formally and informally, both consciously and unconsciously, in schools. Examples of current related issues that impact the daily work of educators (and librarians) include monopolies in educational publishing, family values and community standards, pressure groups, systemic racism, censorship, freedom of expression on professional and policy issues, and imposed technology in schools. Emergent issues in the latter category include the experimental imposed student wearing of radio frequency ID. A February 22, 2005, *L.A. Times* article reported that in the Northern California farm town of Sutter (population 2,885)

> every student at Brittan Elementary School had to wear a badge the size of an index card with their name, grade, photo—and a tiny radio identification tag. The purpose was to test a new high-tech attendance system. . . . Known as radio frequency identification, RFID for short, the technology has been around for decades. But only lately have big markets blossomed. Radio identification has been embraced by manufacturers and retailers to track inventory, deployed on bridges to automatically collect tolls and used on ranches to cull cattle. The microchips have been injected into pets. But applying that technology in conjunction with people prompts an outcry from civil libertarians and privacy advocates. Proposals to use the high-tech ID tags in U.S. passports, Virginia driver's licenses and even San Francisco library books have drawn sharp fire. . . . (Lubow, 2005)

A library spin on the same technology reported in a March 22, 2005, *Berkeley Daily Planet* article stated:

> Facing growing anger from residents and librarians over plans to lay off workers and implement tracking devices on materials, the Berkeley Public Library Board of Trustees has selected a veteran of local political battles to join its ranks. If approved by the City Council Tuesday, Ying Lee, 73, . . . Lee said she is opposed to the board's decision last year to install radio frequency identification devices (RFIDs) on the library's 500,000 volume collection. RFIDs are expected to make checkout more efficient, but opponents fear that they could be used by government authorities to track patrons. (Rosenzweig, 2005)

Ideologically, the intercultural information ethics community finds strong support in self-identified activist segments of the library community who share a special commitment to the protection of civil liberties and civic identities. But even in less activist contexts, such as basic library advocacy, from the umbrella organization, the International Federation of Library Associations and Institutions (IFLA), down to national, provincial/state, and local associations around the world, library rhetoric and policy on intellectual freedom recognizes the inherent relationship between human rights and freedom of expression. This powerful connection is embedded in Article 19 of the *United Nations Declaration of Human Rights* (1948), which states: "Everyone has the right to freedom of opinion and expression; this right includes freedom to hold opinions without interference and to seek, receive and impart information and ideas through any media and regardless of frontiers."

Building on this, by virtue of contemporary library core values (Access, Confidentiality/Privacy, Democracy, Diversity, Education and Lifelong

Learning, Intellectual Freedom, Preservation, The Public Good, Professionalism, Service, Social Responsibility [American Library Association, 2004]),
it is librarianship's responsibility to contribute critically to the global discourse of information ethics, as it pertains to the following articles of the *Universal Declaration of Human Rights* of particular relevance to information
work: respect for the dignity of human beings (Art. 1); confidentiality (Art.
1, 2, 3, 6); equality of opportunity (Art. 2, 7); privacy (Art. 3, 12); right to
freedom of opinion and expression (Art. 19); right to participate in the cultural life of the community (Art. 27); and right to the protection of the moral
and material interests concerning any scientific, literary, or artistic production (Art. 27) (International Center for Information Ethics, 2005). This
emphasis reinforces UNESCO's (2004) statement on *Human Rights Research*,
which emphasizes "the promotion and protection of economic, social and
cultural rights, especially the right to education, the right to take part in cultural life and the right to enjoy the benefits of scientific progress and its applications." In essence, it stresses "the indivisibility, interdependence, interrelation and equal importance of all human rights (civil, cultural, economic,
political and social)."

Issues of human rights violations have received increased attention in
the twenty-first century and the events of September 11, 2001, which "triggered the adoption of legislation, policies, and practices in the United States
and around the world, including Canada, the European Union, China, Russia and various African countries. The consequences of such initiatives are
relevant not only to individuals and institutions in those countries but have
broader and more far-reaching impacts as well. In particular, such legislation,
policies, and practices have tremendous implications for such issues as access
to information, privacy, civil liberties, and intellectual freedom" (Caidi,
2005). And in May 2005, the Council of Europe's Committee of Ministers
adopted the "first international framework declaration on human rights and
the rule of law in the Information Society. The Declaration updates the
principles of the European Convention on Human Rights for the cyber-age
and covers issues such as censorship, the protection of private information,
education on assessing information quality, media ethics, using IT for democratic purposes and freedom of assembly in cyberspace. It also considers
means of national and international cooperation by stakeholders such as
Internet Service Providers, hardware and software makers, governments and
society"(Declaration on Human Rights and Rule of Law in the Information
Society, 2005).

In check, in April 2005, a group of approximately sixty Canadian and
American library and information studies educators formed a special interest group (SIG) on information ethics for the Association for Library and
Information Science Education (ALISE). The idea behind the new SIG is
to give critical attention to ethical reflection in the context of library and

information studies education. At this point in ALISE's history, there is a strong interest in dedicating consistent formal space in the annual conference program and yearly activity to the subject of information ethics and related areas. The SIG's charter (approved at the April 14–15, 2005, ALISE board meeting) identifies as its charge to: (1) promote the study of information ethics in the LIS curriculum; (2) support pluralistic dialogue about ethical considerations both within the global library and information studies community and with partner communities (education, journalism, computer science—informatics, philosophy, law, management, and so on); and (3) serve as a clearinghouse for teaching, research, and service resources in information ethics.

In general, the SIG aims to promote ethical reflection on twenty-first-century information work to spark interest in and support of librarianship's responsibilities to the better attainment of human rights in the context of the knowledge society. In specific, it wants to promote pluralistic ethical reflection in library and information studies education with special emphasis on the following goals for ethics for information specialists, as outlined by the International Center for Information Ethics (2005): (1) to be able to recognize and articulate ethical conflicts in the information field; (2) to activate the sense of responsibility with regard to the consequences of individual and collective interactions in the information field; (3) to improve the qualification for intercultural dialogue on the basis of the recognition of different kinds of information cultures and values; and (4) to provide basic knowledge about ethical theories and concepts and about their relevance in everyday information work.

To complicate matters, while the subject of library ethics is on the rise, most librarians around the world are engaged in work that carries no sanctions when professional ethics are violated. A recent study by Pnina Shachaf (2005) indicates that only three places (Portugal, Sri Lanka, and the UK) have formal sanctions on their books for librarians who violate their code of professional ethics. In the U.S. context, Shirley Wiegand's legal analysis of the U.S. Library Bill of Rights bluntly concluded: "The ALA has no authority over library administrations" (Wiegand, 1996, p. 83). Thus, action, coalition, and alliance take special importance. As Martha Smith observed, "Although UNESCO seeks to influence members states, it does not exert governing or enforcement authority. Therefore persuasion and consensus building are its primary tools" (Smith, 2001, p. 534). Like UNESCO, IFLA is a leader, not an enforcer. Accordingly, in her opening address at the 2004 IFLA conference in Buenos Aires, IFLA President Kay Raseroka stated: "The first experiences of IFLA in worldwide advocacy, within the framework of the World Summit of the Information Society, have demonstrated the need and power of cooperation; with other international organizations, and amongst ourselves as national member associations. These are only the first steps to

influence governments to establish and maintain democratic information services, and to live up to the Universal Declaration of Human Rights"
(Raseroka, 2004, p. 2).

Persuasion and consensus building within librarianship are basic characteristics of the critical library movement (also known in North America as
progressive librarianship, activist librarianship, socially responsible librarianship, and radical librarianship). This international movement has a network
base in such nations as Africa, Argentina, Austria, Germany, Mexico, South
Africa, Sweden, the UK, and the United States. (It is emergent in Canada
through the online face of the Web site http://www.librarianactivist.org/,
which draws attention to school library issues.) The critical library movement dates back to the 1930s in the North American context, where it has
evolved hand-in-hand with the ethos of intellectual freedom. Since the
adoption of the original Library's Bill of Rights in 1938, this discourse gained
significant momentum in the late 1960s/early 1970s in the United States and
elsewhere in the 1980s. In the past fifteen years, the decentralized and mul-
tidirectional technology and communications infrastructure of the Internet
has greatly enhanced relationship building, grassroots democratic organizing,
and the development of "new citizenship groups" around the discourse and
practice of progressive librarianship (Friedland, 1996, p. 207). There is little
doubt that the critical library movement is building unprecedented momentum in the twenty-first century.

The newly minted August 28, 2004, manifesto Declaration from Buenos
Aires On Information, Documentation and Libraries recognizes that "information, knowledge, documentation, archives, and libraries are communal
cultural goods and resources. They are based upon and promoted by democratic values, such as: freedom, equality, and social justice, as well as tolerance,
respect, equity, solidarity, communities, society, and the dignity of individuals" (2004). Yet historically, it has been argued, marginalized populations,
such as indigenous peoples, women, oral communities, and political radicals
(i.e., "the least socially and politically favored" [Declaration from Buenos
Aires, 2004]) have not been represented by the world's cultural and civic
identities. In this critical view, cultural workers, such as educators, publishers, librarians, archivists, and documentalists have both consciously and
unconsciously participated in tasks and policy elaborations that have resulted
in concessions, absences, omissions, biases, negations (e.g., misrepresentation
of racialized and immigrant cultures), broken cultural protocols, and discon-
nects "between the way peoples are presented in mainstream" culture,
"including library materials" and the way people "present themselves and
their own culture" (IFRT, 2005).

These records are not (until very recently, in some cases) well apparent
in the cultural and literary canons, the subject headings of the Library of
Congress or the Dewey Decimal Classification systems (less so with the Uni-

versal Decimal Classification) (which critical library and information workers worldwide acknowledge continue to discriminate by "sex, race, ethnicity,
ideology, economic status, social class, disabilities, migration, sexual orientation, religion, and language" [Declaration from Buenos Aires, 2004]), the
mostly middle-class library systems worldwide that organize their collections
by these knowledge systems, the epistemological foundations of these knowledge systems, global information policies informed by the discourses of capital, community value/family value–based school curricula, propagandistic
textbooks of political regimes, or the ashes of cultural destruction brought
about by violence. Also important to consider are the "complicated and
sometimes conflictive relationships among nation, regime, recorded expression, and national bibliography. . . . Legal deposit, in particular, is shadowed
by historical overtones of state censorship and control. It's easy to combine
the goals of projecting a nation's collective memory with those of controlling
dissent" (Hazen, 2004, p. 4). For example:

> The PALIAct Stand: Progressive African Library & Information Activists'
> Group (PALIACT) "recognises the right to relevant information as a basic
> human right. This right must be enshrined in the constitution of all African
> Countries and be endorsed as an active programme by the African Union.
> The struggle for a relevant information service is intimately linked with the
> political struggles of the people for organising a society that ensures that
> material, social, cultural and political needs of the people are met. PALIAct
> believes that the opportunity for making fundamental changes created as a
> direct result of political victories in the early period of struggle for liberation
> was lost. The opportunity that history had brought to our doorsteps to pro-
> vide a people-orientated information service was lost. Instead of challeng-
> ing the very basis on which library and information services were built, we
> allowed ourselves to be manipulated into making merely quantitative
> changes in library services, but failed to make any qualitative changes. The
> classes who were served by the colonial library service continued to be
> served and the needs of working people who had always remained outside
> the remit of such services remained unmet. Their experiences, their cul-
> tures, their very language remained outside the walls of impressive library
> buildings. Thus the advantage gained in the early period of struggle for a
> society and an information system which served the needs of all its people
> was lost. The struggle for such an information service continues to date."
> (Durani, 2005)

The spirit of the PALIAct Stand reinforces the essence of the above-
mentioned UNESCO statement on Human Rights Research. It also begs the
startling question posed by Rafael Capurro: "What is information science
for?" (Capurro, 1992, p. 84). In his conclusion, Capurro warned: "An information economy that seeks to reduce 'information' to an exchange value

without taking into account the different 'forms of life' in which it is grounded is no less dangerous than a blind exploitation of nature. In designing tools, we are designing . . . ways of being. . . . Information science . . . must accomplish a self-reflection in a formal-interpretive as well as in a cultural-historical way. It has to resist the temptation to become a purely technical heuristics or a meta-discipline embracing ethics and politics" (Capurro, 1992, pp. 90–93). Shiraz Durani, for example, noted: "What librarians do—and don't do—is not merely an academic question. It affects our understanding of our natural and social environment, which, taken in its totality, affects our world outlook, affects what we think and what we do . . . British libraries are in danger of using a commercial version of a 'global library' much like McDonald restaurant outlets which serve the same product in every part of the world. While this approach may be a useful one in ensuring a standard level of service, and a useful model for maximizing profits for the McDonald chain, it is disastrous for libraries if they want to root themselves in their local communities. It is essential that a new model of needs-based library service is developed at policy level and implemented" (Durani, 2004, p. 1).

These emphatic words evoke the following questions as a subtext for this work. What are the implications (epistemological, institutional, societal, historical, political, economic, and legal) of forgotten, buried, and contaminated memories of individuals, societies, and institutions? Of a flattened cultural record that reflects standardization, generalization, and homogenization? How can opportunities provided by communications technologies, interconnectivity, and the global digital network be applied to improve upon discriminatory knowledge practices to make them for everybody, not just for some? To what extent can improved practices redress the failed promotion of cultural distinctiveness, cultural literacy, cultural democracy, and democratic education? How can people working in the information and communication technologies fields (and sharing the principle that knowledge and information access is free, open, and egalitarian for everybody [Declaration from Buenos Aires, 2004]) consciously improve knowledge practices to facilitate human rights conditions, such as: critical and free inquiry, freedom of expression, authentic opinion, free decision making, free dissent, the democratization of information and knowledge, and the prerequisite promotion of literacy (in all its forms)?

Strategies, of course, are both apparent and emergent. One concrete example is wikis. Like other forms of social software (e.g., e-mail, blogs or weblogs, social bookmarks, photo sharing, groups, taste sharing, instant messaging, instant relay chat, Internet forum, social networking, real time social networking, collaborative real-time editing, and even cc), wikis value communities (Good, Harder, & Binkley, 2005). The premier example, Wikipedia (an international project managed by volunteers, with the scope of creating a free encyclopedia), has the political goal "to pursue freedom over content and information." It "relies on the political principle to extend freedom" and to change society "by giving control over content to everyone." The political significance of the project is in its: large-scale collaboration; free content; internationalization; bridging of the global divide; removal of property and contract as the organizing principles of collaboration; and, ridding "of subjectivity by showing the discussion around an article and the way it constructs itself through time and the various contributions of Wikipedians" (Muela, 2005a). The basic design principles of wiki are: open, incremental, organic, mundane, universal, overt, unified, precise, tolerant, observable, and convergent. (Wikipedia, 2005). Smaller scale similarly styled projects (e.g., Latin America's Raecpedia, produced under the UNESCO umbrella) contribute to the rethinking of social problems (e.g., governance, sustainable development, women and gender, multicultural and multiethnic issues) from critical and pluralist perspectives in the context of global interconnectivity.

These new resources interplay with the growing international interest in open access and open content. For example, open access journals and open access online archives (for scientific and scholarly publications) that "can be read by anyone free of charge and without restrictions on the internet" (Muela, 2005b). Open access, it has been articulated, "is not just a protocol, but a philosophy of sharing and building an infrastructure of local and independent data and service providers" (Peters, 2005). Emergent technical and social strategies are carrying out some (or all) of the collaborative principles of the free software movement. The Web is a favorable open space for the development of "effective possibilities for collaboration and reciprocal enrichment, not only between the development teams and the users but between the users themselves, as well" (Navarro, 2004, p. 4). Web forums such as webBBS (or Weblogs) and newsgroups are "rich in the productive traffic of knowledge." In this exchange of experiences is invention, which, undoubtedly, contributes to technological development and new possibilities for software use. "But above all, it allows the constitution and broadcasting of know-how among users," and cyberspace "is the unlimited area where this fantastic collective intelligence is displayed" (Navarro, 2004, p. 4.). Furthermore, in hacker philosophy, work takes on the discussion of, and the development pattern for, free software as an "alternative model and quite different from" the development of traditional software (Navarro, 2004, p. 5). Even though hackers (and hacktivists) have a culture of individuals devoted to programming with passion, they also believe in a duty to share information and work (Navarro, 2004, p. 5).

But there are significant challenges in this open arena. These include: the European Union attempt to enforce the 1992 directive to tax libraries to lend books (Library and Intellectual Property Group, 2004), and the development of: standards for metadata, ontologies, annotation, and curation; middleware for data collection, sharing and integration; tools for data mining, visualization, analysis, modeling, and collaborative research (Capurro, 2005, May 18). Most importantly, Gustavo Navarro warns: "Outside the software's domain, open source projects remain relatively marginal and novel. Thus comes the question of how projects like [raecpedia] and Wikipedia will be maintained in the future. To what extent will the generosity that is inherent in the domain of these networks at present become wealth in the future?" (Navarro, 2004, p.7).

This prompts consideration of the librarian as "publisher" in addition to "facilitator" of access. Kevin Stranack voiced support for librarians to move into open access publishing, not merely "hosting and providing related support services" (Muela, 2005c). Pioneer feminist library publisher Celeste West identified and acted on this break from tradition as early as 1972, when she founded Booklegger Press, the first American women-owned library press in the United States Booklegger defined an alternative library culture that worried less about the library as a keeper of the cultural record, and more about the library as an active agent for change. "To counteract censorship by distribution of information," she noted, "is to move towards intellectual freedom."

The long-term success of the above-mentioned strategy depends upon the development and sustaining of virtual communities that support social change. For instance, the coalition and action of information ethics and global information justice groups worldwide via cyber-activism/Internet activism, electronic citizenship, e-democracy/digital democracy, and other new forms of social movement, civic engagement, and community building, which strive to accommodate social transformations and aim to harness knowledge to compel action rather than inaction. For example, the following WIPO Manifesto for Transparency, Participation, Balance and Access:

> Dear Colleague: The following open letter will be sent to WIPO, the World Intellectual Property Organization, calling for TRANSPARENCY, PARTICIPATION, BALANCE and ACCESS in its work. Prior to a large and ambitious publicity campaign, your sign-on to this letter is essential. WIPO is locking NGOs out of its negotiations, using tactics to isolate those governments who stand up for you, and hiding the evidence by deleting it from their website. The mentioned letter goes into great detail on this. If you are a computer programmer or politician; if you are ill, if you have an audio/visual or motor impairment, if you are a student, academic, information or knowledge worker, librarian, or citizen concerned about access to information and knowledge and the absence of balance between rightsholders and the public interest within developed countries and mainly in developing/least developed countries, please take a moment to read this and consider signing into it. (Muela, 2005d)

Our CLA Statement on Intellectual Freedom (1974–) directs that "[l]ibraries should resist all efforts to limit the exercise of [our] responsibilities while recognizing the right of criticism by individuals and groups." The phrase "should resist" implies an activist agenda in which the library is a point of resistance (Rosenzweig, 2002, p.1). It is here, for example, that librarians (in consultation with partners) can conceptualize and reconceptualize their core values, issues, alliances, and where and how they can take stands on policy development for issues that are, not incidentally, of serious concern to teachers. An ever-expanding set of issues reads like a catalogue: post 9/11 surveillance; library disaster relief; cultural destruction; hate speech; Internet access and child protection; pressures arising from family values and community standards; censorship; imposed technologies (e.g., RFIDs); public access to government information; privatization; self-censorship (or inside censorship); negative catalogue entries and descriptors; media conglomeration; the politics of public space; attacks on fair use copying; legislation; information rights; right to read anonymously; impermanent and restricted access to purchased electronic records; academic freedom; freedom of expression on professional and policy issues; systemic racism; international relations; biometrics; labor; outsourcing; bibliocide (or the de-accessioning of books); GATS and TRIPS; cutting of teacher librarian positions; intellectual property; serving the poor, homeless, and people living on fixed income; socially responsible investing; anonymity, privacy, and confidentiality; humane library space; human security; national security policies; the global tightening of information and border controls; transborder data flow; censorship powers of national customs departments; and so on.

In closing, Will Weaver (professor of English, Bemidji State University, Minnesota) (2005) recently posted the following to the ALA's Social Responsibilities Round Table (SRRT) listserv:

> The Bemidji, Minnesota, school board hearing on Plainsong was held last night. A packed house, a three hour meeting, lots of passionate testimony. It was a general victory for free access to reading, though with some loss: the book was removed from the 9th grade classroom but retained for 10–12. Its place in the school library was secured as well. However, the book challenge was a wake up call to those of us in this community who take good books— and freedom to teach them—for granted. Nowadays everything is political and ideological. Past freedoms that we assumed must be re-visited and re-articulated. This whole incident has had a galvanizing effect on we who write and teach. We will be increasingly watchful of candidates for ANY elected office—especially school and library boards.

Weaver's words bring us full circle to the opening of this chapter. The work of teachers and librarians share overlapping ethical ground and are inextricably linked, as are "the indivisibility, interdependence, interrelation and equal importance of all human rights (civil, cultural, economic, political and social)" (UNESCO, 2004).

Librarians and teachers coexist front and center in life, not on the margins of society. Librarians and teachers in Canada (and elsewhere) are in the midst of post-9/11 surveillance, the firebombing of the United Talmud Torah School library in Montreal and other forms of cultural destruction, hate speech, pornography, Internet access and child protection, family values, pressure groups, censorship, imposed technologies, access to government records, privatization, and, of course, just recently, the case of "Vancouver gay bookstore Little Sisters Book and Art Emporium" and its challenge of the censorship powers of Canada's Customs department (Gay bookstore, 2005). The list goes on and there is much work to be done in the attainment of education for human rights and global citizenship.

Studying library activism worldwide indicates that our "mutual advocacy" depends upon such conditions as: intention; ability to publicly finance our work; freedom of expression within our own ranks; increased support for teacher and librarian employees who take risks in the defense of academic freedom and intellectual freedom; respect for cultural distinctiveness, cultural literacy (in all its forms), and cultural democracy; desire to redress omissions, absences, and negations in history, memory, human legacy, and cultural and civic identities; and progress in opposing commodification of information, "corporate globalization, privatization of social services, monopolization of information resources, profit-driven destruction (or private appropriation and control) of cultural artifacts and the human record" (Rosenzweig, 2002, p.5).

That said, it is evident that librarians face two highly loaded challenges: (1) their action, coalition, and alliances in a profession that is largely guided by an ethical framework that carries no sanctions when violated, and (2) their ability to negotiate the enduring dilemma about what constitutes library work.

NOTE

In her November 2004 plenary at the at the Shared Dialogue and Learning: International Conference on Educating for Human Rights and Global Citizenship, Ratna Ghosh (McGill University) firmly cautioned that access to education is not enough, if the message of education is not what it should be. The message of inquiry-based learning is a good one—but only if educators and librarians share in the telling.

REFERENCES

Abram, S. (2004). President's message—Influence: it takes a fine hand. *Feliciter*, 50(5), 173.

American Library Association (ALA). (2004). Core Values Task Force II report. Retrieved on May 6, 2005 from http://www.ala.org/ala/oif/statementspols/corevaluesstatement/corevalues.htm.

ALA. (1997). Resolution on IFLA, Human Rights, and Freedom of Expression. http://www.ala.org/ala/iro/awardsactivities/resolutionifla.htm.

Bailey, E. (2005, February 22). California town give brave new world an F. When an elementary school required students to wear radio frequency IDs, some parents saw the specter of Big Brother. *LA Times*, p. B1.

Book and Periodical Council. (2004). *Freedom to read kit: 20th anniversary issue*. Retrieved on May 6, 2005 from http://www.freedomtoread.ca/docs/2004/ kit2004.pdf.

Branch, J., & Oberg, D. (2004). *Focus on inquiry: A teacher's guide to implementing inquiry-based learning*. Edmonton, AB: Alberta Learning.

Caidi, N. (2005, January 25). *Call for papers: Special issue of Government Information Quarterly on national security policies and implications for information flow*. Toronto: Faculty of Information Studies, University of Toronto. Retrieved on May 6, 2005, from http://www.fis.utoronto.ca/faculty/caidi/cfp/GIQ_CFP.pdf.

Canadian Library Association. (1985, November 18). *Statement on intellectual freedom*. Retrieved May 6, 2005, from http://www.cla.ca/about/intfreed.htm.

Capurro, R., & HjØrland, B. (2003). The concept of information. *Annual Review of Information Science and Technology, 37*, 389.

Capurro, R. (1992). What is information science for? A philosophical reflection. In P. Vakkari & B. Cronin (Eds.), *Conceptions of library and information science: Historical, empirical, and theoretical perspectives* (p. 84). London: Taylor Graham.

Capurro, R. (2005.). Listserv posting. From: rafael@capurro.de. To: icie@zkm.de. Date: 18 May 2005. Subject: [icie] First International Conference on e-Social Science. Forum of the IFLA Social Science Libraries section.

Chartered Institute of Library and Information Professionals (CILIP). (2005). Margaret Watson appointed as chair of the new CILIP ethics panel. Retrieved on May 6, 2005, from the CILIP Web site: http://www.cilip.org.uk/aboutcilip/ newsandpressreleases/archive%202005/news050309.htm.

Declaration from Buenos Aires on information, documentation, and libraries. (2004). *Social Forum on Information, Documentation, and Libraries*. Retrieved May 6, 2005, from http://www.inforosocial.org/declaration.html. The attendees at the First Social Forum on Information, Documentation and Libraries: alternative action programs from Latin America for the information society, held in Buenos Aires from August 26–28, 2004, was called by the Social Studies Group on Library Science and Documentation (Argentina) and the Study Circle on Political and Social Librarianship (Mexico).

Declaration on human rights and rule of law in the information society. (2005). Listerv Posting. From: kmccook@tampabay.rr.com. To: SRRT Action Council srrtac-l@ala.org. Date: 10 Jun 2005. Subject: Declaration on human rights and rule of law in the Information Society.

Durani, S. (2004). Submission to culture, media, and sport committee (Session 2003–04. 26 October 2004. New Inquiry: Public Libraries. 19 November 2004), 1.

Durani, S. (2005). Re: Africa Liberation Library Project—expression of interest. Listerv Posting. From: shiraz.durrani@blueyonder.co.uk. To: eddyobp2000@yahoo.co.uk. Date: 19 Feb 2005. Subject: RE: AFRICA LIBERATION LIBRARY PROJECT—EXPRESSION OF INTEREST. Appeared in PLGNET-L Digest 2056.

Friedland, L. A. (1996). Electronic democracy and the new citizenship. *Media Culture & Society, 18*, 185–212.

Gay bookstore denied court funds. (2005, February 23). *Index on Censorship*. Retrieved May 6, 2005, from http://www.indexonline.org/en/indexindex/articles/2005/1/ canada-gay-bookshop-denied-court-funds.shtml.

Good, K., Harder, G., & Binkley, P. (2005). Social bookmarking and Wikis. NEOS mini-conference, Edmonton, Alberta, June 3, 2005. http://www.neoslibraries.ca/content.aspx?p=592.

Hazen, D. (2004). National bibliography in a globalized world: The Latin American case, 70th IFLA General Conference and Council—22–27 August 2004—Buenos Aires, Argentina, 4. *La bibliografa nacional en un mundo globalizado: el caso de America Latina*.

Hopkins, C. (n.d.) Librarians and teachers. Message posted to plgnet-l@listproc.sjsu.edu.

IFRT New Orleans Program 2006. Listserv posting. From: kellypw@umich.edu. To: pam@jeffersoncountylibrary.org. Date: 31 May 2005. Subject: FW: IFRT New Orleans Program 2006.

International Centre for Information Ethics (ICIE). (2005). The field. Retrieved on May 6, 2005, from http://icie.zkm.de/research.

Library and Intellectual Property Group, Spanish Federation of Archives, Museology, and Library and Information Science (FESABID). (2004). Report on public lending by libraries. Retrieved May 6, 2005.

Lubow, D. (2005, February 15). Listerv posting. Subject: RFID's in the schools. To: SSRTAC-L@ala.org.

Muela-Meza, Z. M. (2005a). Listserv posting. From: zapopanmuela@yahoo.com. To: Progressive Library International Coalition lib-plic@yahoogroups.com. Date: 31 Mar 2005. Subject: The political importance of the Wikipedia Project: the only true Encyclopedia of our days. Wikipedia: towards a new electronic Enlightenment Era? Tuesday 16th November 2004. by Jean-Baptiste Soufron. http://soufron.free.fr/soufron-spip/article.php3?id_article=71.

Muela-Meza, Z. M. (2005b). Listerv posting. From: zapopanmuela@yahoo.com. To: Progressive Library International Coalition lib-plic@yahoogroups.com. Date: 22 Mar 2005. Subject: Finnish government endorses Open Access scientific publishing.

Muela-Meza, Z. M. (2005c). Listserv posting. From: zapopanmuela@yahoo.com. To: Progressive Library International Coalition lib-plic@yahoogroups.com. Date: 21 Mar 2005. Subject: Changing roles of librarians in an open access world.

Muela-Meza, Z. M. (2005d). Listserv posting. From: zapopanmuela@yahoo.com. To: Progressive Library International Coalition lib-plic@yahoogroups.com. Date: 10 Mar 2005. Subject: Request for endorsement: Open Letter to the United Nation's (U.N.) World Intellectual Property Organization (WIPO).

Navarro, G. (2004). Self-organization in Open Source Communication Networks. Red Académica Electrónica de CLACSO-RAEC (CLACSO's Electronic Academic Network-EANC-) case. *International Journal of Information Ethics* (IJIE), *2*, 1–9. Retrieved May 6, 2005, from http://container.zkm.de/ijie/ijie/no002/ijie_002_21_navarro.pdf.

Peters. Listerv posting. From: peters@earlham.edu. To: Biblio-Info-Sociedad@yahoogrupos.com.mx. Date: 30 March 2005. Subject: Invitation to speak at Wikimania Conference, August 5–7, 2005, Frankfurt, Germany.

Raseroka, K. (2004). World Library and Information Congress opening address, 70th IFLA General Conference and Council—22–27 August 2004—Buenos Aires, Argentina, 2.

Rosenzweig, M. (2002). What progressive librarians believe: An international perspective. *INNOVATION*, *22*, 1–5.

Rosenzweig, M. (2005). Listerv posting. To: SSRTAC-L@ala.org. Date: 23 March 2005. Subject: Berkeley fighter against RFIDs.

Save Library and Information Studies, Inc. (n.d.). Save library and information studies. Retrieved on May 6, 2005, from http://www.savelibinfostudies.org/index2.htm.

Schachaf, P. (2005). A global perspective on library association codes of ethics. Paper presented at the ALISE 2005 conference. Retrieved May 6, 2005, from http://ella.slis.indiana.edu/~shachaf/ALISE%202005.ppt.

Smith, M. (2001). Global information justice: Rights, responsibilities, and caring connections. Library Trends, *49(3)*, 519–537.

United Nations. (1948, December 10). Universal declaration of human rights. Retrieved on May 6, 2005, from http://www.un.org/Overview/rights.html.

United Nations Educational, Scientific and Cultural Organization (UNESCO). (2004). Human Rights research. Retrieved May 6, 2005, from UNESCO Web site: http://portal.unesco.org/shs/en/ev.php-URL_ID=3515&URL_DO=DO_TOPIC&URL_SECTION=201.html.

Weaver, W. (2005). Listerv posting. To: srrtac-l@ala.org. Date 15 March 2005. Subject: Report on Bemidji PLAINSONG Challenge.

Wiegand, S. (1996). Reality bites: The collision of rhetoric, rights, and reality, and the Library Bill of Rights. Library Trends, *45(1)*, 75–86.

Wiki Design Principles. http://c2.com/cgi/wiki?WikiDesignPrinciples.

SIXTEEN

Reconstructing the Legend

Educating for Global Citizenship

Graham Pike

EDUCATING FOR GLOBAL CITIZENSHIP is not a new idea. It has been pursued, in various ways, for more than half a century. In the UK, for example, the Council for Education in World Citizenship has vigorously promoted the concept in schools since 1939 (Heater, 1984). The development education, global education, and world studies movements have all made significant contributions, especially in teacher education and curriculum development, resulting in a wealth of sophisticated resources and teaching ideas. In Canada, nongovernmental organizations and teachers' associations have been to the fore in advocating for a global perspective in the school curriculum, assisted notably by funding from the Canadian International Development Agency (CIDA), which established global education projects in eight provinces and one territory from 1987 to 1995 and now supports school-based projects through its Global Classroom Initiative. The recent resurgence of interest in citizenship education, especially in Europe, has provided another platform, as academics debate the meaning of citizenship in the age of globalization and classroom teachers strive to determine the most effective approach to engaging young people in the world around them.

What has been the resulting impact of more than half a century of activity, over a period of time in which the world itself has witnessed remarkable and tumultuous change, characterized by an explosion of interdependence and interconnectedness among nations and cultures? In surveying the educational landscape in Canada, it is hard to spot the legacy of all this endeavor in the current discourse and preoccupations of educators. Global education, the term most widely understood in Canada, is not at the forefront of politicians' calls for additional funding or of parents' concerns about their children's learning deficiencies. Sadly, it is rarely even on their lists. A recent survey of global education activity across the country indicated that global education was not a current priority for schools, school boards, or teacher education programs (Pike & Houghton-Mooney, 2004). There are few gatherings of global educators at regional or national conferences; there appears to be little active research and there is no dedicated journal in which to disseminate ideas. Of course, there are pockets of interest and activity in most provinces, often led by nongovernmental organizations or individual teachers with passion and commitment. No doubt, too, there are some elements of "global education," without the term being used, being practiced in classrooms up and down the country, where teachers are endeavoring to promote greater environmental awareness, or develop students' conflict resolution skills, or ensure equitable consideration of the needs of minority groups. Indeed, most provincial curricula would seem to lend support, in places, to some of global education's basic goals, though it appears that reductions in educational expenditure have severely limited the provision of resources and professional support that is required to facilitate the implementation of these goals (Pike & Houghton-Mooney, 2004). In short, the result of more than twenty years of global education advocacy in Canada amounts to little more than the key elements that were there at the beginning: small groups of dedicated teachers and grassroots organizations determined to buck the prevailing educational trends in order to promote better understanding of an increasingly complex and troubled world. In the post-9/11 era, it seems the urgent need for greater global literacy has gone largely unheeded.

At the theoretical level, there is no shortage of models and visions of education for global citizenship. Among these are Heater's concept of the "multiple citizen" (Heater, 1990); Selby's description of "plural and parallel citizenship" (Selby, 1994); and Hébert's construction of "a new flexible citizenship" (Hébert, 1997). From the field of multicultural education, Lynch (1992) suggests that "education for active global democracy" is the real challenge for educators; and Banks (2001) depicts "globalism and global competency" as the sixth and ultimate stage in individuals' development of cultural identity. From a peace education perspective comes Boulding's idea of "building a global civic culture" (Boulding, 1988). Nussbaum (1996) makes a strong case, from a philosophical viewpoint, for teaching children to see themselves as global citizens in her defense of "cosmopolitan education." Noddings (2005) emphasizes the importance of caring in the education of global citizens. Two relatively full, research-based models of global citizenship are described by Griffith (1998) and by Cogan and Derricott (1998), who prefer the term *multidimensional citizenship*. Nongovernmental organizations, including Oxfam (no date) in the UK, the Canadian Council for International Cooperation (1996, 2004), and the Bahá'í International Community (no date), have also published their visions of global citizenship. International support comes from UNESCO's (1995) *Declaration and Integrated Framework of Action on Education for Peace, Human Rights and Democracy.*

If there is a need for a global perspective in education, a proposition that perhaps few would contest as a general principle, and the theoretical frameworks abound, why do we see such sparse activity on the ground? This, I believe, is the key question for global educators today. Why is the cry for global literacy muted, drowned out by the cries for other "literacies," such as information, scientific, and technological literacy? These, too, are vitally important, but are they so much more important than an understanding of the forces that shape our lives and an ability to play an effective role in determining our individual and collective futures? Surely, there exists a strong degree of mutual interest: just as a global perspective without the tools of basic literacy would likely result in frustration and alienation, so literacy without a global perspective limits our understanding of our lives and communities and restricts the possibilities for building lasting change. After twenty-five years' work as a global educator, I wish I could furnish convincing ripostes to the questions posed above. All I can suggest, however, is that we have failed to fully explore and appreciate the problematic concept of global citizenship and the challenges it poses for educators.

THE PREVAILING LEGEND

A fundamental principle of global citizenship is that an individual's awareness, loyalty, and allegiance can and should extend beyond the borders of a nation to encompass the whole of humankind, an idea variously termed "post-nationalist consciousness" (Ignatieff, 1993) or "the cosmopolitan ideal" (Kingwell, 2000). This is the bedrock upon which other dimensions of global citizenship, such as rights, responsibilities, and participation, are built. It is frequently argued that such consciousness is no more than due acknowledgment of the realities that link all humans in an interlocking network of global systems. Herein lies a major difficulty. As Ignatieff (1994) points out, the reality may take on the appearance of a gigantic global village, but individual citizens do not live in a global village; they live, for the most part, in their own culture, surrounded by the customs, the language, the people, and the legends that make them feel "at home." The global village does not feature in the prevailing legend through which most people make sense of their lives. It is not a concept, however much it affects our daily living, that has taken root within the fundamental belief systems that govern our thoughts and actions. It is not deeply embedded within the values framework that determines our decision making on critical issues of rights, equity, and justice. For most people, it is not sufficient to simply know about events happening in other countries, or that more of our personal goods come from overseas, or that our communities are becoming more infused by ideas, practices, and people from other places. More important for understanding global citizenship is our *consciousness* of global reality (Dower, 2003), of how the global village concept fits into the legend that we have woven about ourselves.

Legends blend fact and myth into powerful stories that shape our cultures and our lives. Their messages, often steeped in morality, help us to make sense of who we are and how we fit in. Just as legends about heroes and villains helped us understand our developing selves in childhood, so legends about the world assist in our understanding of where we fit in the global system: rich or poor, free or fettered, powerful or weak, fortunate or disadvantaged. They tell us how the world works—the economic, political, cultural, and ecological operations of the global system. As legends become rooted in a culture, especially a dominant culture, they are notoriously resistant to change and new versions are subject to repeated denial, as Copernicus and Darwin discovered. I believe we are in a similar position today as we struggle to rewrite the story about the place of the human species on the planet where we live. Global educators are among small groups of people from all walks of life in multiple localities—"conspirators," as Ferguson (1982) called them—who are suggesting revisions to the prevailing legend that has guided human development since the industrial and scientific revolutions, a legend shaped by patriarchy and colonialism, and driven by the free market forces of capitalism. The new versions being offered are deeply troubling to many, as they require a rejection of the very ideas and practices that have underwritten the most incredible expansion of human population and human achievement ever seen, practices such as the short-term exploitation of the earth's resources, the confident reliance on technological solutions, and the relentless pursuit of economic growth. The new versions are uncomfortable as, for those in positions of power and influence, they do not seem to fit the reality of the world around them: a world characterized by unbridled consumption, increasing personal liberty, and the astonishing hallmarks of human ingenuity. The fact that this reality, the dominant legend, fails to acknowledge the stories of poverty and oppression, or the tales of traditional subsistence living, that portray the lives of billions of people around the world, provides strong motivation for persistent denial and the creation of "feelgood" measures such as development aid and humanitarian assistance. From a position of power, it is safer to tinker with a few minor details than to radically alter the plot.

The role of global educators, and other allies in the conspiracy for global change, is to help weave the fabric of the new legend. The task is formidable: the legend needs to be more inclusive and more visionary, to allow a majority of the world's people to find themselves represented within it, and to ensure that future generations can be written in. Key to this task is the spread of global consciousness, or the promotion of an ethos of global citizenship

(Pike, 2001) within our educational institutions. It could be argued, with some justification, that global educators, among others, have been attempting this for some time and have had some success. Environmental awareness among students is almost certainly greater than it was twenty-five years ago; it is probably true that young people have more exposure to what's happening in the world than they used to, though perhaps resulting more from the influences of the mass media than from education; undeniably, youth have more opportunities to become involved in cross-cultural dialogue and to have a voice on issues of international concern; and, of course, the Internet puts the world, literally, at their fingertips. However, I would argue that the collective impact of such developments is as yet insufficient in strength and focus to make the breakthrough required to reconstruct the prevailing legend. In this chapter, I will suggest three major challenges to a more profound understanding of global citizenship and then offer some practical strategies for educators.

TOWARDS THE GLOBAL SOUL: THREE MAJOR CHALLENGES

A Lack of Plausible Alternatives to the Prevailing Legend

"We are," suggested Danish poet Piet Hein some forty years ago, "global citizens with tribal souls" (cited in Dower, 2003, p. 145). The realities of our interdependence, a phenomenon that grows and deepens with the multiple impacts of globalization, are still not felt where it truly matters: in our hearts and souls. Indeed, the more obvious our interdependence appears to become, the more strident are our attempts to deny its very existence. In the UK, once the hub of a global empire, parochialism appears to be spreading: foreign news has been drastically cut on the main television channels; fewer people are learning foreign languages; and while more Britons are traveling abroad than ever before, the favored destinations are places where they can rub shoulders with people like themselves (Jacques, 2004). In the United States, the current dominant global power, the government's principal response to the tragedies of 9/11 has been to seal its borders, to further isolate its people from the disturbing differences of other cultures and peoples. In France, an obvious display of cultural difference has been made illegal through the ban on religious dress in schools. On a global scale, despite decades of media coverage of famines, diseases, and other catastrophes that afflict the world's poor, the gap between the richest and poorest quintiles of the global population continues to widen inexorably. This results in "a fragmentation of our shared reality," suggests Homer-Dixon (2003, p.15). "Never before have we been so connected together on this planet and never before have we been so far apart in our realities." In other words, we are investing copious and valuable resources in shoring up the dominant legend and resisting alternative versions.

Why is it so difficult to admit to the existence of other realities? Why is it so hard to expand our notions of loyalty, fairness, and justice to those outside our own cultural circles? How can we encourage the slow, and hesitant, transition from tribal to global souls? Such are the questions that development agencies and social justice groups have been debating for many years. Their answers have led to several strategies for promoting a public response, such as presenting shocking images of emaciated or stricken children, making the "personal" connection through child sponsorship, using the mass appeal of media stars, and preying on our sense of guilt and shame. All have had limited success in prompting short-term humanitarian assistance, but they have failed to instigate long-term solutions to global problems. Doubtless, there are many reasons for this lack of real success. A key reason, I would suggest, is the failure to provide believable and desirable alternatives to the "business as usual" scenario for the future, or the prevailing legend. The versions of reality portrayed in much of the narrative that feeds our perceptions of the wider world are cloaked in catastrophe, chaos, and hopelessness. Rarely are we nourished by the countless stories of achievement, stability, and richness that are also part of the everyday realities of people around the world, or the visionary initiatives, such as the Grameen Bank in Bangladesh or the Green Belt movement in Kenya or the Sarvodaya model of community sufficiency in Sri Lanka, that provide inspiration for the rest of us. At best, we hear of dogged perseverance in the face of unending hardship. It is difficult to find a space in our legend for such bleakness. Moreover, it is problematic to construct a new and more inclusive legend if, by so doing, we would seem to be curtailing the chances of our own satisfaction and survival. It is safer to put up the barricades and try to ignore the problems that fester outside.

Few Real Incentives for Change

Access to knowledge about global issues and events has grown exponentially over the past two decades, due to the proliferation of television channels (including those, such as Al-Jazeera, that give very different versions of reality) and the extraordinary explosion of the Internet. Ignorance, for those in the wealthy nations at least, is no longer excusable on the basis of limited access to information. These developments in global communications have also facilitated the capacity of individuals to take action in pursuit of solutions to global problems in ways that were previously unthinkable. The international campaign against the proposed Multilateral Agreement on Investment (MAI), a global investment treaty that would have expanded the powers of transnational corporations, was significantly aided by having the full text of the treaty scanned and put on the Internet (Clarke & Barlow,

1997). Dower (2003) argues, however, that an increased knowledge about the world and a greater ability to act at a distance are not sufficient in themselves to lead people into action. Motivation is also needed, a "commitment to a global ethic, first to the idea that human beings matter anywhere and so whatever evils befall people anywhere are, in principle, of relevance" (p. 20). A global ethic is integral to the new legend, but how do we encourage its development? What forms of motivation will entice more than the few who are already committed to a global ethic to see the relevance of evils and problems beyond their own national borders? How do we foster the second component of Dower's notion of a global ethic, a sense of personal responsibility for doing something, however little, about the problems we face? In the rich world, at present, the incentives for taking personal responsibility for global change are often far from enticing. My local hydro company gives me the opportunity to contribute to the development of renewable energy production through paying a premium on my monthly bill. This is a penalty, not an incentive, and it is unlikely to hasten the growth of renewable energy sources. After OPEC doubled the price of crude oil in 1973, the public demanded smaller cars and governments introduced energy conservation measures; as the prices of crude oil fell over subsequent years, the North American market for larger vehicles and SUVs grew and the illusion of abundant and problem-free energy returned. Through a lack of vision and leadership, an opportunity was lost to capitalize on a global phenomenon that could have led to significant changes in transportation systems and, consequently, less environmental damage. Interventions that result from such global crises may bring about short-term changes in behavior but they are unlikely to result in longer-term transformation—a new legend—unless there is an incentive that provokes a parallel shift in underlying attitudes and beliefs. An understanding of the current legend, a vision of alternatives and an incentive to modify existing behavior are all prerequisites for the development of a global ethic.

INSUFFICIENT APPRECIATION FOR THE
POTENTIAL OF INDIVIDUAL ACTION

Motivation for change is driven not only by desire but also by possibility. The willingness to aid the plight of Africa's starving children is tempered by the belief that, for whatever reasons, little will change in the long term. After all, such tragedies have been written into the current legend over several decades without the emergence of a viable alternative future for that continent. Consequently, the "business as usual" story may be perpetuated as much by a belief that change is not possible as it is by a view that it is not desirable. Critical to the development of the new legend is an enhanced understanding of the potential for action, whether through the established democratic channels or by other measures. A fundamental component of this understanding is a conviction that the actions of individuals, working in harmony, do make a difference, even at the global level. The MAI treaty was eventually thrown out when governments were forced to realize its negative implications for democratic decision making by the concerted, and coordinated, efforts of individual citizens. Moreover, it is equally important for citizens to realize that non-action—whether by design or by default—also has an impact on the global system, generally to perpetuate the status quo.

The omnipotent forces of economic globalization have afforded global citizens, especially the wealthier ones, a highly significant, and largely ignored, role to play in the weaving of the new legend: that of the consumer. As Saul (1995) has pointed out, corporate success in the global marketplace depends upon individuals' desire for inner comfort, for the satisfaction of desires through consumption of goods and services. In affluent societies, consumerism has become a means by which we search for answers to a fundamental need, a sense of identity and belonging (O'Sullivan, 1999). This can be viewed negatively, a corruption of the lofty ideals of civic engagement that does not lead to happy and meaningful lives (Kingwell, 2000). On the other hand, global consumerism presents limitless possibilities for individuals to use their buying power to influence the decisions of transnational corporations, the drivers of the global economy, and thereby to clothe the satisfaction of individual needs in a global ethic. The Fair Trade movement, though still a tiny player on the global scene, has indicated the potential for change through more informed consumerism. As global society becomes more profoundly interconnected, the opportunities for motivated individuals to make a difference—through thoughtful consumerism or other means—present new avenues for active global citizenship.

THE ROLE OF GLOBAL EDUCATORS

Reconstructing the legend is not a task for education alone. The prevailing story is so deeply embedded within the social and institutional structures that govern our lives that multiple players—including government, media, business, and civil society—are required to work in harmony if significant change is to occur. However, I do believe that education has a pivotal role to play because schools, and other educational institutions, have unique opportunities to present other versions of reality and to help students explore alternative visions of the future. Indeed, the broadening of horizons, the development of critical thinking and the weighing up of differing and conflicting beliefs are all essential features of a sound education. Schools can also be model communities: they can articulate a preferred vision of global society and demonstrate apposite attitudes and behaviors; they can encourage responsible student participation and illustrate the power of collaborative action. How, then, can global educators hope to have more impact on the educational landscape than has been apparent over the past twenty-five years? How can we elevate global literacy to the top of the stack of perceived essential literacies for the twenty-first century? I do not underestimate the enormity of the task, but we have to do better than we have done in the past. We need to move beyond the current practice of infusing the prevailing legend with a global perspective: global education has to challenge the assumptions underpinning the dominant story; it has to disorient and bewilder the reader, and thereby precipitate the search for alternative versions. In the remainder of this chapter, I would like to offer for consideration some ways in which the challenges identified earlier could be addressed.None of the strategies outlined below is new. Most have been well articulated by global educators in the past; all are derived from my own experiences in working with students and teachers. Although these are not new ideas, they are worth restating in that they are often overlooked, even if they have space in the formal curriculum, or are crowded out by the ceaseless pressures of competing demands on the school timetable. It's a classic "Catch-22" situation: if they are not part of the current legend, they are not viewed as important by educators; yet education has a responsibility to ensure that they become part of the new legend.

DEVELOP GLOBAL THINKING

More than two hundred years of intellectual and social development based on the mechanistic thinking of the rational-industrial worldview have left their mark on our ability to conceptualize whole systems, to understand the big picture, to think about the long-term implications of present actions. Recent estimations indicate that human consumption is 20 percent higher than the earth's carrying capacity and continues to grow (Living Planet Report, 2004). Our "loss of the cosmological sense," suggests O'Sullivan (1999), is at the root of many global crises we face, notably our inability to live sustainably within the limits of the planet's resources. More cynically, Kingwell (2000) contends that the forces of economic globalization demand that we remain disconnected, lest we should understand the less wholesome practices of the global labor market and decide to reduce our consumer spending. Global thinking is not in the interests of the global market.

The mechanistic worldview pervades our school systems, thereby perpetuating difficulties in global thinking for at least another generation. The compartmentalization of knowledge into rigid disciplines, the favoring of analytical over synthetic or relational thinking skills, the dearth of global, holistic, and futures' perspectives in practically every area of the curriculum, an obsession with the "hard" sciences and concurrent suspicion of the "soft"—and more integrative—arts; such priorities within education reflect our collective inability—and, perhaps, our lack of will—to think globally. My research among global education practitioners suggests that even they find it difficult to release themselves from the shackles of worldviews that perceive nations and cultures as separate and distinct. Global education itself is imbued with mechanistic thinking (Pike, 2000). To develop global thinking, we have to tear down the artificial walls of the curriculum, to help students understand how the separate pieces fit together, how to recognize connections and relationships between various social and global phenomena, how to think long term and see the interrelationship of past, present, and future. Global thinking is fundamental to sustainability: without a full understanding of global interdependencies, and how present decisions will likely affect future generations, it is impossible to know how to live sustainably. Seeing the big picture is also critical to acknowledging the coexistence of differing versions of reality, thereby nurturing alternatives to the prevailing legend and providing incentives for change.

Foster Interest in Local Action

The current interest in citizenship education in Western democracies would seem to stem, in part at least, from a concern over declining rates of participation in civil society, especially in the formal democratic process. Voter turnout at significant elections is falling; disenfranchisement—actual and perceived—among minority groups is rising; cynicism toward the political process and apathy among young people are widely reported. In the absence of any instruments of world government (which do not feature in most models of global citizenship), active participation at a local level is of paramount importance. National citizenship continues, albeit imperfectly and despite citizens' lack of engagement, because the necessary civil and political structures are in place. Global citizenship is virtual; its essence depends upon the collective participation of citizens worldwide to give substance to an otherwise unrealizable ideal.

An understanding of the link between local action and global change is critical to actualizing the full potential of global citizenship. For most citizens, of any age, action at the global level is not possible; for young people, in particular, it is necessary that we scale down the global issues and explore their local manifestations, both to aid understanding and to provide realistic opportunities for action. Opinion polls suggest that Canadian youth are increasingly worldminded, yet increasingly frustrated with their perceived lack of power to influence decision makers on matters that concern them (O'Neill, 2004). This "democratic deficit" presents schools with a real opportunity—and a responsibility—to exploit students' interests and concerns and to channel their enthusiasms into practical action projects that can be seen to make a difference. Experiential learning, whether acquired through volunteering in the local food bank, constructing a butterfly garden, or helping out in a Seniors home, is a powerful tool for illustrating the potential of individual and collaborative action and for instilling the motivation for active and life-long participation in the democratic process. However, as Hart (1992) has noted, schools' attempts at encouraging active participation among students, and thereby refining the necessary skills of global citizenship, are often more tokenistic than meaningful. From the school's perspective, action projects are often viewed as "extra-curricular," as add-ons to the real business of education; for many students, however, such projects are where real learning takes place, where their interests and skills come together in a way that provides a meaningful and lasting experience.

ENHANCE APPRECIATION OF COMPLEXITY AND AMBIGUITY

Implicit in the dominant legend is a belief that simple solutions can be found to complex problems. In the search for alternative energy sources or a cure for cancer, the goal is to find *the* answer that will allow us to continue living in much the same way as before, rather than having to rewrite the legend. Such thinking is dangerously naive, failing to recognize that the problems we face are complex and multilayered and that there are multiple potential solutions, each one having consequences that should be carefully considered. Nowhere is the quest for "right answers" more evident than in our education systems. The idea of a formal curriculum establishes the view that there exists a body of knowledge that every student should understand (and, by implication, that everything outside that body is less worthy). Current fads for standardization and accountability further narrow the learning opportunities for students by making it more difficult for individual interests, either those of the student or teacher, to be pursued beyond what is prescribed in the curriculum. As the content of the curriculum expands to include new areas that are deemed essential, such as information technology, so the possibility for exploring any topic or theme in depth diminishes. Complex problems and ambiguous situations demand a dedication of time and effort that will lead to profound understanding; schools are rarely able to establish the conditions in which such learning can occur.

Understanding complexity is more likely to be achieved through student-directed experiential learning than through a teacher- or textbook-driven formal lesson. The kind of action projects suggested above are often good vehicles for encouraging students to research a topic in depth, to uncover the hidden complexity, and to make informed choices from a range of possible courses of action. The learning that results—the knowledge, skills, and self-confidence gained—can then be applied in other real-life situations in the future. Through exposure to complex situations, it is likely that students will not be able to find a satisfactory solution to every problem, or will be faced by a host of alternative, and perhaps conflicting, solutions. Such experiences offer tremendous opportunities for learning about the multidimensional nature of problem solving and for building up tolerance for ambiguity—an acceptance of the view that "right answers" are hard to find, but there are successful ways to live with and manage problems while seeking out better solutions. Appreciating complexity and ambiguity is fundamental to the emergence and acceptance of new versions of the prevailing legend, which are unlikely to reveal simple solutions to global problems or to indicate a straight and clear road to future development.

RECOGNIZE THE SIGNIFICANCE OF THE MEDIA AGE

Perhaps the most profound change of the last half-century has been the growth in the accessibility of information to ordinary people. Even acknowledging that the "information revolution" does not yet extend to most of the world's poor, the transformation brought about by television and electronic communications is far-reaching. The legends of our time are shaped increasingly by the mass media; indeed, the very fact that these legends can now be global in scope, rather than being framed by local and national contexts, is due largely to the media's capacity to bring the real stories of other cultures and peoples so vividly into our lives. To a considerable degree, our schools have failed to adapt to the reality of the media age. Despite decades of child-centred learning theories, we still tend to organize education based on the factory model of schooling that Charles Dickens criticized a century and a half ago. We authenticate knowledge gained from teachers and textbooks and we devalue knowledge and experience that comes from other sources. Thus, we create the gulf—for many students—between the school as a place where learning is artificially and painfully constructed and elsewhere, where the real legends are woven.

Our failure to address the power of mass media is disturbing on two counts. First, we miss out on helping young people utilize the most extensive source of ideas and information about the world that has ever been made accessible. The possibilities for delving into, and interacting with, the lives of people in distant places through electronic media are truly extraordinary. We fail, too, to exploit the potential of "media heroes" to promote desired change: perhaps the most influential catalysts for raising public awareness of global issues over the past twenty years have been rock stars (e.g., Bob Geldof, Bono), television and film personalities (e.g., Michael Moore, Oprah), and royalty (e.g., Princess Diana, Queen Noor). Second, and perhaps more importantly, we fail to grasp the opportunity to nurture global citizens who have the knowledge and skills required to critically evaluate the role that the media play in shaping the prevailing legend. The media, of course, provide not just information but a whole package of values, assumptions, and biases that insidiously determine how we perceive and understand the world. The skills of media literacy, enabling students to analyze how the media construct reality and how this influences their perceptions of themselves and others, are among the most critical tools for active and aware global citizens. These skills are required to enable us to break out of the constricting mental mold that the dominant legend has built in order to seek viable alternatives.

Demonstrate Commitment to a Global Ethic

The knowledge and skills identified in the four points above are deemed crucial to enabling students to better understand the complex world in which they live and to constructively participate in shaping its future. One question remains, however: How do schools encourage a real commitment to a global ethic, the notion that individuals should exercise responsibility for what happens not only to themselves and people around them but also to other people and other species anywhere? The development of a "global moral community" (Dower, p. 26) presents the biggest challenge. Nussbaum recognizes the need for education to give due recognition to the people closest to us and with whom we identify, but she argues that "we should also work to make all human beings part of our community of dialogue and concern . . . and give the circle that defines our humanity special attention and respect" (Nussbaum, 1996, p.9). Such a commitment can only be achieved, in my view, through schools actively, patiently, and persistently practising the principles that underlie it. Given the wide array of other influences on young people's attitudes and behaviors, there can be no guarantee that the demonstration of a global ethic in schools will have the desired impact on individual students, but it remains the best option.

The most difficult area for schools in making this commitment pertains to values and beliefs. A standard view to hold is that the role of formal education is to provide information upon which individuals can make their own decisions, not to advocate particular viewpoints. Even some who might be regarded as "global educators" share this view (Jickling, 1992). Yet Canadian schools routinely advocate positions on a variety of social and moral issues, through policies and practices that promote healthy lifestyles, encourage environmental conservation, outlaw gender and racial discrimination, promote the nonviolent resolution of conflict, and ignore religious affiliations and beliefs. Many (though not all) of these positions already support the principles of a global ethic; the main change would be to widen the circle of concern to include all human beings and other species. The implications, of course, are far-reaching, requiring schools to give priority in their curriculum goals to the development of global literacy, to be more proactive in fostering students' involvement as local and global citizens, and to be seen to act responsibly on a number of other fronts (for example, reducing consumption of goods and services to meet sustainability targets; ensuring that the goods they buy support healthy environmental and labor practices; modeling collaborative work habits and democratic decision making). Such initiatives pose considerable challenges to schools in an educational climate which is dominated by short-term, narrowly focused goals that emanate from, and tend to support, the dominant legend. But if our educational institutions cannot be catalysts in constructing the new legend, from where is that impetus likely to come?

REFERENCES

Bahá'í International Community (no date). World citizenship. A global ethic for sustainable development. New York

Banks, J. A. (2001). Cultural diversity and education. Foundations, curriculum, and teaching. Boston: Allyn & Bacon.

Boulding, E. (1988). Building a civic culture. Education for an interdependent world. Syracuse: Syracuse University Press.

Canadian Council for International Co-operation (1996). Global citizenship: A new way forward. Report from the CCIC Task Force on building public support for sustainable development. Ottawa.

Clarke, T., & Barlow, M. (1997). MAI. The multilateral agreement on investment and the threat to Canadian sovereignty. Toronto: Stoddart.

Cogan, J. J., & Derricott, R. (1998). Citizenship for the 21st century. An international perspective on education. London: Kogan Page.

Dower, N. (2003). An introduction to global citizenship. Edinburgh: Edinburgh University Press.

Ferguson, M. (1982). The Aquarian conspiracy. Personal and social transformation in the 1980s. New York: Granada.

Griffith, R. (1998). Educational citizenship and interdependent learning. London: Jessica Kingsley Publishers.

Hart, R. (1992). Children's participation: From tokenism to citizenship. Innocenti Essays No 4. Florence: UNICEF International Child Development Centre.

Heater, D. (1984). Peace through education. The contribution of the Council for Education in World Citizenship. London: Falmer Press.

Heater, D. (1990). Citizenship. The civic ideal in world history, politics, and education. London: Longman.

Hébert, Y. (1997). Citizenship education: yes, but how? Towards a pedagogy of social participation and identity formation. Paper presented at the Canadian Society for the Study of Education conference, St. John's, Newfoundland, June.

Homer-Dixon, T. (2003). Human adaptation and the ingenuity gap. Brock Education, 12(2), 1–22.

Ignatieff, M. (1993). *Blood and belonging. Journeys into the new nationalism*. Toronto: Viking.

Ignatieff, M. (1994). Cited in Abley, M., Enigma variations: Michael Ignatieff. *Canadian forum, 826*, 5–9.

Jacques, M. (2004). The problem with abroad. *Guardian weekly*, August 27–September 2, p. 5.

Jickling, B. (1992). Why I don't want my children to be educated for sustainable development. *Journal of Environmental Education, 23(4)*, 5–8.

Kingwell, M. (2000). *The world we want. Virtue, vice, and the good citizen*. Toronto: Viking.

Lynch, J. (1992). *Education for citizenship in a multicultural society*. London: Cassell.

Noddings, N. (Ed.). (2005). *Educating citizens for global awareness*. New York: Teachers College Press.

Nussbaum, M. (1996). Patriotism and cosmopolitanism. In J. Cohen (Ed.), *For love of country: debating the limits of patriotism*. Boston: Beacon.

O'Neill, M. (2004). *New horizons: Engaging Canadians as active global citizens*. Ottawa: Canadian Council for International Co-operation.

O'Sullivan, E. (1999). *Transformative learning. Educational vision for the 21st century*. New York: Zed.

Oxfam (no date). A curriculum for global citizenship. Oxford.

Pike, G. (2000). Global education and national identity: In pursuit of meaning. *Theory into Practice, 39(2)*, 64–73.

Pike, G. (2001). Citizenship education in a global context. A paper presented at the annual conference of the Canadian Society for the Study of Education, Université Laval, May 24.

Pike, G., & Houghton-Mooney, S. (2004). Regional global education centres: a feasibility study. A report prepared for the Canadian International Development Agency. University of Prince Edward Island.

Saul, J. R. (1995). *The unconscious civilization*. Concord: Anansi.

Selby, D. (1994). Kaleidoscopic mindset. New meanings within citizenship education. *Global education, 2*, 20–31.

United Nations Educational, Scientific and Cultural Organisation (1995). *Declaration and integrated framework of action on education for peace, human rights, and democracy*. Paris: UNESCO.

WWF International (2004). Living planet report 2004. Geneva: WWF International.

Threads of My Life

(Spanish Original)

Hilaria Supa Huaman

Buenas noches. Empezamos con una oración. Pónganse de pie por favor.
Pachamama Pachakamaq
Imploro que sea presente con nosotros. Y a todos nuestros antepasados que nos iluminan con todo su sabiduría, el equilibrio y el amor.Pido que todos los seres humanos que sean blancos, negros, indios, de toda cultura entendamos el equilibrio. Somos juntos todos. Somos hermanos. No hay ninguna clase de discriminación cuando no diferencias. Somos iguales, tenemos los mismos sentimientos. En el equilibrio hay el amor, el respeto, el auto-estima. De querernos, tal como somos. No tenemos que avergonzarnos de nosotros. Hay que querernos.

Que cada uno nos entendimos. Que haya la comprensión. Que entramos en el equilibrio del entendimiento. Gracias Pachamama. (Madre Diosa Divina) Gracias Pachakamaq. (Padre Dios Divino)

En los tiempos de los abuelos, se formaron a la gente desde el vientre de la madre, a los hijos y las hijas se educaba. Se les hablaba. Les decía al nuevo ser, "eres inteligente, eres bueno de corazón." En quechua es *sama sonco*. Se decían a los nuevos seres—ser noble, sea de buena corazón, sea buen trabajador. En las noches conversaron con los niños, las mujercitas, los varoncitos, ambos, les conversaban de muchas cosas. Así formaron, educaron a los niños. Así se formaron los lideres, los sabios.

Fue en la unión de la pareja que el amor esta sembrado. Hemos vivido siempre así. Con un buen ejemplo de los padres para los hijos, en el amor, en el trabajo de ser honestos, de ser dignos, de ser sabios. Así las generaciones resistieron la invasión. Eso todavía existe en muchas comunidades. Es el respeto de los hombres y las mujeres mutuamente, nos da el equilibrio. La dignidad es la personalidad de cada ser.

¿Por qué estamos perdiendo eso? Tenemos que recuperarlo. En mi comunidad las mujeres se preguntaron como lograron operarnos, ¿porque hemos dejado que nos hace eso? Somos fuertes, ¿Qué paso?

Somos muy nobles. Cuando las enfermeras vinieron a las casas, nos hemos tratado con amor, con respeto, como siempre lo hacemos. Hemos confiado en ellas. Hemos visto con ellas el progreso, una forma de sacarnos de la miseria maternal. Nos han engañado.

Las mujeres que primero se operaron fueron los que tiene confianza con la posta medica. Esa gente empezó a convencer al pueblo mismo. Ellas se arrepienten hoy, preguntan, ¿Por qué acepte? No han aceptado, fueron obligadas. ¿Por qué me hicieron, porque me engañaron? ¿Quién manda a engañarnos?

En los 10 anos desde que se operaron muchas mujeres, las veo envejeciéndose prematuramente. Con la ligadura ya no son jóvenes, tienen una profunda tristeza. Las mujeres tratan de esconder el dolor. Recién vinieron unos periodistas Franceses. Cuando las mujeres contaron sus cuentos, lloraron juntos con los periodistas. Cada vez que yo reúno con las mujeres conversamos y lloramos. No demostramos a la gente nuestro dolor. Si no silenciosamente cargamos nuestro dolor. Pero sí, recamos a la Pachamama y a Pachakamaq.

Hay que hacer un tratamiento psicológico. Están golpeados por los maridos. La justicia se hace caso. No hay justicia en las ligaduras. En el Perú las mujeres no encontramos justicia. Las mujeres que están agredidos por la ligadura están maltratados de su salud y por sus esposos. Cuando las mujeres van a cejarse a la justicia, no le hacen caso. Tampoco encontraron justicia por el abuso que le hicieron a los derechos humanos—el derecho a vivir sano y derecho a vivir con la felicidad, el derecho a vivir con el trabajo, el derecho a vivir dignamente.

En mi comunidad dos mujeres ligadas dejaron a sus familias. Por los insultos, los maltratos, su carácter ha cambiado, son traumatizados. Toda la comunidad se sienta apenados; ese hecho hace daño a la comunidad. Muchas familias han vendido sus animales para curarse, quedaron sin animales, sin medio para vivir. Hay muchos huérfanos.

De las doce mujeres que fueron los que anunciaron los hechos, una de ellas su marido volvió alcohólico. Le pegaba a su mujer y al fin de suicidado dejando la mujer con siete hijos. Ella vive a nueve horas de la posta medica. Se fue trayendo sus hijos al Centro de Salud para hacer controlar. La enfermera le habla sobre la esterilización. Ella no acepta. La enfermera fue a su casa a decir a su esposo que la mujer tenia que hacerse la ligadura y si no se hacia le mandaba el hombre a la cárcel. Desde allí, va la mujer al Centro siempre con miedo. No quería hacerse. Tal día, la llamaron adentro, cuando se dio cuenta, trato de escapar, a diez mujeres se encerraron, hicieron la ligadura. El día siguiente se fue a pie a su comunidad, se fue sin explicación, sin medicamentos. Camino las nueve horas en el sol, en el camino se infecta su herida. Después de 3 o 4 días en la casa, regreso a al posta. Decía señorita estoy mal. La enfermera le dije "cochina, mentirosa, por eso es enferma, cochina. La enfermera le pega una inyección, sentía que su pierna se adurmicio, la mandaron a casa, camino las nueve horas, no podría caminar más. Le había, poniendo la inyección, hincado en el nervio de la nalga. La mujer se vuelve invalida. Vendieron los animales para tratar de curarla, al final su marido se enveneno, ya no podrían más. Ella se queda sola, con sus dolores, con su pena. No puede trabajar, sus hijos no pueden estudiar. Tenia que mandarlos a la ciudad para trabajar en las casas como servidumbre doméstica.

Todos hemos nacido dignos. Siempre hay dignidad del espíritu, lo que no hay es economía. Entre los diez anos, década de los derechos humanos, entre 1995 y 2005 hay mas familias, mas pobreza. Entres hombres y mujeres ambos. ¿De donde viene? Los que tienen mas dinero quieren más. Matan a la gente, vota la comida, malgaste el dinero. Mientras que muere la gente de pobreza y de hambre. No conocen otros mundos. Somos fuertes, por eso sobrevivimos. No saber dónde sacar un pan para comer, cuando no tienes casa, no tienes nada. Necesitamos una buena inversión para que haya producción. De que vas a vivir si no hay producción. En todos aspectos, ¿de qué vivir? Hay que vivir ¿No? Cuando no hay economía, no hay producción. No hay economía, eso es cierto.

Siempre existió antes la producción, para siempre. No conocíamos el dinero, Si, había producción. Así se vivía en el equilibrio. Antes se producía sin ningún abono. Sin ninguna química se producía natural y se respetaba a la naturaleza. Por eso teníamos cosecha para alimentarnos sanamente y vivir sanamente.

Existía el auto-estima. Uno debe conocerse—de donde eres, porque viniste, que haces. Es querer a uno mismo. Sentirse capaz de todo. Sentirse inteligente, servicial. Sentirse el amor en el corazón. Compartir el amor y también quererse a uno mismo. Necesitamos de todos. Necesitamos también de los malos. Para conocerlos, para cambiarlos. A los hombres blancos hay que curarlos.

Termino con un cuento del oso. Es del mundo de ojupacha [el mundo de abajo, de adentro entre los tres mundos de la cosmología andina]. Todo lo que vota la gente, el oso lo limpia. Hemos venido a Canadá dos hermanos Peruanos y yo. Queríamos ver el oso, hemos llamado al oso al campamiento. Vino a visitarnos un oso negro. Estuvimos felices conociendo, mirando el oso. Pero se quedo tres días en el campamiento; empezó a comer la basura. Al final los hombres blancos lo mataron a balazos al oso. Me sentía mal, me sentía culpable para haber llamado al oso. ¿Qué hay de aprender de eso? No debemos de votar basuras. Somos los culpables por votar basuras.

Cada ser humano tiene basura adentro en el corazón. Mientras que vive en la oscuridad, tiene basura. Para que no mueran mas ositos, ningún animal. Para que no nos estemos matando a nuestra naturaleza. Se mete la basura por ser débiles, sin amor, sin espíritu. Cuando somos débiles puede entrar fácil el mal espíritu que se llama la basura. Si uno es fuerte con el amor y con la fe, y con un espíritu fuere, llenos de amor no podrán entrar ninguna basura.

Hay que hacer recordar a los niños y a los abuelitos. Hacer recordar la sabiduría. El conocimiento al respeto a la naturaleza. Hay que enseñar a los niños. Los abuelos tienen que enseñar a los niños su sabiduría, sus experiencias. Los abuelos son los mejores libros. Son los profesores de la vida.
Yo recabo a Pachamama y Pachakamaq. Ayúdanos a que seamos fuertes. Gracias.

Contributors

ALI A. ABDI is Professor of Education and International Development at the University of Alberta in Edmonton, Canada. His areas of research include International Education; Globalization, Citizenship and Human Rights Education; Social Foundations of Education. His articles have appeared in such academic journals as *Comparative Education, Compare: A Journal of Comparative Education, Western Journal of Black Studies, International Education, McGill Journal of Education, Horn of Africa Journal,* and *Cultural Studies.* He is the author, co-author or co-editor of several books including *Culture, Education and Development in South Africa* (2002), *Education and the Politics of Difference* (2004), *Issues in Africa Education* (2005), and *African Education and Globalization* (2006).

NIGEL DOWER is Honorary Senior Lecturer and former Senior Lecturer in Philosophy at the University of Aberdeen School of Divinity, History, and Philosophy. He has also taught in Zimbabwe and the United States. He was Visiting Professor at the University of Akureyri, Iceland in 2004, and at Colorado State University, Fort Collins in 2006. His research interests focus on the ethics of international relations, development, and the environment. Apart from numerous articles and chapters, he has written *World Ethics: The New Agenda* (2007), *World Poverty—Challenge and Response* (1983), *World Ethics—The New Agenda* (1998), *An Introduction to Global Citizenship* (2003), and edited *Global Citizenship: A Critical Reader* (2002), and *Ethics and Environmental Responsibility* (1989). He has served as President of the International Development Ethics Association (IDEA), and as convener of the Development Ethics Study Group of the Development Studies Association (DSA). He is a member of the Educational Advisory Board for the Earth Charter and the IUCN Ethics Specialist Group.

DEREK G. EVANS teaches and consults on strategic evaluation, conflict transformation, and human rights. He is a former Executive Director of Naramata

Centre, one of Canada's foremost retreat and experiential learning centres (1999–2004). During the 1990s, he served as Deputy Secretary General of Amnesty International, with responsibility for research, policy and strategic direction of the global human rights organization. Evans is a Fellow of the Canadian Academy of Independent Scholars and an Institute Associate of the Wosk Centre for Dialogue at Simon Fraser University. His most recent book is *Before the War: Reflections in a New Millennium* (Northstone, 2004).

RATNA GHOSH is James McGill Professor and William C. Macdonald Professor of Education at McGill University in Montréal, Canada. The first woman Dean of the Faculty of Education she has received several awards and honours such as the Order of Canada, Order of Quebec, Fellowship in the Royal Society of Canada and the European Academy of Arts, Sciences and Humanities. *Time* Magazine had a full page profile (2003) on her as one of "Canada's Best in Education." She was President of the Shastri Indo-Canadian Institute. Her publications in books, journals and encyclopaedias focus on social justice issues in relation to education and women.

SHIBAO GUO is an assistant professor in the Faculty of Education at the University of Calgary and an affiliated researcher with the Prairie Centre of Excellence for Research on Immigration and Integration (PCERII). He holds a Master's degree in adult education from the University of Nottingham and a doctoral degree in educational studies from the University of British Columbia. His research focuses on citizenship and immigration, Chinese immigrants, social justice and equity in education, and adult education. He has published in international and Canadian journals, including *Journal of International Migration and Integration, Canadian Journal of University Continuing Education, Canadian Review of Social Policy,* and *Alberta Journal of Educational Research.*

CARL E. JAMES teaches in the Faculty of Education and in the graduate program in Sociology at York University. His research interest on issues of equity in relation to race, ethnicity, class, gender and immigrant status, youth and sports, and multiculturalism also inform the courses he teaches—i.e. Urban Education, Foundations of Education, among others. A former youth worker, James holds a Ph.D. in Sociology, and is a visiting lecturer in the Teacher Training Department at Uppsala University, Sweden. His publications include: *Race in Play: Understanding the Socio-Cultural Worlds of Student Athletes* (2005); *Possibilities and Limitations: Multicultural Policies and Program in Canada* (2005).

JERROLD L. KACHUR is a professor in the Department of Educational Policy Studies at the University of Alberta. He specializes in the international sociology of higher education; social and political theory; and the philosophical anthropology of the human sciences. He has co-authored *Contested Classrooms: Education, Globalization and Democracy in Alberta* (1999) and *Educational Reform and the Role of Teachers' Unions: A Comparison of the United States, Canada, Japan, Korea, Mexico and Argentina* (2000). His research focuses on 1) globalization, empire, and the politics of knowledge and 2) intellectual property rights and the commercialization of higher education. Of late, he has turned his attention toward post-communism in Slavic and Eurasian societies.

DIP KAPOOR is Assistant Professor in International Education at the University of Alberta, Edmonton, Canada and founding member and President of a Canadian development NGO that has been working with Dalit (scheduled caste) and Adivasi (scheduled tribe) communities in eastern India for over a decade. His research interests are in education and development; adult learning/popular education and politicization in indigenous, peasant, and rural-women's movements in the South (post-colonial states); NGO-social movement knowledge/learning engagements; and global/development education. Some of his recent publications appeared in such journals as *Convergence, Journal of Postcolonial Education* and *Development in Practice*.

SHULAMITH KOENIG is the recipient of the 2003 United Nations Prize in the field of human rights and is the Founder and Executive Director of the People's Movement for Human Rights Education. She initiated and spearheaded the call for a decade of human rights education that resulted in the launching of the UN Decade for Human Right Education, 1995–2004. She now leads the Human Rights Cities Initiative and is establishing a network of Regional and International Learning Institutions for Human Rights education.

GRAHAM PIKE is Associate Professor and Dean of Education at the University of Prince Edward Island, where he teaches global and international education to BEd. and graduate students. He has directed many projects in environmental education, global education and human rights education, in partnership with charitable foundations, business corporations, government agencies and non-governmental organizations. His work as a consultant in global education has taken him to more than twenty countries around the world, including substantial work for UNICEF on school improvement projects in the Middle East and Eastern Europe. He has written extensively on global education, including ten co-authored books for teachers.

GEORGE RICHARDSON is an associate professor and Associate Dean (International) in the University of Alberta's Faculty of Education. His research interests include the role of education in national identity formation, citizenship education, multicultural and international education and action research. He is the editor of journal *Canadian Social Studies*, and, among his publications, he is co-editor of *Troubling the Canon of Citizenship Education* (Peter Lang, 2006) and author of *The Death of the Good Canadian: Teachers National Identities and the Social Studies Curriculum* (Peter Lang, 2002).

TONI SAMEK is Associate Professor, School of Library & Information Studies, University of Alberta. Her interests and contributions are in the areas of critical librarianship, intercultural information ethics, global information justice, human rights, intellectual freedom, and social responsibility. Toni is the author of the 2001 book Intellectual Freedom and Social Responsibility in American Librarianship, 1967–1974 *with* McFarland & Company Inc, Publishers and the 2007 book Librarianship and Human Rights: A 21st Century Guide *with* CHANDOS (Oxford) Publishing. Toni chairs the Canadian Library Association's Advisory Committee on Intellectual Freedom and is an Advisory Board Member for the international activist group Information for Social Change. She also is a founding member and first convenor of the Association for Library and Information Science Education's Information Ethics Special Interest Group.

LYNETTE SHULTZ is Assistant Professor and Co-Director of Global Education Network (GEN) in the Department of Educational Policy Studies, University of Alberta. Her interests and contributions are in the areas of education and social justice, children and work, human rights education, community-school partnerships, and organizing for change. Her work has been published in the *Canadian and International Education Journal*, the *Canadian Journal of Public Policy*, the *Journal of Education Policy*, and the *Alberta Journal of Educational Research*. She is frequently an invited speaker on the topics of exploitive child labor and human rights, as well as education and justice.

MAKERE STEWART-HARAWIRA is an Associate Professor at the University of Alberta and the author of *The New Imperial Order: Indigenous Responses to Globalization* (Zed &Huia, 2005). Other recent publications include "Globalization, work and indigenous knowledge under the new imperium" in *Educating the Global Workforce: Knowledge, Knowledge Work, and Knowledge Workers*. L. Farrell & T. Fenwick (Eds: Kogan Page (2007) and "The Two-edged Sword: a perspective from Indigenous peoples," in *National Perspectives on Globalization: A Critical Reader*. Paul Bowles, Henry Veltmeyer, Scarlett Cornellison, Noela Invernizzi and Kwong-leung Tang, (Eds Palgrave Macmillan (2007). Her current research focuses on the intersection of indigenous ontologies, conceptualizations of global citizenship and postmodern imperialism.

HILARIA SUPA HUAMAN is a human rights activist, an active member of several indigenous women organizations. She is currently an elected representative in the Peruvian parliament and belongs to the Union of Peru Party. In 1991 she became a leader in the Women's Federation of Anta (Federación de Mujeres de Anta FEMCA), where she was responsible for education issues. Hilaria Supa has taken part in numerous international women's meetings and has actively promoted her native Quechua language. She has been resolutely lobbying against sterilization of women, accusing the former health minister under Alberto Fujimori, Alejandro Aguinaga, of carrying out a population policy resulting in forced sterilization of Peruvian women.

CORA WEBER-PILLWAX is Associate Professor of international and intercultural education with particular focus on Indigenous perspectives and experiences, critical and interdisciplinary analysis across the social sciences, participatory action research and other forms of community-driven research as well as First Nations and Metis social and educational issues and policies in Canada. Her publications have appeared in such journals as the *Canadian Journal of Native Education* and the *Journal of Educational Thought*. Currently, Professor Weber-Pillwax is leading a five year research project:Healing through culture and language: Research with Aboriginal peoples in Northwestern Canada supported by the Social Sciences and Humanities Research Council of Canada.

Index